SCHOLASTIC

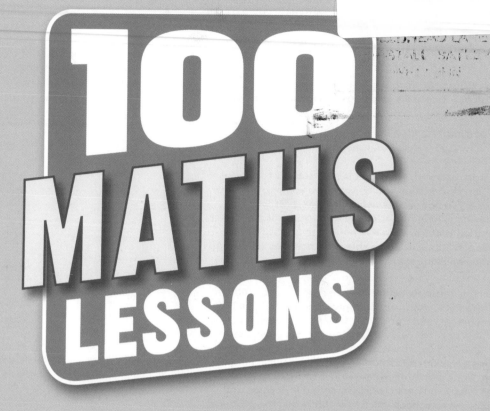

100 MATHS LESSONS

SCHOLASTIC

Book End, Range Road, Witney, Oxfordshire, OX29 0YD
www.scholastic.co.uk

© 2014, Scholastic Ltd

1 2 3 4 5 6 7 8 9   4 5 6 7 8 9 0 1 2 3

British Library Cataloguing-in-Publication Data
A catalogue record for this book is available from the
British Library.

ISBN 978-1407-12771-2
Printed by Bell & Bain Ltd, Glasgow

Due to the nature of the web we cannot guarantee the
content or links of any site mentioned. We strongly
recommend that teachers check websites before using
them in the classroom.

Extracts from *The National Curriculum in Maths, Maths
Programme of Study* © Crown Copyright. Reproduced
under the terms of the Open Government Licence
(OGL). http://www.nationalarchives.gov.uk/doc/open-
government-licence/open-government-licence.htm

Author
Ann Montague-Smith

Series Editor
Ann Montague-Smith

Editorial team
Emily Jefferson, Jenny Wilcox, Mary Nathan and
Margaret Eaton.

Cover Design
Andrea Lewis

Design Team
Sarah Garbett, Shelley Best and Andrea Lewis

CD-ROM development
Hannah Barnett, Phil Crothers, MWA Technologies
Private Ltd

Typesetting and illustrations
Ricky Capanni, International Book Management

Contents

Introduction

About the series

The *100 Maths Lessons* series is designed to meet the requirements of the 2014 National Curriculum, Mathematics Programme of Study. There are six books in the series for Years 1–6, and each book contains lesson plans, resources and ideas matched to the new curriculum. These six titles – along with the accompanying *100 Maths Planning Guide* – have been carefully structured to ensure that a progressive and appropriate school curriculum can be planned and taught throughout the primary years.

About the 2014 Curriculum

The curriculum documentation for Mathematics provides a yearly programme for Years 1 to 6 (ages 5 to 11).

The new curriculum goes further than the previous version with times tables to 12 x 12 by Year 4, an early introduction to long division and an increasingly complex understanding of fractions and decimals. The new curriculum also has a strong focus on varied and frequent practice of the fundamentals of maths – mastery of number facts and times tables should be developed throughout the primary phase.

There is a renewed emphasis on reasoning mathematically and solving problems with particular emphasis on multi-step problems and problems in the context of measurement, money and time. The main coverage of the use and application of mathematics however can be found in the aims of the curriculum:

> *The National Curriculum for Mathematics aims to ensure that all pupils:*
> - *become fluent in the fundamentals of mathematics, including through varied and frequent practice with increasingly complex problems over time, so that pupils have conceptual understanding and are able to recall and apply their knowledge rapidly and accurately to problems*
> - *reason mathematically by following a line of enquiry, conjecturing relationships and generalisations, and developing an argument, justification or proof using mathematical language*
> - *can solve problems by applying their mathematics to a variety of routine and non-routine problems with increasing sophistication, including breaking down problems into a series of simpler steps and persevering in seeking solutions.*

Terminology

The curriculum terminology has changed; the main terms used are:
- **Domains:** The main areas of mathematical study, such as Number and Geometry.
- **Topics:** These are identified in each weekly planning grid and drill the domains down into 'Place value', 'Addition and subtraction' and so on.
- **Curriculum objectives:** These are the statutory programme of study statements or objectives.

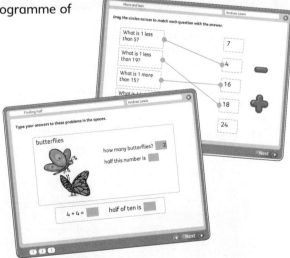

About the book

This book is divided by term and week with a summary heading giving an indication of the week's work. Each week follows the same structure:

Weekly overview

At the start of each week you will find a summary of what is covered, which includes:

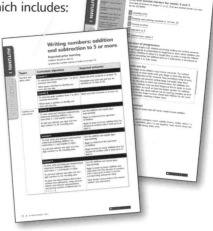

- **Expected prior learning:** What the children are expected to know before starting the work in the chapter.
- **Weekly planning grid:** A lesson-by-lesson breakdown of the coverage of each week – by 'topic', 'curriculum objectives' and 'expected outcomes'.
- **Oral and mental starters:** Suggested activities that might be used from the bank of starters that follow each half-term's lessons.
- **Overview of progression:** A brief explanation of the expected progress that children should make through each week's work.
- **Watch out for:** Possible mathematical misconceptions with ideas for addressing them.
- **Creative context:** How the week's work could link to other 2014 curriculum areas.
- **Vocabulary:** Key vocabulary to introduce or consolidate. (Words in bold also appear in the glossary, see CD-ROM notes on page 7.)
- **Preparation/You will need:** A full list of resources required from book and CD, as well as any general class resources requiring preparation. (A full resource list is given on page 255.)
- **Further practice:** Ideas for consolidating learning using additional resources or practical activities.

Lessons

Each half term contains six weeks' work. Each week contains five lessons. Each lesson includes the following:

- **Curriculum objectives:** A list of the relevant objectives from the Programme of Study.
- **Success criteria:** Expected outcomes for the lesson written as 'can do' statements.
- **You will need:** List of required resources.
- **Whole-class work:** Ideas for working together as a class.
- **Group/Paired/Independent work:** Teaching notes for paired, groups or independent work.
- **Differentiation:** Ideas to support children who are not sufficiently fluent with concepts or to challenge children to apply their understanding (see 2014 National Curriculum aims for further information on the approach to differentiation).
- **Progress check:** 'Mini-plenaries' to enable teachers to check progress throughout the lesson.
- **Review:** Opportunity to reflect on children's learning, and address any misconceptions.

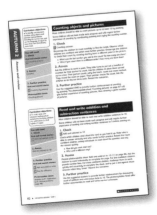

Assess and review

At the end of each half term are activities designed to assess children's understanding or mastery of key curriculum objectives. These can be conducted during the half-term's lessons or at the end, in an 'assess and review week'.

There are four curriculum objectives covered in each half–term. Each section includes ideas to:

- Check progress using appropriate starter activities.
- Assess children's learning using a mix of activities, problems and puzzles.
- Provide further practice activities to consolidate their understanding.

Oral and mental starter activities

In each half term a bank of oral and mental starters is provided. These can be used flexibly to address particular requirements, though suggestions are made within each weekly overview as to which starters might be used across a week's lessons. Each starter includes modelled teacher questions to probe children's ability to recall facts, rehearse strategies or apply learning.

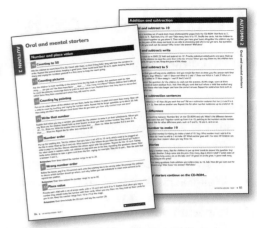

Photocopiable pages

At the end of each chapter, you will find a bank of photocopiable pages linked to the 'Assess and review' section. These sheets offer an 'I can...' statement at the bottom to allow self-assessment of pupil progress towards a particular curriculum objective. Ask the children to colour in the traffic lights next to each statement green, amber or red to reflect their confidence with the objective. There is also space for comments. Additional sheets, linked to the lessons, can be found on the CD-ROM (see page 7 for further information).

Equipment list

This provides an overview of all of the classroom resources required to teach each year's lessons. The resources are broken down by mathematics topic.

Vocabulary list

This provides a list of all key vocabulary to introduce or consolidate over the course of the year. Words appearing in bold type also appear in the glossary (see page 7 for further information).

■SCHOLASTIC

About the CD-ROM

The CD-ROM contains:

- Printable versions of the photocopiable sheets from the book and additional photocopiable sheets as referenced in the lesson plans.
- Interactive activities for children to complete or to use on the whiteboard.
- Interactive teaching resources such as 'Number grids' and 'Pattern squares', designed to support whole–class teaching.
- Printable versions of the lesson plans and the oral and mental starters.
- Digital versions of the lesson plans with the relevant resources linked to them.

Getting started

- Put the CD-ROM into your CD-ROM drive.
    - For Windows users, the install wizard should autorun, if it fails to do so then navigate to your CD-ROM drive. Then follow the installation process.
    - For Mac users, copy the disk image file to your hard drive. After it has finished copying, double-click it to mount the disk image. Navigate to the mounted disk image and run the installer. After installation the disk image can be unmounted and the DMG can be deleted from the hard drive.
- To complete the installation of the program, you need to open the program and click 'Update' in the pop-up. **NB** This CD-ROM is web-enabled and the content needs to be downloaded from the internet to your hard-drive to populate the CD-ROM with the relevant resources. A web connection is only required on first use, after which you will be able to use the CD–ROM without any connection. If at any point any content is updated you will receive a pop-up message upon start–up when you are next connected to the web. You will then have the option to update the content as required.

Navigating the CD-ROM

There are two options to navigate the CD-ROM, either as a Child or as a Teacher.

Child

- Click on the 'Child' button on the first menu screen. In the second menu click on the relevant year group (please note only the books installed on the machine or network will be accessible. You can also rename year groups to match your school's naming conventions via Teacher > Settings > Rename Books area.)
- A list of interactive activities will be displayed; children need to locate the correct class or year group and click 'Go' to launch.
- There is the opportunity to print or save a PDF of the results of each activity on completion.

Teacher

- Click on the 'Teacher' button on the first menu screen and you will be taken to a menu showing which of the *100 Maths Lessons* titles you have purchased. From here, you can also access the credits and 'Getting started' information
- To enter the product, click 'Next' in the bottom right of the screen.
- You can then enter a password (the password is: login).
- On first use:

    - Enter as a Guest by clicking on the 'Guest' button.
    - If desired, create a profile for yourself by adding your name to the list of users. Profiles allow you to save favourites and to specify which year group(s) you wish to be able to view.
    - Go to 'Settings' to create a profile for yourself – click 'Add user' and enter your name. Then choose the year groups you wish to have access to (you can return to this screen to change this at any time).
      Click on 'Login' at the top of the screen to re-enter the CD-ROM with your new profile.
- On subsequent uses you can then select your name from the drop-down list.
- The 'Guest' option will always be available if you, or a colleague, prefer to use this.
- When you have set up your profile, you can then save activities or lessons in 'Favourites'.

For more information about how to use the CD-ROM, please refer to the 'Help' file which can be found in the teacher area of the CD-ROM. It is displayed as a red button with a question mark inside, on the right-hand side of the screen just underneath the 'Settings' tab.

Counting

Expected prior learning

Children should be able to:

- count to at least 5
- count out objects to at least 5.

Topic	Curriculum objectives	Expected outcomes
Number and place value	**Lesson 1**	
	To count to and across 100, forwards and backwards, beginning with 0 or 1, or from any given number.	Know the number names and recite them in order to 10, then extend to 20 and beyond, from and back to 0 or 1.
	Lesson 2	
	To count to and across 100, forwards and backwards, beginning with 0 or 1, or from any given number.	Know the number names and recite them in order to 10, then extend to 20 and beyond, from and back to 0 or 1.
	Lesson 3	
	To identify and represent numbers using objects and pictorial representations including the number line, and use the language of: equal to, more than, less than (fewer), most, least.	Count reliably up to ten objects.
	Lesson 4	
	To identify and represent numbers using objects and pictorial representations including the number line, and use the language of: equal to, more than, less than (fewer), most, least.	Count reliably up to ten objects. Compare two sets and use the vocabulary of more than, less than, fewer than, the same number as.
	Lesson 5	
	To identify and represent numbers using objects and pictorial representations including the number line, and use the language of: equal to, more than, less than (fewer), most, least.	Count reliably up to ten objects. Compare two sets and use the vocabulary of more than, less than, fewer than, the same number as.

■SCHOLASTIC

Preparation

Lesson 1: copy 'Number cards 0–20', one set for each pair

Lesson 2: copy 'Number cards 0–20', one set for each pair

You will need

General resources
'Number cards 0–20'

Equipment
Counting objects, such as cubes; interlocking cubes

Further practice

Photocopiable sheets
'Counting how many'

Oral and mental starters for week 1

See bank of starters on pages 41 to 42. Oral and mental starters are also on the CD-ROM.

1 Counting to and from 10 then 20

2 Take turns counting

3 Counting circle

4 Count objects to 10

Overview of progression

Children will practise counting to at least 20. At first, they may falter during the counting, but with help should extend their knowledge of counting numbers to 20 during the week. They will also count out objects, up to ten at this stage. Check that the children count out objects by coordinating the touch, say the number, and move the item out of the way. This will help the children to see what has been counted so far, and what still needs to be counted. It also avoids counting objects twice.

Watch out for

For those children who lack confidence in saying the counting numbers, count with them, ensuring that your voice can be heard. This will help the count to continue even though the children may have stopped counting. Repetition will help the children to begin to remember the counting numbers. Some children may, when counting objects, count an object twice, or miss one out altogether. Encourage them to line the objects up, then follow the 'touch, say, move' strategy outlined above. Once the objects are counted, suggest that they count them again, but in a different order, just to reinforce that the quantity has not changed even though the counting order has.

Creative context

Use rhymes and stories which involve counting, especially ones where the children can join in. For example, 'One, two, buckle my shoe', with actions, and recited with a good rhythm will help the children to use number names to 20.

Vocabulary

compare, counting numbers to at least 20, fewer, more, the same number as

Lesson 1 **Oral and mental starter** 1

Curriculum objectives
● To count to 20, forwards and backwards, beginning with 0 or 1, or from any given number.

Success criteria
● I can count to at least ten.

You will need

General resources
'Number cards 0–20'

Differentiation

Less confident learners

Limit the starting numbers to zero, one, two and three. Decide whether the children should count up to 10, 15 or 20, depending on their confidence with these counting numbers.

More confident learners

Decide whether the children should extend the count beyond 20 to 25 or 30 and back to 0.

Main teaching activities

Whole-class work: Remind the children that they are already good at counting to and from ten. Explain that in this lesson they will extend their counting to 20. Start with 0 and count all together to 20, then back again. Keep the count going at a good pace and with a steady rhythm. If the count falters, say the number for the children in order to keep up the pace. When the children are confident with this, repeat the activity, this time starting with any small number.

Group work: Ask the children to work in groups of four. They take turns to pick up a number card from the shuffled pack, which is placed face down on the table. The child who picks up the card says the number. He or she then counts individually around the table from that number to 20 and back to 0. The next child turns over a card, and the activity is repeated.

Progress check: Ask questions such as:

● *What comes after 6? Before 9?*
● *Count back 5 from 15. What number will you get to?*

Review

Ask the children to count together from 0 to 20 and back again. Keep the pace sharp, again providing the next number if a child falters. Ask probing questions such as:

● *What number comes before/after ...?*
● *Count on 6 from 11. What number will you get to? Who would like to count that aloud?*

■ SCHOLASTIC

Curriculum objectives

● To count to 20, forwards and backwards, beginning with 0 or 1, or from any given number.

Success criteria

● I can count to at least ten and back again.

You will need

General resources

'Number cards 0–20'

Differentiation

Less confident learners

Decide whether to limit the number range to up to ten to begin with.

More confident learners

Encourage children to count to at least 30 and back.

Lesson 2

Oral and mental starter 2

Main teaching activities

Whole-class work: Repeat the whole-class activity from Lesson 1, this time counting individually around the class.

Group work: Repeat the group work activity from Lesson 1, this time asking the children to count back from their starting number to 0, then up to 20 or beyond, then back to their starting number.

Progress check: Choose a group of children and ask them to respond to questions such as:

- Which number comes after 5... 8... 12... 19...?
- Which number comes before 7... 13... 14...?
- How did you work this out?

Repeat this for other groups, adapting the questions to appropriate number ranges for the less and more confident.

Review

Invite the children to count around the class from a starting number to 20 and back again. Ask questions such as:

- What number comes next after ...?
- What number comes before ...?
- How do you know that?

Invite the more confident children to count on to up to 30 and back again. Ask them to repeat this and encourage the other children to join in the count.

Curriculum objectives

● To identify and represent numbers using objects.

Success criteria

● I can count up to ten objects.

You will need

Equipment

Counting objects, such as cubes

Differentiation

Less confident learners

Limit the size of the count to up to about six by providing larger items to be counted. Check that the children count carefully and coordinate the 'touch, move and count' process.

More confident learners

Decide whether to provide smaller items, so the children can pick up more of them.

Lesson 3

Oral and mental starter 3

Main teaching activities

Whole-class work: Put out six items (such as cubes) on a table, counting them aloud as you place them. Invite a child to count them, touching and moving each item as he or she counts it. This will partition the set, so that the children can see clearly which items have been counted and which are still to be counted. Repeat this for quantities from about five to about ten.

Group work: Ask the children to work in pairs. They take turns to take a small handful of counting objects from the container and count them. Their partner checks to make sure that the count is correct. Encourage the children to touch and move an item as they say each counting number.

Progress check: Ask questions of pairs of children such as:

- What was the last number in the count? So how many toys are there?
- There are five here. If I put one more with them, how many will there be? Someone count to check.
- What if I take one away? Now how many are there?

Review

Invite various children to put out some items and to count them using the 'touch, move and count' method (check that they do this in a coordinated way). The other children can join in the count by pointing and saying the numbers. Ask probing questions:

- What was the last number we said? How many are there here? How do you know that?
- What if I put out one more/one fewer? How many would there be then? Someone show me.

Curriculum objectives
● To identify and represent numbers using objects and pictorial representations.

Success criteria
● I can count on in ones to add.

You will need
General resources
'Number cards 0–20' (0–9 cards)
Equipment
Interlocking cubes; individual whiteboards

Differentiation
Less confident learners
At this stage the children can use the cubes only to model the additions and write the answer in a number sentence.

More confident learners
Encourage the children to work mentally only, by counting on from the larger number.

Main teaching activities

Whole-class work: Ask a child to count out seven cubes and to make a tower with them. Ask another child to count out five cubes and make a tower. Invite the children to stand and hold out their towers so that everyone can see them. Ask: *Which tower has more cubes? How do you know that? Which tower has fewer cubes? How did you work that out?*

Now ask all the children to make their own tower using up to ten cubes. Ask them to compare their tower with a partner. Say, for example: *Which tower has more? How can you tell? And which tower has fewer? Who has the same number of cubes as their partner? How do you know that?*

Paired work: Ask the children to work in pairs and to each take a handful of cubes. This time they count their cubes. Ask them to compare how many they have and to decide who has more and who has fewer. They repeat this another five times.

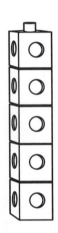

Progress check: Invite two children to come to the front of the class and to make a different tower with the cubes. Ask them to put their tower by their partner's tower. Ask all the children, for example:

- *Who has more cubes in their tower?*
- *Who has fewer?*
- *How do you know that?*

Review

Make a tower of seven cubes. Ask the children to count as you make the tower. Now ask the children to make their own tower that has more cubes than yours. Say, for example: *How many cubes do you have? Is that more or fewer than my tower? How do you know that?*

Repeat this for the children to make a tower with fewer than seven cubes and ask the same questions.

Now add another cube to your tower and ask the children to count how many cubes there are with you. Invite them to each make a tower that has the same number of cubes as yours. Repeat all of this, using different quantities of cubes for the tower, up to ten cubes. Ask:

- *How many cubes did you use?*
- *Is that more... fewer than my tower?*
- *How do you know that?*
- *How many cubes do you need to use to make a tower with the same number as my tower?*

Curriculum objectives

● To identify and represent numbers using objects and pictorial representations.

Success criteria

● I can count up to ten objects.
● I can compare two sets.
● I can find which has more and which has fewer.

You will need

Equipment

Counting objects, such as cubes

Differentiation

Less confident learners

Keep the quantities between five and seven.

More confident learners

Encourage the children to work with quantities beyond ten.

Lesson 5

Oral and mental starter 4

Main teaching activities

Whole-class work: Put out ten cubes and ask the children to count them as you place them on the table. Ask them to shut their eyes and remove two cubes. When they open their eyes ask: *Are there more or fewer than ten cubes now? How do you know that?* Repeat this for other starting numbers.

Paired work: Ask the children to work in pairs. They take turns to take a handful of cubes, then say 'more' or 'fewer'. Their partner counts how many cubes there are. Then they take a handful that contains more or fewer than that number.

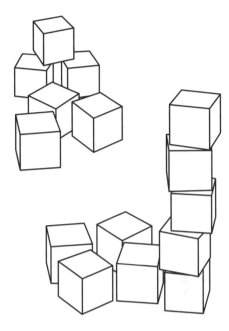

Progress check: Put out nine cubes as before. Then, without the children seeing, remove two cubes. Ask:

- *Are there more or fewer than nine cubes now?*
- *How can you tell that?*
- *Watch as I put a cube back. Are there more or fewer than nine now?*
- *What if I put another cube back. How many are there now?*

Review

Repeat the paired activity with the whole class. A child takes some cubes and the class counts together how many cubes are taken. Then the child says 'more' or 'fewer' or 'the same number' and the other children count out an appropriate number of cubes. Say, for example:

- *How many did you count out?*
- *Is that more or fewer or the same number as these (pointing to the cubes the child counted)?*
- *How do you know that?*

Repeat several times and check that children understand the vocabulary of comparison.

Writing numbers; addition and subtraction to 5 or more

Expected prior learning

Children should be able to:

● know the number names, in order, to at least 10.

Topics	Curriculum objectives	Expected outcomes
Number and place value	**Lesson 1**	
	To read and write numbers from 1 to 20 in numerals and words. When given a number, to identify one more and one less.	Read and write numerals to at least 10. Recognise one more and one less for numbers to 10, then to 20.
	Lesson 2	
	To read and write numbers from 1 to 20 in numerals and words. When given a number, to identify one more and one less.	Read and write numerals to at least 10.
Addition and subtraction	**Lesson 3**	
	To read, write and interpret mathematical statements involving addition (+), subtraction (−) and equals (=) signs. To add and subtract one-digit and two-digit numbers to 20, including zero.	Use the addition and equals signs appropriately. Begin to understand the operation of addition. Begin to know by heart: addition facts for all pairs of numbers with a total up to at least 5.
	Lesson 4	
	To read, write and interpret mathematical statements involving addition (+), subtraction (−) and equals (=) signs. To add and subtract one-digit and two-digit numbers to 20, including zero.	Use the addition and equals signs appropriately. Begin to understand the operation of addition. Begin to know by heart: addition facts for all pairs of numbers with a total up to at least 5.
	Lesson 5	
	To read, write and interpret mathematical statements involving addition (+), subtraction (−) and equals (=) signs. To add and subtract one-digit and two-digit numbers to 20, including zero. To solve one-step problems that involve addition and subtraction, using concrete objects and pictorial representations, and missing number problems such as $7 = \square - 9$.	Use the addition and equals signs appropriately. Begin to know by heart: addition and subtraction facts for all pairs of numbers with a total up to at least 5 and the corresponding subtraction facts. Solve simple word problems that involve addition and subtraction.

■SCHOLASTIC

Week 3

Topics	Curriculum objectives	Expected outcomes
Addition and subtraction	**Lesson 6**	
	To add and subtract one-digit and two-digit numbers to 20, including zero.	Begin to know by heart: addition and subtraction facts for all pairs of numbers with a total up to at least 5.
	Lesson 7	
	To add and subtract one-digit and two-digit numbers to 20, including zero.	Begin to know by heart: addition and subtraction facts for all pairs of numbers with a total up to at least 5.
	Lesson 8	
	To add and subtract one-digit and two-digit numbers to 20, including zero.	Begin to know by heart: addition and subtraction facts for all pairs of numbers with a total up to at least 5.
	Lesson 9	
	To add and subtract one-digit and two-digit numbers to 20, including zero.	Begin to know by heart: addition and subtraction facts for all pairs of numbers with a total up to at least 5.
	Lesson 10	
	To solve one-step problems that involve addition and subtraction, using concrete objects and pictorial representations, and missing number problems such as $7 = \Box - 9$.	Solve addition and subtraction word problems for numbers up to 6.

Preparation

Lesson 1: copy 'Numbers to 10'

Lesson 2: copy 'Butterfly numbers'

Lesson 4: copy 'Add it up'

Lesson 8: copy 'Addition and subtraction to 6'

Lesson 10: copy 'Word problems: addition and subtraction to 6'

You will need

Photocopiable sheets

'Numbers to 10'; 'Butterfly numbers'; 'Add it up'; 'Addition and subtraction to 6'; 'Word problems: addition and subtraction to 6'

General resources

'Number cards 0–20'; interactive activity, 'More and less'

Equipment

A washing line and pegs; interlocking cubes; containers for cubes; two blank dice marked 1, 1, 2, 2, 3, 3 and 2, 2, 3, 3, 4, 4 for each pair; 1–6 dice marked with numerals

Further practice

Photocopiable sheets

'Adding to 5'; 'Subtracting within 5'

Oral and mental starters for weeks 2 and 3

See bank of starters on pages 41 to 42. Oral and mental starters are also on the CD-ROM.

3 Counting circle

5 Reading and ordering numerals to 10, then 20

6 Writing numbers

7 Add facts to 5

9 Subtract facts within 5

Overview of progression

This fortnight begins with children practising reading and writing numerals to 10 and beyond, in preparation for beginning to learn about addition and subtraction. Addition to about 6 is taught first, in order to help the children to begin to remember the addition facts to 5. Subtraction is introduced at the end of week 2 as 'take away'.

Watch out for

At this stage some children may reverse numerals. Try 'writing' the numeral on their backs with your finger so that they feel the shape and direction of the numeral. Also, providing a tray of sand, where children can practise writing large numerals, helps them to see the direction in which the numeral faces. For addition and subtraction, children may use their fingers at first in order to count. Encourage them to count on from the larger number for addition. For subtraction, the same method can be used by counting up from the smaller to the larger number. Check that children do not count twice, for example, counting a finger twice.

Creative context

Encourage children to invent and tell stories which involve addition and subtraction.

Vocabulary

add, altogether, answer, compare, count, explain, leaves, makes, minus (−), number sentence, operation, plus (+), put together, read, record, show me, sign, subtract, sum, take away, total, write

Curriculum objectives
● To read and write numbers from 1 to 20 in numerals.
● When given a number, to identify one more and one less.

Success criteria
● I can write numbers to 10.

You will need

Photocopiable sheets
'Numbers to 10'

General resources
'Number cards 0–20'

Equipment
Washing line and pegs

Differentiation

Less confident learners

You may prefer these children to attempt the first part only of photocopiable page 'Numbers to 10' initially; this involves writing only the numerals to 10. If the children find these difficult, encourage them to recite the numbers from 0 or any small number to 10, forwards and backwards.

More confident learners

These children could try the second part of photocopiable page 'Numbers to 10', which has number tracks containing higher numbers to 20.

Lesson 1   Oral and mental starter 3

Main teaching activities

Whole-class work: Explain that this lesson will help the children to remember the written numerals 0 to 10, and extend up to 20. Show them the large number cards. Explain that you would like them to read the number on each card with you, and then you will ask someone to peg the card onto the washing line so that all the cards go onto the line in order. Begin with 0, 1, 2 and so on. When all the numbers are on the line, invite individual children to remove the cards, saying for example:

- *Jon, take the card that has the number one more than 5... 9... 13...*
- *Salma, find the number that is one less than 8... 1... 14...*
- *Which number is 1 before 1... 3... 12... 20...?*

When the children are confident with this, remove all the cards from the line and give them out to the children. Ask those holding a card to peg their cards back on the line in the correct order, starting with 0.

Independent work: Ask the children to complete photocopiable page 'Numbers to 10' from the CD-ROM. They should trace a set of numerals, then fill in the missing numerals on simple number tracks. Check that they trace and write in the writing direction.

Progress check: Ask individual children to answer questions such as:

- *Which number comes next?*
- *How do you know that?*
- *Would this number fit next?*
- *Why/why not? Tell me why you are sure about that.*

Review

Invite 21 children each to hold one of the set of large numeral cards (0–20). Ask them to take turns to peg their card onto the washing line, until all of the cards are in order. Say:

- *Which number is one more/one less than ...?*
- *Mei Mei, point to the number that is one more/one less than....*

Point to the numbers in order, asking the children to say each number as you point to it.

Curriculum objectives
● To read and write numbers from 1 to 20 in numerals.
Success criteria
● I can read and write numbers to at least 10.

You will need
Photocopiable sheets
'Butterfly numbers'
General resources
'Number cards 0–20'; interactive activity 'More and less'
Equipment
Washing line and pegs

Differentiation
Less confident learners
Work with the children using a number track or counting objects to support their understanding.
More confident learners
Offer these children the interactive activity 'More and less' on the CD-ROM, which includes numbers up to 30.

Lesson 2 — Oral and mental starter 3

Main teaching activities

Whole-class work: Repeat the whole-class activity from lesson 1. This time, count around the class individually as well as all together. Ask: *What number is one more than... / one less than...?*

Independent work: Ask the children to complete photocopiable page 'Butterfly numbers' from the CD-ROM. This involves writing the numbers that are 1 more and 1 less than some given numbers to 20.

Progress check: Remove the numerals from the washing line. Invite a child to choose a number and to hold it up for everyone to see. Ask:

- *What is this number?*
- *What number is one more than this? Find the number for me from the cards.* (Child holds the number up, next to the child holding the starting number.)
- *What number is one less than this? Find the number for me from the cards.* (The original number. Child holds the number up, next to the child holding the starting number.)

Repeat for another starting number.

Review

Write table headings on the board or flipchart as shown below. Write a number in the 'My number' column and invite a child to write in the other two numbers. Repeat this for different numbers, taking account of the range of abilities within the class. Ask questions such as:

- *Which number is one more/one less than ...?*
- *How do you know that?*
- *Choose your own number. Now, what is one more/one less than that?*
- *How did you work that out?*

One less than	My number	One more than

Curriculum objectives
● To read, write and interpret mathematical statements involving addition (+) and equals (=) signs.

Success criteria
● I can write addition sentences using numbers and signs.
● I can work out additions up to a total of 7.

You will need
Equipment
Interlocking cubes; two blank dice marked 1, 1, 2, 2, 3, 3 and 2, 2, 3, 3, 4, 4 for each pair; 1–6 dice marked with numerals

Differentiation
Less confident learners
Provide two 1, 1, 2, 2, 3, 3 dice so that the totals are smaller. Make sure that the children are clear about what is meant by 'larger' and 'smaller' numbers, so they count on from the larger number each time.

More confident learners
Decide whether to replace one or both dice with 1–6 dice. This will give totals up to 12. Encourage the children to devise their own method of recording.

Lesson 3 — Oral and mental starter 5

Main teaching activities

Whole-class work: Explain that in today's lesson, the children will be learning a new way to add small numbers mentally. Write on the board: 2 + 3 = and ask the children to read this number sentence to you.

Check that they can read the signs + and =. Ask: *How could we work out this sum?* Children may suggest: counting out two and then three cubes, then counting them all; counting on fingers. *What if we put the larger number first, then count on? Do you think that would work? Let's try it.* Rewrite the number sentence as 3 + 2 =.

Ask the children to put the 3 in their heads, and count on two: *3, 4 and 5. So 3 add 2 is 5.* Write 5 after the = sign. Use cubes to demonstrate that this is the correct answer: combine a three-rod with a two-rod and count all the cubes.

Repeat this for other number sentences, such as 2 + 4 and 1 + 3. Ask:

- *What is 2 add 4?*
- *How did you work that out?*
- *Did anyone use a different way to find the answer?*
- *Find the answer to 1 add 3.*

Group work: Ask the children to work in pairs. They roll two dice each time (a 1, 1, 2, 2, 3, 3 dice and a 2, 2, 3, 3, 4, 4 dice) to generate an addition sentence. Remind them to put the larger number first and count on. They can record their sums in the form: 3 + 1 = 4, and so on.

Progress check: Ask questions of all the children such as:

- *I have a 4 on one dice and a 2 on the other. Use your cubes. What is the total of 4 add 1?*
- *Tell me one of your addition sentences, but not the total.*
- *Who has worked out the total for those two numbers?*
- *Do you agree?*

Review

Invite some children from each ability group to write one of their sums on the board. Ask the other children to work out the answer, counting on from the larger number. Ask questions such as:

- *Which is the larger number?*
- *How do you know that?*
- *What if you counted on from the smaller number – would you get the same answer?*

Now say: *There are four bricks in this pot. I put one more in. How many bricks are there in the pot now? How did you work that out?*

Curriculum objectives
- To read, write and interpret mathematical statements involving addition (+) and equals (=) signs.

Success criteria
- I can write the add (+) and equals (=) signs correctly.
- I can say some addition sentences to 6.
- I can solve some addition problems.

You will need

Photocopiable sheets

'Add it up'

Differentiation

Less confident learners

Ask an adult to work with these children in a group. They take turns to demonstrate how they calculated the answers.

More confident learners

Check that if the children need to count on they always count on from the larger number.

Lesson 4   Oral and mental starter [6]

Main teaching activities

Whole-class work: Repeat the whole-class activity from lesson 3. Use, for example, 4 + 1, 3 + 2, 5 + 1. Ask:
- *How did you work out the answer?*
- *Who 'knows' the answer? Well done!*

Independent work: Provide copies of photocopiable page 'Add it up' from the CD-ROM for each group (one per child).

Progress check: Ask each group separately to look at the answer to the first question on their sheet. Ask:
- *What is the number sentence?*
- *How did you work out the answer?*

Check that the children are confident with what they have been asked to do.

Review

Choose some of the sums and ask individual children to explain how they worked out the answer. Check that the children are using effective mental strategies. Ask: *How did you find the answer? Did anyone find this using a different way? Who 'knows' the answer?*

Curriculum objectives
- To read, write and interpret mathematical statements involving addition, subtraction and equals signs.
- To solve one-step problems that involve subtraction, using concrete objects.

Success criteria
- I can write the add (+) and equals (=) signs correctly.
- I can say some subtraction sentences to 6.
- I can solve some subtraction problems.

You will need

Equipment

Interlocking cubes; a 1, 1, 2, 2, 3, 3 dice for each pair

Differentiation

Less confident learners

Decide whether to ask the children to subtract the dice score from 4, then 5, each time.

More confident learners

Decide whether to provide a 1–6 dice and ask the children to subtract from 8, then 9.

Lesson 5   Oral and mental starter [6]

Main teaching activities

Whole-class work: Make a tower of six interlocking cubes and say: *How many will be left if I take away 2? How can we work this out?* Invite the children to suggest ways of finding the answer, such as taking away two cubes and counting what is left. More confident learners may suggest counting back 2 from 6.

Remove two cubes from the tower, and count with the children what is left. Say the sentence together: *6 take away 2 leaves 4.* Now ask them to put 6 'in their heads' and count back 2: *6, 5, 4. So 6 take away 2 leaves 4.* Write this on the board as a number sentence: 6 − 2 = 4. Explain that the '−' sign means 'take away'.

Group work: Provide each pair with a 1, 1, 2, 2, 3, 3 dice. Ask them to roll the dice and subtract the score from 6 each time. They should write a number sentence for each subtraction. They can repeat this for subtractions from 7.

Progress check: Say, for example, *Count back 4 from 6. What is 6 take away 4?* Ask the children to work mentally, saying the subtraction sentence together, then demonstrating with cubes to confirm the answer. Ask *How did you work this out? Is there another way?*

Review

Invite some pairs of children to write one of their subtraction sentences on the board, without the answer. Invite the others to find the answer mentally. Ask: *How did you work that out?* Now invite the children to listen to a subtraction story: *There are four children in the sweet shop. Two go outside. How many are left in the sweet shop?* Ask the children to suggest their own subtraction story for the numbers 3 and 2.

Curriculum objectives
● To subtract one-digit numbers to 5.

Success criteria
● I can find answers to subtraction from up to 6.

You will need

Equipment
Five interlocking cubes for each child

Differentiation

Less confident learners
If children are unsure, ask them to put their towers down on the table, and take away the cubes in front of their partner. They then count back from the starting total to find what is left. They can check by counting the tower left on the table.

More confident learners
Decide whether to extend the starting quantity to 6.

Lesson 6   Oral and mental starter 7

Main teaching activities

Whole-class work: Explain that this lesson is about counting back to find the answer to a subtraction sentence. On the board write: 5 − 2 = ☐ and together read this subtraction sentence. Make a tower of five cubes, with the children counting aloud each cube that is added to the tower. Now take away two cubes, and show the children the tower that remains and the two cubes that have been removed. Say together: *Put 5 in your heads. Now count back 2 with me: 5 and 4, 3. So 5 take away 2 leaves 3.* Repeat this for other subtractions, such as 4 − 3, 5 − 1, and so on. Ask:

- *How did you work this out?*
- *Did anyone 'know' the answer? That is very good!*

Paired work: Ask the children to work in twos. They each need five interlocking cubes, paper and pencils. Explain that they take turns to make a tower of cubes, but hide it behind their backs or in their laps so that their partner cannot see the tower. They say how many cubes they have used. Then they remove some of the cubes and tell their partner how many they have taken away. Their partner uses counting back to find how many are left. Ask the child with the cubes to show their partner what is left. They both write the subtraction sentence. Ask them to repeat this, taking turns, until they have written ten subtraction sentences.

Progress check: Ask for example:

- *What subtraction sentence did you just make?*
- *How did you find the answer?*
- *Someone tell me another subtraction sentence.*

Use this sentence to count back together so that everyone finds the answer. For example, for 4 − 2, say: *Put 4 in your heads. Now count back 2: 4 and 3, 2. So 4 take away 2 leaves 2.*

Review

Put out six cubes and ask the children to count these with you. Now, hide the tower behind your back and take away two cubes. Say: *I took away 2 cubes. How many cubes are left?* Say together: *Put 6 in my head. 6 and 5, 4. So 6 take away 2 leaves 4.* Repeat this for other subtractions from 6. Ask questions such as:

- *How many cubes did we start with?*
- *How many are left?*
- *What is the subtraction sentence? Write it on the board.*

Curriculum objectives
● To subtract one-digit numbers to 6, including zero.
Success criteria
● I can find answers to subtraction from up to 6.

You will need
Equipment
Interlocking cubes

Differentiation
Less confident learners
If children are unsure, ask them to try the activity with just four cubes, then move to five, then six. Check that they understand how to count back to find the answer.

More confident learners
Encourage the children to try to recall answers.

Lesson 7
Oral and mental starter 7

Main teaching activities

Whole-class work: Repeat the activity from lesson 6, this time increasing the quantity to 6.

Paired work: Children will need six cubes, paper and pencils. Ask the children to take turns to make a tower of six cubes. Their partner says a subtraction sentence, starting with 6, such as 6 take away 3. They both write the subtraction sentence, and calculate the answer together by counting back 3. There are seven possible subtraction sentences, including $6 - 0$; encourage the children to find all of the possibilities.

Progress check: Ask the children to say the subtraction sentences that they have found. Say:
- *Try this again, counting back from 6 in your heads.*
- *Is this the same answer?*

Review

On the board, write the number sentences. Begin by writing $6 - 1 =$ and ask for the answer. Repeat this for $6 - 2$, $6 - 3$ and so on to $6 - 6$. Now write above the first one $6 - 0$, and say:
- *What is 6 take away 0?*
- *What does 0 mean?*
- *What is 5 take away 0?*
- *So, if I take away 0 from, say 8 what would the answer be?*

Curriculum objectives
● To add and subtract 1-digit numbers to 7, including zero.
Success criteria
● I can add and subtract numbers to 7.
● I am beginning to know addition and subtraction facts to 5.

You will need
Photocopiable sheets
'Addition and subtraction to 6'

Differentiation
Less confident learners
Decide whether to ask an adult to work with this group. The children work together to find the solutions. The adult asks the children to say each number sentence aloud.

More confident learners
Ask the children to try to recall the answers. They draw a spot beside any answers that they 'know'.

Lesson 8
Oral and mental starter 9

Main teaching activities

Whole-class work: Explain that in this lesson the children will be adding and subtracting up to 6. Explain that you would like them to do this mentally. Say for example: *What is 2 add 3? How did you work that out? Is there another way?* Review the counting on from the larger number together: *2 add 3: put the larger number first and count on. So 3 and 4, 5. 2 add 3 is 5.* Repeat this for other examples. Now say *What is 5 take away 2?* Review counting back from the larger number.

On the board write:

$2 + 3 = 5$ $5 - 2 = 3$

Ask the children if they can make another addition sentence with the numbers 2, 3 and 5. Write up $3 + 2 = 5$. Now ask if there is another subtraction sentence with these numbers. Write up $5 - 3 = 2$. Explain that from three numbers that make an addition sentence, there is always one more addition sentence, and two subtraction sentences that can be made.

Independent work: Provide each child with photocopiable page 'Addition and subtraction to 6' from the CD-ROM. They complete each number trio.

Progress check: Ask questions such as:
- *If I know that $3 + 1 = 4$, what other addition sentence can I make?*
- *Tell me two subtraction sentences that use 3, 1 and 4.*

Review

Write on the board $5 + 1 = \square$. Ask: *What is 5 add 1?* Write the answer 6. Say:
- *Tell me another addition sentence that uses 5, 1 and 6.*
- *Tell me two subtraction sentences that use these three numbers.*
- Repeat this for other number trios such as 4, 3 and 7.

Curriculum objectives
● To add and subtract one-digit numbers to 7, including zero.

Success criteria
● I can add and subtract up to 7.

You will need
Equipment
Interlocking cubes

Differentiation
Less confident learners

If children need further help, provide interlocking cubes so that they can model the number sentences. Encourage them to check by counting up or back as before.

More confident learners

Challenge the children to repeat this for 8.

Lesson 9 — Oral and mental starter 9

Main teaching activities

Whole-class work: Repeat the whole-class activity from Lesson 8, this time with facts up to 7. Encourage the children to use counting up or back strategies to find solutions.

Paired work: Ask the children to take turns to choose a number less than 7 such as 4. They write two addition and two subtraction sentences, such as $4 + 3 = 7$; $3 + 4 = 7$; $7 − 3 = 4$; $7 − 4 = 3$. They repeat this until they have five sets of four number sentences.

Progress check: Ask questions such as:
● *What were the two starting numbers, 7 and ...?*
● *How did you work out your answers?*
● *Try to find another number trio for 7.*

Review

Invite the children to give examples of their number sentences. Write these with the number trio above, onto the board. Now ask the more confident learners to give some examples for 8, such as 2, 6 and 8. Encourage the other children to find solutions by counting up from the larger number to 8 for addition, and back from 8 for subtraction. Ask questions such as:

● *How did you find that answer?*
● *If you know that $1 + 7 = 8$ what other addition sentence can you make?*
● *What subtraction sentences can you make?*

Curriculum objectives
● To solve one-step problems that involve addition and subtraction, using concrete objects and pictorial representations, and missing number problems.

Success criteria
● I can find answers to addition word problems up to a total of 6.
● I can find answers to subtraction word problems with a starting number of 6.

You will need
Photocopiable sheets
'Word problems: addition and subtraction to 6'

Differentiation
Less confident learners

Provide interlocking cubes to help the children to calculate the answers.

More confident learners

Encourage the children to use recall to find the answers where they can. Ask them to put a spot next to the answers that they 'knew'.

Lesson 10 — Oral and mental starter 7 9

Main teaching activities

Whole-class work: Explain that you will say a problem. Say: *There are three cats on the table. There are two cats under the table. How many cats is that altogether?* Ask whether they need to add or subtract. *How do you know that?* Discuss how the word 'altogether' makes this an addition problem. Invite the children to calculate the answer and to say how they worked it out.

Repeat for: Five cats are on the table. One cat goes under the table. How many cats does that leave on the table? How do you know whether to add or subtract? (The word 'leave' shows that it is a subtraction problem.) Calculate the answer and say how you worked it out.

Independent work: Provide photocopiable page 'Word problems: addition and subtraction to 6' from the CD-ROM. Read the problems through together. Remind the children of the counting on strategy for addition, and the counting back strategy for subtraction.

Progress check: Check that children can read the words in the problem. If necessary read the words again, problem by problem. Ask, for example:
● *What does the word 'altogether' tell us about this problem?*
● *What word tells you that this is a take away problem?*

Review

Write this problem onto the board: *There are six hens in the hen house. Four hens go to sleep. How many hens do not go to sleep?*

Ask:
● *What sort of problem is this?*
● *Which words tell you that this is a take away problem?*
● *What is the answer? How did you work that out?*

Repeat for another problem, such as: *There are three hens on the perch. There are three hens on the floor. How many hens are there in total?*

Addition to totals to 10

Expected prior learning

Children should be able to:

- count out quantities to 10
- use quantities and objects
- add and subtract two single-digit numbers and count on to find the answer.

Topic	Curriculum objectives	Expected outcomes
Addition and subtraction	**Lesson 1**	
	To read, write and interpret mathematical statements involving addition (+), subtraction (−) and equals (=) signs. To add and subtract one-digit and two-digit numbers to 20, including zero. To represent and use number bonds and related subtraction facts within 20.	Understand the operation of addition and of subtraction as 'take away'. Begin to know by heart: • addition and subtraction facts for all pairs of numbers with a total up to at least 5 and the corresponding subtraction facts. • addition facts for all pairs of numbers with a total up to at least 10, and the corresponding subtraction facts. Use the strategy for addition: put the larger number first and count on in ones.
	Lesson 2	
	To represent and use number bonds and related subtraction facts within 20.	Begin to know addition facts for all pairs of numbers with a total up to at least 10. Use the strategy for addition: put the larger number first and count on in ones.
	Lesson 3	
	To represent and use number bonds and related subtraction facts within 20.	Begin to know addition facts for all pairs of numbers with a total up to at least 10. Use the strategy for addition: put the larger number first and count on in ones.
	Lesson 4	
	To represent and use number bonds and related subtraction facts within 20.	Begin to know addition facts for all pairs of numbers with a total up to at least 10. Use the strategy for addition: put the larger number first and count on in ones.
	Lesson 5	
	To solve one-step problems that involve addition and subtraction, using concrete objects and pictorial representations, and missing number problems such as $7 = \square - 9$.	Solve simple word problems that involve addition and subtraction.

Preparation

Lesson 1: prepare number cards 0–9

Lesson 2: copy and prepare 'Add facts 6 to 10', one set per pair; copy and enlarge 'Add facts 6 to 10' to A3 before cutting, to make a teaching set of cards

Lesson 4: copy 'Missing numbers (1)'; copy and enlarge 'Missing numbers (1)' to A3

You will need

Photocopiable sheets
'Add facts 6 to 10'; 'Missing numbers (1)'

General resources
'Number cards 0–20'

Equipment
Interlocking cubes; individual whiteboards

Further practice

Photocopiable sheets
'Addition to 9 and 10'; 'Addition to 10'

Oral and mental starters for week 4

See bank of starters on pages 41 to 42. Oral and mental starters are also on the CD-ROM.

3 Counting circle: extend the count to 30 and more

7 Add facts to 5

8 Write the answer for addition to 5

Overview of progression

During this week the children will extend their knowledge of addition to totals up to 10. They will learn to count on from the larger number for addition. At first, they may well find using their interlocking cubes helpful, followed by using fingers as they count on. Encourage them to begin to develop a mental number line for counting on, and to move from using fingers and concrete materials. There are links with subtraction within lesson 4, in that children are counting up to find a missing number. This work leads into the next week's work on subtraction.

Watch out for

Some children may still count all rather than counting on from the larger number. Provide experience of counting all, using interlocking cubes. Then repeat the addition, counting on from the larger number so that the children understand that this gives the same answer and is a more efficient and effective method.

Creative context

Encourage the children to say and write number stories in sentences.

Vocabulary

add, altogether, equals, how many are gone?, how many are left/left over?, how much less is...?, leave, make, minus, plus, sign, subtract, sum, take away, total

Curriculum objectives

● To read, write and interpret mathematical statements involving addition (+), subtraction (−) and equals (=) signs.
● To add and subtract one-digit and two-digit numbers to 20, including zero.
● To represent and use number bonds and related subtraction facts within 20.

Success criteria

● I can count on in ones to add.

You will need

General resources

'Number cards 0–20'

Equipment

Interlocking cubes; individual whiteboards

Differentiation

Less confident learners

At this stage the children can use the cubes to model the additions and write the answer in a number sentence.

More confident learners

Encourage the children to work mentally only, by counting on from the larger number.

Lesson 1   Oral and mental starter 3

Main teaching activities

Whole-class work: Explain that this lesson is about addition up to 10 and that the children will use the strategy of 'put the larger number in your heads and count on in ones' for addition. Write on the interactive whiteboard $6 + 2 = \square$ and ask the children to read this with you as *6 add 2 equals*. Put out a tower of six cubes and ask a child to count and confirm how many that is. Now add a tower of two cubes. Ask a child to count how many there are in total. Explain that it is not necessary to count from the beginning because we already know that we have six cubes. Together, say *6, and 7 and 8*, as you point to the additional two cubes. Say *6 add 2 equals 8*.

Ask: *Which is the larger number, the 6 or the 2?* Say: *Put the 6 in your heads. Now count on 2. So 6, and 7, 8. 6 add 2 equals 8.*

Repeat this for other examples where the total is 10 or less, such as 3 + 4, 7 + 2, and so on. Model each addition with cubes first, then repeat by counting on from the larger number. The children can write the answers onto their whiteboards and hold them up for you to see when you say: *Show me*.

Paired work: Ask the children to work in pairs with a set of 1–9 number cards. Ask them to shuffle the cards, and then take turns to draw the top two cards. They model the addition with interlocking cubes and count on from the larger tower number in order to find the answer. They check their answer by counting on in ones from the larger number. They write an addition sentence to record what they have done.

Progress check: Invite pairs to show the additions they have written and the corresponding cube towers. Ask children to explain their methods. Ask: *Which number did you count on from? Why? Which symbol do we use to show 'add'?*

Review

Explain that you will say some addition number sentences. Ask the children to use the strategy 'counting on in ones from the larger number' to find the answer. Say, for example: *What is 4 add 2? Which number did you start with? Why was that?* Say together: *4 add 2 is 4 and 5 and 6. So 4 add 2 equals 6.* Repeat for other examples, such as 5 + 2, 2 + 4, 3 + 5. Ask each time:

● *Which is the larger number?*
● *So how did you find the answer?*

Curriculum objectives
● To represent and use number bonds within 10.
Success criteria
● I can count on from the larger number to add.
● I can write an addition number sentence.

You will need
Photocopiable sheets
'Add facts 6 to 10'
Equipment
Interlocking cubes

Differentiation
Less confident learner
Provide interlocking cubes for the children to model the answers.
More confident learners
Encourage them to write down any answers that they can now recall, then check by counting on.

Lesson 2
Oral and mental starter 7

Main teaching activities

Whole-class work: Remind the children of the addition strategy 'put the larger number in your heads and count on in ones'. Ask them to use this to calculate 6 + 3. Now say for example: *Add 3 to 5. What is 6 plus 2? What is 5 add 1? What is the sum of 2 and 7? How many are 4 and 6 altogether?* Encourage the children to explain how they worked out the answers.

Paired work: Provide each pair with a set of cards from photocopiable page 'Add facts 6 to 10' from the CD-ROM. They take turns to draw a card, and then count on from the larger number to find the answer. They write an addition number sentence for each card.

Progress check: Pick one of the cards, and ask a pair who found that total to explain what they did. Ask: *Did anyone do it in a different way?* Invite children to show the calculation they have found most difficult so far.

Review

Use a teaching set of cards from photocopiable page 'Add facts 6 to 10'. Ask the children to work mentally to find the answer for each card that you show. Ask questions such as:
- *How did you work that out?*
- *Who remembered the answer? That's good.*

Curriculum objectives
● To represent and use number bonds within 10.
Success criteria
● I can write addition number patterns.

You will need
Equipment
Individual whiteboards

Differentiation
Less confident learners
Encourage them to try to add on in their heads, using their fingers to keep track of the count.
More confident learners
When they have finished this, ask them to find all of the additions with an answer of 10 in the same way.

Lesson 3
Oral and mental starter 8

Main teaching activities

Whole-class work: Write on the board:

Ask the children to help you to complete the chart. When this is done say: *Are there any number patterns that you can see?* Invite children to explain the patterns, such as the first column goes up one each time while the second column of numbers goes down one each time.

$$0 + 7 =$$
$$1 + 6 =$$
$$2 + 5 =$$
$$3 + 4 =$$
$$4 + 3 =$$
$$5 + 2 =$$
$$6 + 1 =$$
$$7 + 0 =$$

Independent work: Ask the children to make a similar pattern for the answer 8, beginning with 0 + 8 = 8. They write this out, adding on in ones to the larger number each time. When they have completed this, ask them to make the pattern for the answer 9.

Progress check: Ask children to hold up what they've done so far. Ask: *What do you notice about your answers?*

Review

Invite various children to explain how they worked out their answers. Say, for example:
- *Who counted on in ones using their fingers/not using their fingers?*
- *Who knew the answer without counting on? Try to remember the answers.*

Curriculum objectives
● To represent and use number bonds and related subtraction facts within 10.

Success criteria
● I can solve addition problems.
● I can count on from the larger number.

You will need
Photocopiable sheets
'Missing numbers (1)'

Differentiation
Less confident learners
Ask an adult to work with this group. Children work together to solve each question. Ask them to say the number sentence, then to count on from the given number up to the answer each time.

More confident learners
Invite the children to find two possible answers for each of the number sentences in the second part of the activity.

Curriculum objectives
● To solve simple problems that involve addition and subtraction, using concrete objects and pictorial representations, and missing number problems.

Success criteria
● I can solve word problems about addition.

You will need
Equipment
Individual whiteboards

Differentiation
Less confident learners
Ask an adult to work with the group to help them to invent their word problems and to find the answers.

More confident learners
Challenge the children to invent four word problems.

Lesson 4   Oral and mental starter 7

Main teaching activities

Whole-class work: Revise the strategy of putting the larger number first and counting on in ones with examples such as $2 + \square = 7$, $3 + \square = 6$. Ask how the children calculated the missing numbers, such as counting up.

Independent work: Ask the children to complete photocopiable page 'Missing numbers (1)' from the CD-ROM.

Progress check: Choose one of the calculations and ask children what method they used. *Did anyone use a different method?* Invite children to say which question they have found most difficult so far, and discuss how they could find the answer.

Review

Use the A3 enlargement of the photocopiable page 'Missing numbers (1)' from the CD-ROM. Invite various children to give answers to the first set of questions and to explain how they calculated each time. For the second set, ask for possible answers. Encourage the more confident children to give two possible answers each time. Ask, for example:

● *Who can find another possible answer?*
● *How did you work that out?*
● *Are there any more answers?*
● *How do you know that?*

Lesson 5   Oral and mental starter 8

Main teaching activities

Whole-class work: Explain that you will be giving the children some problems to solve. Ask: *There are three bananas and four oranges. How many pieces of fruit is that altogether?* Invite the children to say what sort of number sentence they need and write this onto the board. Ask them to calculate the answer. Check that if they don't know the answer, they count on from the larger number. Repeat for another problem such as: *There are two kittens in the red basket and four kittens in the blue basket. How many kittens are there altogether?*

Ask the children for vocabulary that they could use in addition word problems, such as 'add', 'and', 'altogether'. Say: *There are two dog bones on the lawn and six dog bones on the flower bed. How many dog bones are there in total?* Ask: *What word tells you to add?* Ask the children to write their own number sentence and to calculate the answer. Invite a child to give the number sentence and explain how they calculated the answer. Discuss the language used, and which word or words make it clear that the answer is found by adding.

Paired work: Ask the children to invent two word problems and write the number sentences for them on individual whiteboards. Give them a few minutes to do this. Then ask each pair to work with another pair. They take turns to say their word problems for the others to solve.

Progress check: Invite pairs to read out their word problems. *Which word in the problem shows that they have to add?* Ask children to say all the different words they have used for 'add' in their problems so far.

Review

Invite children from each of the groups to say one of their word problems for others to solve. Ask questions such as: *How did you work that out? Is there another way? Which words show that you have to add?*

Properties of shapes

Expected prior learning

Children should be able to:

● recognise given 2D or 3D shapes in the environment, such as matching a cuboid to a cereal packet, or matching the front cover of a book to a rectangle.

Topics	Curriculum objectives	Expected outcomes
Geometry: properties of shapes	**Lesson 1**	
	To recognise and name common 2D and 3D shapes, including: ● 2D shapes [for example, rectangles (including squares), circles and triangles] ● 3D shapes [for example, cuboids (including cubes), pyramids and spheres].	Recognise and differentiate between cube, cuboid, cones, cylinders, pyramids and spheres.
	Lesson 2	
	To recognise and name common 2D and 3D shapes, including: ● 2D shapes [for example, rectangles (including squares), circles and triangles] ● 3D shapes [for example, cuboids (including cubes), pyramids and spheres].	Recognise and differentiate between cubes, cuboids, cones, cylinders, pyramids and spheres. Recognise the faces of 3D shapes and name them, for example, square, rectangle.
	Lesson 3	
	To recognise and name common 2D and 3D shapes, including: ● 2D shapes [for example, rectangles (including squares), circles and triangles] ● 3D shapes [for example, cuboids (including cubes), pyramids and spheres].	Recognise and differentiate between cubes, cuboids, cones, cylinders, pyramids and spheres. Recognise the faces of 3D shapes and name them, for example, square, rectangle.
	Lesson 4	
	To recognise and name common 2D and 3D shapes, including: ● 2D shapes [for example, rectangles (including squares), circles and triangles] ● 3D shapes [for example, cuboids (including cubes), pyramids and spheres].	Recognise and differentiate between cubes, cuboids, cones, cylinders, pyramids and spheres. Recognise the faces of 3D shapes and name them, for example, square, rectangle.
	Lesson 5	
	To recognise and name common 2D and 3D shapes, including: ● 2D shapes [for example, rectangles (including squares), circles and triangles] ● 3D shapes [for example, as cuboids (including cubes), pyramids and spheres]	Recognise which shape comes next in a repeating pattern.

Preparation

Lesson 2: set up group activities as described in lessons 2 and 3

Lesson 3: set up group activities as described in lessons 2 and 3

You will need

General resources

Interactive activity 'Match a shape'

Equipment

A set of 3D shapes (cube, cuboid, pyramid, sphere, cone, cylinder) for each group, and containers for the shapes; sets of 2D shape tiles for each group (square, rectangle, triangle, circle); feely bags; Plasticine®; everyday materials (for model-making); glue; coloured sticky paper; sugar paper; scissors; construction kits; commercial packaging materials; 2D shape tiles (squares, rectangles, circles, triangles)

Further practice

Where children are unsure of the names and properties of 2D and 3D shapes, provide further experience of naming shapes and describing their properties, using, for example, a feely bag containing a shape.

Oral and mental starters for week 5

See bank of starters on pages 41 to 42. Oral and mental starters are also on the CD-ROM.

1	Counting to and from 10 then 20
2	Take turns counting
3	Counting circle
4	Count objects to 10

Overview of progression

Shape is introduced through 3D shapes. Children begin to recognise the shapes, name them, and to identify their properties, such as the shape and name of the faces. This introduces 2D shape. Children make models with the 3D shapes, and with construction kits and everyday materials. They learn about which shapes fit well together, which are good for building, and which are not so good for building. In Lesson 5 they work with 2D shape tiles, making repeating patterns. They name the shapes and identify which shape comes next, and next... in a pattern.

Watch out for

Children may confuse 2D shapes with 3D shapes, such as naming a cube a square, because what they see is the square face. In order to overcome this, encourage them to hold the 3D shape, to examine each of its faces, and to learn that these are properties of the 3D shape, which are described using 2D language. For example, a cube has six square faces, a cuboid has rectangular faces, two of which may be square.

Creative context

Work on patterns using 2D shape tiles can link with work in art. Children can make repeating patterns, using lines, blocks of colour, printing with shapes, and so on.

Vocabulary

build, **circle**, **cone**, corner, **cube**, **cuboid**, curved, **cylinder**, draw, edge, face, flat, group, hollow, make, **pattern**, point, predict, property, **pyramid**, **rectangle**, repeating pattern, set, shape, side, solid, sort, **sphere**, **square**, straight, **triangle**

Lesson 1   Oral and mental starter 1

Curriculum objectives
● To recognise and name common 3D shapes.

Success criteria
● I can name cubes, cuboids, cones, pyramids, cylinders and spheres.

You will need
Equipment
Set of 3D shapes for each group: cubes, cuboids, cylinders, cones, pyramids and spheres.

Differentiation
Less confident learners
Ask each child to work with a more confident talk partner within each group.
More confident learners
Encourage the children to write about the properties of a cube, cuboid, pyramid, sphere, cone and cylinder.

Main teaching activities

Whole-class work: Hold up a cube and ask: *What is this shape called? What can you tell me about this shape?* Encourage the children to describe its properties, such as: It has square faces; all the faces are the same size... Repeat this for other 3D shapes, including a sphere, cone and cylinder. Now introduce the cuboid and its name. Invite the children to tell you what they notice about its properties (such as its flat faces). Discuss how it is similar to, and how it is different from, a cube.

Group work: Provide each group with a set of 3D shapes. Ask the children to look carefully around the classroom and find something in the room that has the same shape as one of the 3D shapes. They should repeat this for each shape, drawing the correct objects under the headings 'cube', 'cuboid', 'cone', 'cylinder', pyramid and 'sphere'.

Progress check: Ask individual children the names of the shapes that they are using, and how they know that. Ask, for example: *What shape is that? How do you know? Find me another.*

Review

Review the shapes that the children drew, asking for examples from the classroom of cubes, cuboids, pyramids, spheres, cones and cylinders. Ask the children to explain how they recognise the items as having those specific shapes. Ask questions such as: *What shape is that? How do you know? What else did you find that was the same shape? What do you know about shapes like this?*

Curriculum objectives
● To recognise and name common 2D and 3D shapes.

Success criteria
● I can name cubes, cuboids, cones, pyramids, cylinders and spheres.
● I can name squares, rectangles, triangles and circles.

You will need
Equipment
A set of 3D shapes for each group, and containers for the shapes; sets of 2D shape tiles for each group; feely bags; Plasticine®; everyday materials (for model-making); glue; scissors; construction kits

Differentiation
Less confident learners
Decide whether to limit the range of shapes to a cube, cuboid, sphere and cone.
More confident learners
Challenge the children to make and describe a model using at least one each of a cube, cuboid, pyramid, sphere, cone and cylinder.

Lesson 2   Oral and mental starter 2

Main teaching activities

Whole-class work: Provide each group with a set of 3D shapes. Say: *I'm thinking of a shape and will describe it. Sort the shapes as I say each property. Put any shapes that do not fit the description back into the container.* Say, for example: *My shape has no curved faces. All its faces are the same shape. All its faces are the same size.* Repeat this for other shapes.

Group work: Children work in groups of four. Choose from this range of activities and the activities in lesson 3. You may wish to use them as a circus of activities for all the children to attempt.

Sort sets of shapes by given properties such as 'Has a curved face' and 'Has six faces'. Record the results by placing the shapes inside labelled circles.

Choose a 3D shape and either describe it orally or write a description of its properties.

Place some shapes inside a feely bag. Children take turns to feel a shape inside the bag and describe this to the group. The group then have to guess the shape.

Progress check: Ask the children to name the shape that they are using or making and to explain how they know it is that shape. For example:
- *What is that shape called?*
- *How do you know that it is a cube... and not a cuboid...?*

Review

Ask the children to describe the properties of the shapes they have been using. Ask individuals questions such as: *Which shapes have flat/curved faces? Which shapes have flat and curved faces?*

Curriculum objectives
● To recognise and name common 2D and 3D shapes.

Success criteria
● I can name squares, rectangles, triangles, circles, cubes, cuboids, cones, pyramids, cylinders, spheres.

You will need
General resources
Interactive activity 'Match a shape'

Equipment
3D shapes; sets of 2D shape tiles; feely bags; Plasticine®; glue; scissors; construction kits

Differentiation
Less confident learners
Work with children on the interactive 'Match a shape'. Concentrate on children's understanding of the shape vocabulary.

More confident learners
Children should complete the interactive 'Match the shape' and justify their decisions.

Curriculum objectives
● To recognise and name common 2D and 3D shapes.

Success criteria
● I can make models with 3D shapes.
● I know the names of the 3D shapes.
● I know the names of the models' faces.

You will need
Equipment
Construction kits; commercial packaging materials; a set of 3D shapes

Differentiation
Less confident learners
Ask an adult to work with the children and encourage them to discuss their work, using the vocabulary of shape.

More confident learners
Ask the children to draw what they have made, showing how the parts fit together.

Lesson 3
Oral and mental starter 2

Main teaching activities

Repeat the whole class activity from lesson 2, this time using 2D shape tiles. Say, for example: *My shape has four sides. All the sides are the same length. What is my shape?* Repeat for other 2D shapes.

Group work: Choose from this range of activities and the activities in lesson 2. You may wish to use them as a circus of activities for all the children to attempt.

Each child in a group has a feely bag containing a set of shapes. They take turns to feel inside their bag and name a shape by touch. The others have to find that shape by touch. When everyone is ready, they bring out their own design, then use the vocabulary of 3D shapes to describe what shapes they have used.

Use a variety of construction kits to make specific 3D shapes. Use Plasticine® to model specific 3D shapes.

Use everyday materials to build models of their own design, then use the vocabulary of 3D shapes to check that they were correct.

Progress check: Ask the children to name the faces of the shape that they are using or making and to explain how they know it is that shape. For example:
● *What is that shape called?*
● *What is the name of this face?*
● *How do you know it is a ...?*

Review

Ask the children to describe the properties of the shapes they have been using. Ask individuals questions such as: *Which shapes are good for making models? Why is that? Think of a rectangle in your head. Can you see it? Tell me about it.*

Lesson 4
Oral and mental starter 3

Main teaching activities

Whole-class work: Remind the children of the work they did on shapes in previous lessons. Hold up a cube and say: *What shape is this? What shape is this face? What shape are all of the faces of a cube?* Agree that each face is a square, and hold up a square tile. Repeat this for a cuboid, using the rectangle tile (and if appropriate, the square as well). Discuss how the cuboid has six faces, with opposite faces matching and all faces either rectangular or square. Hold up the cylinder. The children should observe that the ends are circular. Elicit or explain the idea that the curved surface could be spread out to make a rectangle. Roll up a rectangular sheet of paper into a cylinder, and show the children that the hole at each end is circular. Discuss how the cone has a circle as one face.

Discuss which 3D shapes are good for making models. Ask: *Which shapes have flat/curved faces? Which shapes would be good/bad at the bottom of a tower? Why?*

Group work: The children work in pairs, making a model of a castle with a construction kit and/or commercial packaging materials. Ask them to explain why they have used 3D shapes in particular places, referring to the properties of these shapes.

Progress check: Ask: *Why did you choose to put that shape there? Would this shape have worked just as well? Why do you think that?*

Review

Choose some children to demonstrate what they have made and describe the shapes they have used. Ask: *What shapes can you see? Which have curved/flat faces? Which shapes can you think of that have both curved and flat faces?*

 SCHOLASTIC

Curriculum objectives

● To recognise and name common 2D and 3D shapes, including: 2D shapes [rectangles (including squares), circles and triangles]; 3D shapes [cuboids (including cubes), pyramids and spheres].

Success criteria

● I can make a repeating pattern.
● I can say which shape comes next in a repeating pattern.

You will need

Equipment

2D shape tiles (squares, rectangles, circles, triangles); coloured sticky paper; sugar paper; glue; scissors

Differentiation

Less confident learners

Limit the range of shape tiles to two types initially, so that the children can confidently construct AB or AAB type patterns before moving on.

More confident learners

Challenge the children to make more complex patterns, as shown in the example right.

Lesson 5   Oral and mental starter 4

Main teaching activities

Whole-class work: Use 2D shape tiles. Display a square, rectangle, square and rectangle. Ask: *Which shape should come next? Why?* Now display a square, circle, triangle, square, circle and triangle. Discuss this repeating pattern.

Paired work: Provide shape tiles, scissors and sticky coloured paper. The children work in pairs to make a pattern with the shape tiles. They then cut out the shapes, using the shape tiles as templates, and stick their pattern onto sugar paper. Encourage them to make three different repeating patterns.

Progress check: Invite individual children to 'say' their pattern, such as square, square, rectangle, square. Ask questions such as:

- What would come next in your pattern?
- What would come after that?
- Tell me how you know that.

Review

Review some of the patterns that the children made, choosing examples from each ability range. Ask questions such as: *What shapes are there in this pattern? Who can 'say' the pattern? What comes before/after the ...?*

Make a repeating pattern with some shapes to show the children. Now ask them to shut their eyes. Remove two pieces from the pattern and close the gaps. Say: *Open your eyes. What is wrong with my pattern?* Repeat this for other patterns, checking that the children can 'read' each pattern and identify faults.

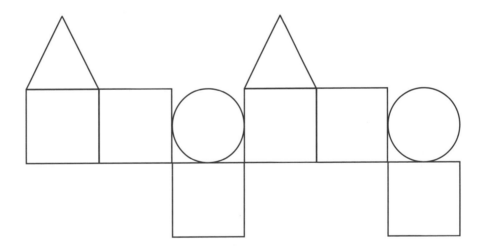

Addition and subtraction to 10

Expected prior learning

Children should be able to:
- read and write addition, subtraction and equals signs
- begin to know addition and subtraction facts to 5.

Topic	Curriculum objectives	Expected outcomes
Addition and subtraction	**Lesson 1**	
	To read, write and interpret mathematical statements involving addition (+), subtraction (−) and equals (=) signs. To add and subtract one-digit and two-digit numbers to 20, including zero.	Write addition and subtraction sentences using +, − and =. Begin to know addition and subtraction facts to 10.
	Lesson 2	
	To read, write and interpret mathematical statements involving addition (+), subtraction (−) and equals (=) signs. To add and subtract one-digit and two-digit numbers to 20, including zero.	Write addition and subtraction sentences using +, − and =. Begin to know addition and subtraction facts to 10.
	Lesson 3	
	To read, write and interpret mathematical statements involving addition (+), subtraction (−) and equals (=) signs. To represent and use number bonds and related subtraction facts within 20. To add and subtract one-digit and two-digit numbers to 20, including zero.	Write addition and subtraction sentences using +, − and =. From a number trio, such as 3, 5 and 8, make two addition and two subtraction sentences. Begin to know addition and subtraction facts to 10.
	Lesson 4	
	To read, write and interpret mathematical statements involving addition (+), subtraction (−) and equals (=) signs. To represent and use number bonds and related subtraction facts within 20. To add and subtract one-digit and two-digit numbers to 20, including zero.	Write addition and subtraction sentences using +, − and =. From a number trio, such as 3, 5 and 8, make two addition and two subtraction sentences. Begin to know addition and subtraction facts to 10.
	Lesson 5	
	To solve one-step problems that involve addition and subtraction, using concrete objects and pictorial representations, and missing number problems such as $7 = \square - 9$.	Solve simple missing number problems using addition and subtraction facts known, and objects or counting on or back to find the missing number.

■ SCHOLASTIC

Preparation

Lesson 1: select sets of number cards 0–10, one set for each pair

Lesson 2: select sets of number cards 0–10, one set for each pair

Lesson 3: select sets of number cards 0–10, one set for each pair

Lesson 4: select sets of number cards 0–10, one set for each pair

Lesson 5: copy 'Missing numbers: addition and subtraction' for each child; copy and enlarge 'Missing numbers: addition and subtraction'

You will need

Photocopiable sheets
'Missing numbers: addition and subtraction'

General resources
'Number cards 0–20'

Equipment
Interlocking cubes

Further practice

Photocopiable sheets
'Addition to 9 and 10';
'Addition to 10'; 'Subtraction from 9 and 10'

Oral and mental starters for week 6

See bank of starters on pages 41 to 42. Oral and mental starters are also on the CD-ROM.

8 Write the answer for addition to 5

10 Write the answer for subtract facts within 5

11 Complements of 10

12 Add facts 6 to 10

Overview of progression

Children begin the week with finding complements to 10, such as 7 + 3, 9 + 1, and 10 − 7, 10 − 9, and so on, then practise using these facts so that they begin to memorise them. They then extend their knowledge with number facts that total up to 10, ordering the facts, so that they begin to see patterns, such as 7 + 0, 7 + 1, and so on, and the corresponding subtraction facts. They solve missing number problems using both complements to 10 facts, and number facts that total up to 10.

Watch out for

Check that where children are counting using concrete materials to find the solutions, they count on from the larger number for addition, and count back for subtraction. Check that they do not 'count all', starting from the beginning each time.

Creative context

Encourage the children, as a class, and as part of English lessons, to invent a number story for each of the complements to ten. These can be simple stories such as four girls walk into the playground. Then six boys walk into the playground. Now there are ten children in the playground altogether. These can be ordered, starting with zero and ten, and placed on the classroom wall.

Vocabulary

add, altogether, answer, as many as, count, difference, equals (=), equal to, explain, first, how many?, how many fewer is ___ than ___?, how many more is ___ than ___?, how many more to make?, how much less is ___?, how much more is ___?, leaves, makes, minus (−), number sentence, ones, operation, **pattern**, plus (+), read, record, second, show me, sign, subtract, sum, take away, tens, the same number as, third, total, what is the difference between?, write

Curriculum objectives
● To read, write and interpret mathematical statements involving addition (+), subtraction (−) and equals (=) signs.
● To add and subtract 1-digit numbers to 10, including zero.

Success criteria
● I can find all addition and subtraction facts to 10.

You will need
General resources
'Number cards 0–20'

Differentiation
Less confident learners
For each card drawn, encourage the children to say the complete addition sentence.

More confident learners
Challenge the children to think of the partner addition sentence. For example, for 6 + 4 they would also say and write 4 + 6 = 10.

Lesson I
Oral and mental starter 8

Main teaching activities

Whole-class work: Ask the children to suggest some addition facts, such as 8 + 2, 6 + 4. Write on the board 0 + ☐ = 10 and ask: *What fits here?* Agree that 0 + 10 = 10. Now write up 1 + ☐ = 10 underneath and ask for the answer. Repeat for all the facts to 10 + 0 = 10.

Now ask the children to look carefully at the facts. Ask: *Can you see some facts which use the same numbers?* Agree that 0 + 10 and 10 + 0, 1 + 9 and 9 + 1... use the same numbers. Ask: *Which fact does not have a partner? What is special about 5 + 5?* Agree that it is a double so it does not have a partner. Before the group activity, remove the recording from the board.

Paired work: The children shuffle a set of 0–10 number cards, take turns to take a card, and say an addition fact that has a total of 10. For example, if they draw the card 6, then they say 6 + 4 = 10. Ask them to write an addition sentence for each card number.

Progress check: Ask the children to look at their addition sentences and then ask:
● *How did you find the number sentence for the card with 7 on it?*
● *What other addition number sentence can we make with the numbers 7, 3 and 10?*
Repeat this for other cards.

Review

Ask addition questions with the answer of 10. For example: *What is 5 + 5? 8 + 2? I have six sweets. My sister gives me another four sweets. How many do I have now?*

Curriculum objective
● To read, write and interpret mathematical statements involving addition (+), subtraction (−) and equals (=) signs.
● To add and subtract 1-digit numbers to 10, including zero.

Success criteria
● I can find all addition and subtraction facts to 10.

You will need
General resources
'Number cards 0–20'
Equipment
Interlocking cubes

Differentiation
Less confident learners
Decide whether to provide 10 interlocking cubes for each child so that they can model the subtraction sentence.

More confident learners
Encourage the children to work mentally, counting back in their heads. Ask them to come up with a problem to match their number sentence.

Lesson 2
Oral and mental starter 9

Main teaching activities

Whole-class work: Repeat the whole-class activity from lesson 1, this time for subtraction from 10. Ask the children to count back from 10 each time to find the answer. Write 10 − 0 = ☐ and ask for the answer. Continue until all the facts to 10 − 10 = ☐ have been completed.

Paired work: Ask the children to work with a partner. They shuffle all the 0 to 10 cards then turn them face down on the table. They take turns to pick up a card, and both write the subtraction sentence and answer. For example, for the card 6, they write 10 − 6 = 4. Ask them to discard the card that they turn over, so that they only choose each card once. Ask the children to work together to find a corresponding addition sentence for each subtraction one. For 10 − 8 = 2 they would write either 8 + 2 = 10 or 2 + 8 = 10.

Progress check: Check that the children are confident with the strategy for subtraction that they are using, whether this is counting back, using cubes, or counting back mentally. Ask, for example:
● *Tell me one of your subtraction sentences.*
● *So for 10 − 8 the answer is 2. What other subtraction sentence can we make with these numbers?*

Review

Invite a child to read one of their subtraction sentences, apart from the answer. The other children calculate the answer. Ask:
● *Do you agree with the answer?*
● *How did you work that out?*
● *Who used a different way?*
● *Tell me another subtraction sentence using those three numbers.*
Repeat this for other subtraction sentences.

Curriculum objectives

● To read, write and interpret mathematical statements involving addition (+), subtraction (−) and equals (=) signs.
● To represent and use number bonds and related subtraction facts within 10.
● To add and subtract 1-digit numbers to 10, including zero.

Success criteria

● I can use the addition, subtraction and equals signs to write number sentences.
● I am beginning to know the answers to addition facts to 10.

You will need

General resources
'Number cards 0–20'

Differentiation

Less confident learners

Ask the children to work with more confident partners, so that they can model the sentences together.

More confident learners

Extend to the 0–9 cards. This will produce additions of numbers up to 9 + 8.

Lesson 3
Oral and mental starter 8

Main teaching activities

Whole-class work: Write these number sentences on the board and invite the children to give the answers.

Ask: *What do you notice about these number sentences?* Encourage the children to say that the numbers added are the same, but in a different order, and that the answer to both number sentences is the same. Repeat this for other examples, such as: 4 + 3 and 3 + 4; 8 + 2 and 2 + 8.

$$2 + 6 =$$
$$6 + 2 =$$

Group work: Provide each pair of children with a set of number cards 0–9. Ask them to turn the cards face up on the table. They take turns to choose two cards each time which total up to, and no more than, 10. They write an addition number sentence.

Progress check: Ask the children to review their number sentences, and then ask:

● *What is 4 + 4?*
● *How did you work this out?*

Check that the children are using addition strategies of counting on from the larger number confidently.

Review

Invite pairs of children to write one of their sum pairs on the board. Discuss that it does not matter which order the numbers are added in. Remind them that if they know, say, 6 + 3 = 9, then they can also work out that 3 + 6 = 9.

Curriculum objectives

● To read, write and interpret mathematical statements involving addition (+), subtraction (−) and equals (=) signs.
● To represent and use number bonds and related subtraction facts within 10.
● To add and subtract 1-digit numbers to 10, including zero.

Success criteria

● I can work out subtraction facts to 10.

You will need

General resources
'Number cards 0–20'

Differentiation

Less confident learners

Ask the children to work with more confident partners, so that they can model the sentences together.

More confident learners

Encourage the children to work mentally, counting back in their heads, to find the answer.

Lesson 4
Oral and mental starter 11

Main teaching activities

Whole-class work: Explain that in this lesson, children will be using take away to find answers, up to 9. Write on the board: 7 − 3 = ☐. Invite a child to explain how they can find the answer and agree that it can be found by counting back 3 from 7. Together say: *7 take away 3: 7 and 6, 5, 4. So 7 take away 3 leaves 4.* Repeat for another example, such as 8 − 6. Check that the children are counting back, and not counting any number twice.

Paired work: The children shuffle the 0–9 number cards. They spread these out face down, then take turns to pick two cards at random. They write a subtraction sentence, for example, for the cards 2 and 7, they write 7 − 2 = ☐

Progress check: Check that the children understand that even if they pick up the smaller number first, they are to take this away from the larger number that they pick up. So, for 2 and 9 they write 9 − 2, and so on. Ask, for example:

● *What is 8 take away 5?*
● *How did you work that out?*

Review

Ask the children to work in groups of three or four. Explain that you will say a subtraction sentence. Ask:

● *What is 8 take away 1?*
● *What is 9 minus 2?*
● *How did you work that out? Who used a different way?*
● *Did everyone in your group use the same method to find the answer?*

Curriculum objectives
● To solve simple problems that involve addition and subtraction, using concrete objects and pictorial representations, and missing number problems.

Success criteria
● I can find the answer to missing number problems.

You will need
Photocopiable sheets

'Missing numbers: addition and subtraction'

Equipment

Interlocking cubes

Differentiation

Less confident learners

Decide whether to ask an adult to work with this group. The children can use interlocking cubes to model each question. Then, with the adult, they count forward or back to the answer from the starting number to find the missing number. They then say the completed number sentence together.

More confident learners

Ask the children to set some addition and subtraction word problems for others to solve independently or during the Review section.

Lesson 5   Oral and mental starter 11

Main teaching activities

Whole-class work: Explain that in this lesson the children will find answers to addition and subtraction where there is a missing number. On the board write: 5 + ☐ = 8. Ask: *What number goes in the box? How can we work this out?* Discuss how by counting up from 5 they can find the missing number. Say: *5 and 6, 7, 8. How many did we count on? So 5 add 3 is 8.* Children may find it helpful at this stage to keep count on their fingers. Repeat this for another example, such as 6 + ☐ = 10.

Now give a subtraction example, such as 8 − ☐ = 4. Ask: *How can we work this out?* Ask the children to count back from 8 to 4, and to keep a count of how many they count back on their fingers. Say together: *8 and 7, 6, 5, 4. So we counted back 4. 8 take away 4 leaves 4.* Repeat for 7 − 2.

Independent work: Provide the photocopiable page 'Missing numbers: addition and subtraction' from the CD-ROM. In these examples, the missing number is always the second number, for simplicity at this stage. Suggest to the children that they count back using their fingers. For those who still need concrete materials provide interlocking cubes.

Progress check: After a few minutes review the first question together. Say:
- *The question reads 5 take away something leaves 3. How did you work this out?*
- *Who used a different way?*
- *Let's count back together to check: 5 and 4, 3. So 5 take away 2 leaves 3.*

Decide whether to review the next question, which is for addition.

Independent work: Children finish the photocopiable sheet. For any child who needs help with this, provide some interlocking cubes, so that they can model each question.

Review

Show the A3 enlargement of 'Missing numbers: addition and subtraction'. Review each question together. Ask, for example, for number 3:
- *4 add something is 8. How did you find the missing number?*
- *Let's count on to check. 4 and 5, 6, 7, 8. So we counted on 4. So 4 add 4 makes 8.*

Repeat this for the other examples. Give extra praise where children 'knew' the answer, so as to encourage rapid recall.

Now say: *Jon has ten marbles. He gives some marbles to Harry. Jon has three marbles left. How many marbles does Harry have?* Discuss ways of finding the answer. Encourage counting back from 10 to 3. Some of the more confident children may have recall of the complement of 10, that is 3 + 7 = 10, and 10 − 7 = 3. Repeat this for another example, such as *Sally has eight grapes. She gives some to Daisy. Now Sally has five grapes. How many does Daisy have?*

Curriculum objectives
● To count to and across 100, forwards and backwards, beginning with 0 or 1, or from any given number.

You will need

1 Check

Oral and mental starter

1 Counting to and from 10 then 20

2. Assess
'Number cards 0–20'

3. Further practice

Oral and mental starters

2 Take turns counting

3 Counting circle

4 Count objects to 10

Counting to and from 10 then 20

Most children should be able to count to 20.

Some children will not have made such progress and will require additional practice of counting to 10, then to 20.

1. Check

1 Counting to and from 10 then 20

Keep the counting pace sharp. Encourage everyone to join in. Observe who counts confidently and who needs further practice. Extend the count to beyond 20 for the more confident children.

- *If I say 7... 13... 19, what is the next number in the count?*
- *Counting back: If I say 15... 10... 3, what is the next number in the count?*
- *If we start counting on 4, what is the next number that we say?*

2. Assess

Provide groups of four children with sets of 0 to 20 number cards. Ask the children to shuffle the cards, then spread the cards out so that all can be seen on the table top. They take the number 10 card and place it on its own. They then take turns to choose a card and place it on the table where they think it will fit in the number line, using the 10-card to help them. Ask them to check where the others in their group place their cards, to ensure that the number line grows correctly. Record the outcomes.

3. Further practice

Use the suggested OMS to provide further reinforcement of counting to 20 and back.

Curriculum objectives
● When given a number, to identify one more and one less.

You will need

1. Check

Oral and mental starter

6 Writing numbers

2. Assess
'Number cards 0–20'

3. Further practice

Oral and mental starters

3 Counting circle

5 Reading and ordering numerals to 10, then 20

General resources

Interactive activity 'More and less'

Photocopiable sheets

'One more and one less (1)'

One more and one less

Most children should be able to say the number that is one more or one less than a given number.

Some children will not have made such progress and will require additional practice counting forwards and backwards.

1. Check

6 Writing numbers

Encourage the children to respond quickly to writing the numbers that are one more or one less. Observe which children are confident, and which need further practice. Extend to numbers to 20 for the more confident children.

- *How did you work that out?*
- *Which number comes next... and next?*

2. Assess

Provide pairs with a set of shuffled number cards 1–19. They take turns to turn over a card and say the number that is one less and then the number that is one more. Their partner checks to see if they agree. Challenge them to work quickly so that they use recall or a mental number line rather than counting to find the answer. They can write their answers on paper, writing headings 'One more', 'Number', 'One less'. Record the outcomes.

3. Further practice

Use the suggested OMS to provide further reinforcement for recalling one more and one less numbers. Using photocopiable page 'One more and one less (1)' from page 43 and the interactive activity 'More and less' on the CD-ROM, give further experience of finding numbers that are one more or one less than numbers from 0 to 20.

Curriculum objectives
● To add and subtract one-digit and two-digit numbers to 20, including zero.

You will need
1. Check

Oral and mental starter

7 Add facts to 5

9 Subtract facts within 5

2. Assess
'Number cards 0–20' (cards 1–5)

3. Further practice

Oral and mental starters

8 Write the answer for addition to 5

10 Write the answer for subtract facts within 5

Photocopiable sheets
'Adding to 5'; 'Subtracting within 5'

Add and subtract to 5

Most children should be able to recall the addition and subtraction facts to 5.

Some children will not have made such progress and will require additional practice, using fingers to count on or back, and then mental number lines to find the answers.

1. Check

7 Add facts to 5

9 Subtract facts within 5

Use both oral and mental starters, separately and then together, with addition and subtraction facts to 5 mixed. Observe which children are confident and which need further practice. Extend to facts to 10 for more confident children.

- *Tell me an addition sentence with the answer 4.*
- *Tell me another.*
- *Tell me a subtraction sentence with the answer 4.*

2. Assess

Less confident children may use their fingers or a number line. Provide each pair with number cards 1–5, shuffled. They take turns to turn over a card and write an addition sentence, and then a subtraction sentence that includes the card number. Challenge them to do this quickly, checking each other's answers. Check that they use the symbols +,− and = correctly. Record the outcomes.

3. Further practice

Use the suggested OMS to provide further reinforcement for developing recall of facts to 5. The listed photocopiables on pages 44 and 45 give further practice in reading number sentences and finding answers to facts to 5.

Curriculum objectives
● To recognise and name common 2D and 3D shapes, including: rectangles (including squares), circles and triangles; cuboids (including cubes), pyramids and spheres.

You will need
1. Check

Oral and mental starter

13 Find that 3D shape

2. Assess
Sets of 3D shapes, such as cubes, cuboids, spheres, pyramids, cylinders and cones; opaque bags

3. Further practice

Oral and mental starters

14 Which shape is it?

15 Feely bag shape

Properties of 3D shapes

Most children should be able to name the common 3D shapes.

Some children will not have made such progress and will require more practice at naming the shapes and recognising them by their properties.

1. Check

13 Find that 3D shape

Encourage the children to explain how they know that, for example, a cube is a cube and not a cuboid. Observe which children are confident and which need further practice. Extend the more confident children by including shapes such as a cylinder and a cone.

- *How do you know this is a cube?*
- *Which shapes have six faces?*
- *Which shape has six rectangles for faces?*

2. Assess

Ask the children to work in pairs, with a set of 3D shapes in an opaque bag. They take turns to hold a shape and say some of its properties. Their partner says the name of the shape once they recognise it. Less confident children may still say a 2D name for a 3D shape, such as 'square' for 'cube'. Give further experience of recognising the faces of a shape, naming those and saying the shape's name. For the more confident children include a cone and cylinder in the bag. Record the outcomes.

3. Further practice

Use the suggested OMS to provide further reinforcement for developing understanding of shapes and their properties.

Oral and mental starters

Number and place value

Counting to and from 10 then 20

Ask the children to sit in a circle. Count together from zero up to 10. At first you may do much of the counting. As the children become more confident, quicken the pace slightly of the counting, and ask the children to lightly tap on their knees as they count.

Take turns counting

Ask the children to count together with you from 0 to 10 and back again. When they are confident with this, count again – but this time each child takes a turn to say the next number. Carry on up to 10, then back to 0, back up to 10 and so on until everyone has had a turn. Keep the pace sharp.

Counting circle

Ask the children to sit in a circle and count together from 0 to at least 20 and back again. Now ask them to count around the circle, starting from 0. If a child falters, say the number yourself to keep the counting pace sharp. Ask: *If Paul says 5, who will say 10?*

Now, starting with any small number, ask the children to count around the circle to at least 20 and back. Ask questions, e.g. *If I count on 5 from 7, what numbers will I say? If I count on 6 from 9, on what number will I stop?*

Count objects to 10

Give each child a laminated copy of 'Work Mat' from the CD-ROM. Provide ten cubes for each child. Say: *Count out five cubes onto your mat. Check there are five by counting again. Put one back into the pot. Count how many are on your mat now. Put two more onto your mat. How many cubes are there now? (and so on.)*

Repeat this for different starting numbers, keeping the quantity of cubes to between 3 and 10. Invite various children to answer your questions. Check that the children use the 'touch, move and count' process.

Reading and ordering numerals to 10, then 20

Shuffle some 0–9 number cards. Explain that you will hold up a number card. Ask the children to put their hands up to read the number. Ask the child who answers correctly to stand at the front of the class and hold the number card. Repeat this until all the number cards are being held.

Now ask the children to help you to order the cards. Agree where zero goes. Now say: *What number comes next? Who is holding that number?* Continue until all the number cards are in order.

Writing numbers

Explain that when you say a number, you would like the children to write it on their whiteboards. When you say *Show me*, the children should hold up their boards to show you their written number. Say: *Write 3... 8... 10... 15... Show me. Write the number that is one more than ___ . Show me. Write the number that is one less than ___ . Show me.* Extend to 'teens' numbers.

Addition and subtraction

7 Add facts to 5

Use the cards from photocopiable page 'Add facts to 5' from the CD-ROM. Explain that you will hold up a card and would like the children to show you the answer using their fingers. Encourage the children to respond quickly, so that they can demonstrate that they are beginning to recall these facts.

8 Write the answer for addition to 5

Repeat OMS 7 'Add facts to 5'. This time the children write their responses on their individual whiteboards. When you say *Show me*, they hold their boards up for you to see their answers.

9 Subtract facts within 5

Use the cards from photocopiable page 'Take away facts to 5' from the CD-ROM. Explain that you will hold up a card and would like the children to show you the answer, using their fingers. Encourage the children to respond quickly, so that they can demonstrate that they are beginning to recall these facts.

10 Write the answer for subtract facts within 5

Repeat OMS 9 'Subtraction facts within 5'. This time the children write their responses on their individual whiteboards. When you say *Show me*, they hold their boards up for you to see their answers.

11 Complements of 10

Show the teaching set of the cards from photocopiable page 'Complements of 10' from the CD-ROM. Explain that you will hold up a card and you would like the children to show you the answer by holding up their fingers. For example, for the card '4 + ☐ = 10', they would hold up six fingers.

12 Add facts 6 to 10

Provide the children with individual whiteboards and pens. Explain that you will show them an addition sentence. Ask them to write answers on the whiteboards and to hold up their boards when you say *Show me*.

Geometry

13 Find that 3D shape

Put a set of 3D shapes on each table, including cube, cuboid, sphere and pyramid. Explain that you will say the name of a shape. The children in groups identify the shape. When you say *Show me*, one of the children holds up the shape. Ask questions such as *How do you know that this shape is a ...? How many faces does it have?*

14 Which shape is it?

Explain that you will say some properties of a shape that you have hidden in a bag. Ask the children to put up their hands when they think they recognise the shape. Say, for example, for a cube:
- *My shape has six faces.*
- *All the faces are the same shape.*
- *All the faces are the same size.*

Ask questions about the shape, such as:
- *What shape are the faces?*
- *What other shape has six faces?*
- Repeat for other shapes.

15 Feely bag shape

Ask a child to feel the shape hidden in a bag. The other children ask questions until they can say which shape it is. Repeat for other shapes. Ask questions such as: *Which shapes have six faces? Which shape has no flat faces? Which shape has triangles for some of its faces?*

Name: _____   Date: _____

One more and one less (1)

- Write the number that is one more.
- Write the number that is one less.

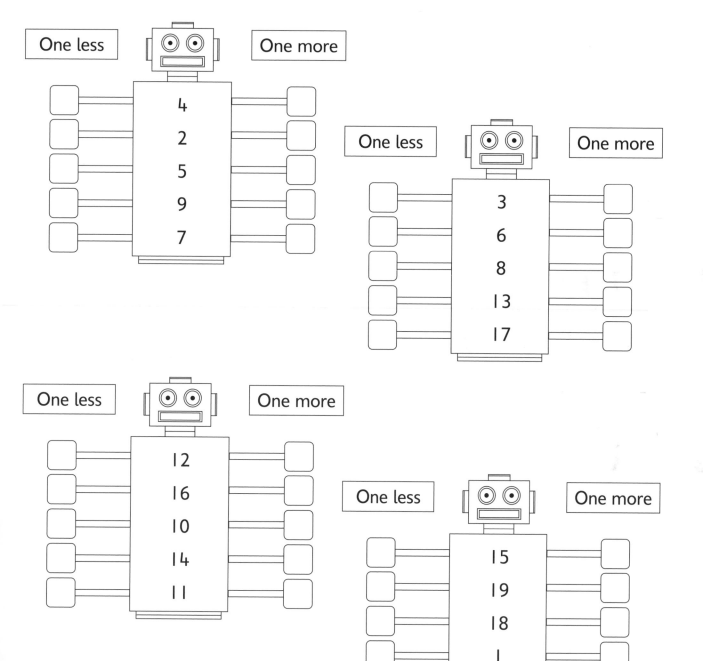

Adding to 5

- Add the numbers on the cars.
- Join the car to its answer on the petrol pump.

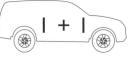 1 + 1

 4

 0 + 1

2

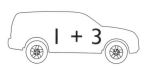 1 + 3

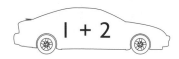 1 + 2

 4

5

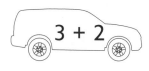 3 + 2

2

 2 + 0

 5

 3 + 0

1

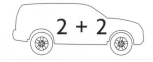 2 + 2

 4

5

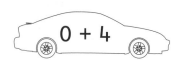 0 + 4

 3

3

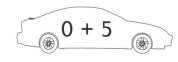 0 + 5

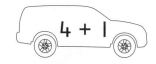 4 + 1

4

 3

I know all addition facts with a total up to 5.

How did you do?

PHOTOCOPIABLE

SCHOLASTIC
www.scholastic.co.uk

Name: _____ Date: _____

Subtracting within 5

- Find the answer to each take away.
- Join the puppy to the answer on the basket.

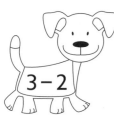 $3 - 2$

 3

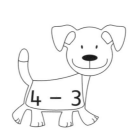 $4 - 3$

 0

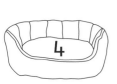 4

 $3 - 1$

 0

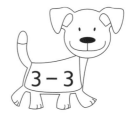 $3 - 3$

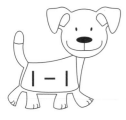 $1 - 1$

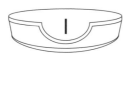 1

 $3 - 0$

 1

 2

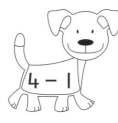 $4 - 1$

 $5 - 1$

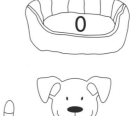 0

 $5 - 3$

 $5 - 4$

 2

 $5 - 2$ / 3

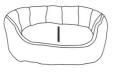 1

 5

 $5 - 5$

 3

 $5 - 0$

I know all subtraction facts up to 5.

How did you do?

Name: _____   Date: _____

Counting how many

- Write how many in the box.

I can count to at least ten.

How did you do?

PHOTOCOPIABLE

Counting and number order

Expected prior learning

Children should be able to:

- count to at least 30 and back
- count objects to 10
- read and write numbers to 10.

Topic	Curriculum objectives	Expected outcomes
Number and place value	**Lesson 1**	
	To count to and across 100, forwards and backwards, beginning with 0 or 1, or from any given number. To count, read and write numbers to 100 in numerals, count in multiples of twos, fives and tens.	Count to 50 and back in ones. Use ordinal number to compare and order numbers.
	Lesson 2	
	To count to and across 100, forwards and backwards, beginning with 0 or 1, or from any given number. To count, read and write numbers to 100 in numerals, count in multiples of twos, fives and tens.	Count to 50 and back in ones. Use ordinal number to compare and order numbers.
	Lesson 3	
	To identify and represent numbers using objects and pictorial representations including the number line, and use the language of: equal to, more than, less than (fewer), most, least. To read and write numbers from 1 to 20 in numerals and words.	Count objects and pictures to 20. Use the vocabulary of comparing quantities and numbers. Read and write number digits up to 20.
	Lesson 4	
	To identify and represent numbers using objects and pictorial representations including the number line, and use the language of: equal to, more than, less than (fewer), most, least. To read and write numbers from 1 to 20 in numerals and words.	Count along a number line. Use the vocabulary of comparing quantities and numbers. Read and write number digits up to 20.
	Lesson 5	
	To identify and represent numbers using objects and pictorial representations including the number line, and use the language of: equal to, more than, less than (fewer), most, least. To read and write numbers from 1 to 20 in numerals and words.	Count along a number line. Use the vocabulary of comparing numbers. Read and write number digits up to 20.

Preparation

Lesson 2: copy and enlarge 'Ordering'; copy 'Ordering' for each child to A3

Lesson 3: prepare the transparent containers of items to be estimated; copy 'Estimate and count' per child

Lesson 4: prepare number cards 0–30, one set of all cards per group; copy the appropriate version of 'Number monsters' for each child

Lesson 5: prepare number cards 0–20, one set of all cards per pair; prepare number cards 21–30 for more confident children; draw a blank number line onto an A3 sheet of paper, one per group

You will need

Photocopiable sheets

'Ordering'; Estimate and count'; 'Number monsters'

General resources

'Work mat'; 'Number cards 0–20'; interactive teaching resource 'Number line'

Equipment

Blank number lines; a big book or poster; reading book for each child; interlocking cubes; set of about eight transparent containers that contain, for example, 20 cubes, 15 counters, 10 dice, 26 marbles, 18 pieces of pasta, 14 conkers, 30 beads and 23 buttons; picture (from a big book or poster) of items that can be counted; about 30 counters for each pair of children; about 20 cubes for each child; washing line and pegs

Further practice

Photocopiable sheets

'Counting pictures'; 'Ordinal numbers'

Oral and mental starters for week 1

See bank of starters on pages 84 to 85. Oral and mental starters are also on the CD-ROM.

16 Counting to 50

17 Counting pictures

19 Write that number

Overview of progression

Children begin the week with counting to 50 and back. They use ordinal numbers to describe the position of a person or an object, in a line. They count objects to 20, using the coordinated touch, count, and move method, and count pictures by pointing. They place numbers to 20 on a number line, and read and write number digits to 20.

> ### Watch out for
> Check that children count each object just once, and recognise that the last number in the count represents how many there are. If children are unsure about the placement of numbers on a number line, work with numbers to 10, then gradually extend this to up to 20.

Creative context

Children can use their counting skills in, for example, science, counting in topics such as minibeasts.

Vocabulary

add, altogether, answer, compare, count, explain, leaves, makes, minus (−), number sentence, operation, order, **pattern**, plus (+), read, record, show me, sign, subtract, sum, take away, total, write

Curriculum objectives
- To count to 50, forwards and backwards, beginning with 0 or 1, or from any given number.
- To count, read and write numbers to 50 in numerals.

Success criteria
- I can count to 50 and back.
- I can use numbers to show position.

You will need

Equipment

A big book; a reading book for each child

Differentiation

Less confident learners

Work with these children as a group, using a big book that they can all see.

More confident learners

Challenge the children to find the pages, words and letters between the eighth and the twelfth.

Lesson 1   Oral and mental starter 16

Main teaching activities

Whole-class work: Ask five children to stand at the front of the class, in a line. Invite the other children to count them, going from left to right. Now ask: *Who is first? Who is second? Who is last in the line? Who is between the third and the fifth...?*

Repeat this with a line of ten children. Say: *Sangeeta, change places with the fifth person; Tom, change places with the person between the sixth and the eighth...*

On the board, show the children how to record using numerals: 1st, 2nd, 3rd, 4th....

Group work: Ask the children to work in pairs. They will need a reading book and some paper for recording. Ask them to find the tenth page in the book and then to record the tenth letter on that page and the tenth word on that page. They can repeat this for eighth, twelfth, fifteenth and twentieth.

Progress check: Ask ten children to stand in a line. Invite the other children to say who is 1st, 2nd, 9th, and so on. Check that they understand that they can count to find the ordinal number position.

Review

Use a big book. Invite individuals to help you find the fifth page, word and letter. Repeat with, for example, the sixth, ninth, eleventh.... Each time, ask a child to write the ordinal number on the board: 5th, 6th, 9th, 11th....

Count to 50 and back. Keep the pace sharp by asking the children to quietly tap their knees in time with the count.

Curriculum objectives
- To count to 50, forwards and backwards, beginning with 0 or 1, or from any given number.
- To count, read and write numbers to 50 in numerals.

Success criteria
- I can count to 50 and back.
- I can use numbers to show position.

You will need

Photocopiable sheets

'Ordering'

General resource

'Work mat'

Equipment

Interlocking cubes

Differentiation

Less confident learners

Complete the activity as a group. Encourage the children to use positional vocabulary.

More confident learners

Put some different-coloured cubes in a line and ask each other questions about the positions of the cubes.

Lesson 2   Oral and mental starter 16

Main teaching activities

Whole-class work: Provide each group with some coloured interlocking cubes and each child with a copy of photocopiable page 'Work mat' from the CD-ROM. Explain that you will ask them to put out a line of cubes. Say: *Put out ten cubes in a straight line, all the same colour. Now take a different-coloured cube and swap it with the sixth cube. Now do the same with the ninth cube.* Repeat this, extending the number of cubes to up to 20.

Group work: Provide copies of the photocopiable page 'Ordering' from the CD-ROM. Read the sheet through together so that the children recognise any new vocabulary. The children work individually to complete the sheet.

Progress check: Invite eight children to stand in a line in front of the class. Ask questions from the photocopiable page: *Who is first? Who is last? Who is next to last? Who is between ... and ...? Who is just in front of ...? What place is ... in?*

Review

Use the A3 version of 'Ordering' to review the activity. Ask questions such as: *Who is one place before/after sixth? Who is last? Who is first? Who is in between fifth place and eighth place?*

Say: *We have been learning to count. How far can you count? How many objects do you think you can count accurately? What do you need to learn to do now? Tell your partner.*

Repeat counting to 50 and back from the starter. Keep the pace sharp by asking the children to quietly tap their knees in time with the count.

Curriculum objectives

● To read and write numbers from 1 to 20 in numerals and words.
● To use the language of: more than, less than (fewer).

Success criteria

● I can read and write numbers up to 20.
● I can count objects and pictures to 20.
● I can count using a number line.

You will need

Photocopiable sheets

'Estimate and count'

Equipment

Set of about eight transparent containers that contain, for example, 20 cubes, 15 counters, 10 dice, 26 marbles, 18 pieces of pasta, 14 conkers, 30 beads and 23 buttons; picture (from a Big Book or poster) of items that can be counted; about 30 counters for each pair of children; about 20 cubes for each child

Differentiation

Less confident learners

Support children's counting using counting objects or number lines.

More confident learners

Suggest that the children try counting the items in twos.

Lesson 3
Oral and mental starter 17

Main teaching activities

Whole-class work: Explain that you have some containers with between 10 and 30 things in each one. You will show the children one container at a time and ask them to estimate how many things there are inside. Begin with the container holding about ten items, and remind the children that they have estimated how many up to about ten in their previous work. Hold up one container and ask: *How many ___ do you think there are?* Write some of the estimates on the board, then ask two children to open the container. One child counts the items, the other checks. Now fill the container, without the children counting, with a different counting material. Ask: *How many do you think there are in the container now? How did you work that out?* Repeat for another container. Ask: *Did you make a good estimate? Were there too many/too few for your estimate?* Discuss how checking helps us to make better estimates.

Paired work: Ask the children to work in pairs. They each need a copy of photocopiable page 'Estimate and count' from the CD-ROM. They take turns to take a handful of counters which they estimate to be up to 20 counters. They record their estimate, then check by counting and writing the count. They put a tick in the third column if they made a good estimate. Encourage them to become more accurate in their estimates as they work.

Progress check: Ask the children to stop working for a moment and say:

- *Did you make a good estimate?*
- *How did you count to check?*

Check that children are spreading out the counters, and using the coordinated touch, count and move method for accuracy.

Review

Discuss how much more accurate the children's estimates became through practice. Invite them to look at another transparent container and estimate how many items are inside it. Ask two children to count the items and check the count. Ask: *Was your estimate close? Who estimated just under/just over the count? When you count, how do you know you have counted everything just once?*

Curriculum objectives
- To identify and represent numbers using objects and pictorial representations including the number line, and use the language of: more than, less than (fewer).
- To read and write numbers from 1 to 20 in numerals and words.

Success criteria
- I can read and write numbers up to 20.
- I can count objects and pictures to 20.
- I can count using a number line.

You will need
Photocopiable sheets
'Number monsters'

General resources
'Number cards 0–20'; interactive teaching resource 'Number line'

Equipment
Washing line and pegs

Differentiation
Less confident learners

Work with children using the interactive number line. Give the children a start number and finish number. Hide the numbers on the line if necessary.

More confident learners

Ask the children to complete their own 'Number monster' using the blank monster on the photocopiable page and selecting their own number range to 30 or beyond.

Lesson 4   Oral and mental starter 16

Main teaching activities

Whole-class work: Explain that you would like the children to help you peg the number cards on the washing line. Say that you have all of the numbers from 0 to 20. Invite individual children to take a card and peg it where they think it should go, taking into account which numerals are still to come. When all the cards are on the line, ask questions such as: *Which number comes between 14 and 16? Tell me three numbers that are between 10 and 16. Which numbers are more than 15 and less than 18?*

Now invite individual children to remove a number card, leaving the numbers 0, 1, 2, 6, 7, 12, 19 and 20 in place. Ask: *Which numbers need to go between 2 and 6? Which numbers are missing between 7 and 12? How do you know? Which numbers go between 12 and 19?*

Group work: Provide each group of four children with a set of 0–20 number cards. They shuffle the cards, then deal them out between them. They hide their own cards. The dealer starts by placing any card on the table (for example, 10). The next child has to place a card that fits on either side (9 or 11). If they cannot do this, they say 'pass' and the next child has a turn. The object of the game is to be the first player to get rid of all their cards. They play this game once. More confident groups can also use numbers 21–30. Now ask the children to play the game again. Encourage them to work quickly so that they use recall of number order to place their cards, rather than counting to find the position of a number.

Progress check: When the children have played the game once, ask questions such as:
- *How did you work out where your card fitted in the number line?*

Now ask two children to stand at the front, holding the 13 and 14 number cards. Ask:
- *What card fits before the 13?*
- *What card fits after 14?*
- *What would be the next card after 15? And the next?*
- *And what card would fit before 12?*
- *What would fit before 11?*

Independent work: Provide copies of the photocopiable page 'Number monsters' from the CD-ROM and ask the children to complete this individually.

Review

Use interactive teaching resource 'Number line' on the CD-ROM to create a number line to 20, and write on these numbers only 8, 10, 11, 15, 18. Ask: *Which numbers come before 8? What is missing between 8 and 10? Which numbers are between 11 and 15? And between 15 and 18? What comes after 18?* Ask the children to explain how they worked out the answers. Some children may have used a mental number line; others may have counted.

Lesson 5

Oral and mental starter 19

Main teaching activities

Whole-class work: Repeat the main activity from Lesson 4. When all the number cards are in place, invite children to remove given numbers, such as: *Take off the number between 16 and 18. Take off the number just before 19... just after 11....* When all the number cards have been removed, shuffle them and invite individual children to place them back, one at a time, where they think that they will fit on the washing line.

Paired work: Ask the children to work in pairs, sitting alongside each other. They will need a set of 0–20 number cards and a blank number line, drawn onto an A3 sheet. Ask them to shuffle the number cards, then take turns to turn over a card. They place this on the table in front of both of them, then write the number onto their number line, counting from zero to find its correct place. They repeat this, turning over and placing a card where they think it fits, and writing in the number on their number line, until all the cards are placed, and the numbers 0 to 20 are written onto their number lines. In case they write in a number in the wrong place, it would be helpful to have some erasers handy.

Progress check: Stop the children after a few minutes and ask questions such as:
● *What number comes just before 14?*
● *And what number comes just after 14?*
● *What would come next?*
● *How did you work that out?*

Review

Use the washing line and number cards to 20 again. Give out the cards to some of the children. Those without a card take turns to say a missing number from the number line. The child holding the card quickly places it on the washing line. Make this a game, to be completed as quickly as the children can. When all the cards are in place, remove them, shuffle them, then give them out again, ensuring that those children who did not have a card to hold last time do this time. Repeat the activity.

Ask:
● *Is this number in its correct place?*
● *How do you know?*
● *So which number would fit next?*

Now ask the children to shut their eyes. Swap over two number cards so that they are in the wrong place. Ask the children to open their eyes and to spot what is wrong with the number line. The child who answers correctly, corrects the number line. Repeat this several times.

Place value and comparing quantities and numbers

Expected prior learning

Children should be able to:

- read and write numbers to at least 10
- use counting on and counting back to find a number.

Topic	Curriculum objectives	Expected outcomes
Number and place value	**Lesson 1**	
	To read and write numbers from 1 to 20 in numerals and words. When given a number, to identify one more and one less.	Begin to recognise and use place value in numbers to 20. Use mental methods to find the number that is one more or one less than a given number, for numbers to 20.
	Lesson 2	
	To read and write numbers from 1 to 20 in numerals and words. When given a number, to identify one more and one less.	Begin to recognise and use place value in numbers to 20. Use mental methods to find the number that is one more or one less than a given number, for numbers to 20.
	Lesson 3	
	To read and write numbers from 1 to 20 in numerals and words. When given a number, to identify one more and one less.	Begin to recognise and use place value in numbers to 20. Use mental methods to find the number that is one more or one less than a given number, for numbers to 20.
	Lesson 4	
	To identify and represent numbers using objects and pictorial representations including the number line, and use the language of: equal to, more than, less than (fewer), most, least. When given a number, to identify one more and one less.	Compare two sets and use appropriate vocabulary. Use mental methods to find the number that is one more or one less than a given number, for numbers to 20.
	Lesson 5	
	To identify and represent numbers using objects and pictorial representations including the number line, and use the language of: equal to, more than, less than (fewer), most, least. When given a number, to identify one more and one less.	Compare two sets and use appropriate vocabulary. Use mental methods to find the number that is one more or one less than a given number, for numbers to 20.

Preparation

Lesson 1: prepare a 10 and 1–9 arrow cards for each child

Lesson 2: prepare a 10 and 1–9 arrow cards for each child

Lesson 3: prepare arrow cards for each child; copy 'Two-spike abacus', one per pair; copy and enlarge 'Two-spike abacus' to A3

Lesson 4: prepare labels 'more', 'fewer' and 'the same', one set per pair

Lesson 5: copy 'One more and one less (2)', one per child; copy and enlarge 'One more and one less (2)' to A3

You will need

Photocopiable sheets
'One more and one less (2)'

General resources
'Two-spike abacus'; interactive teaching resource 'Number line'

Equipment
Arrow cards; straws; elastic bands; interlocking cubes; counters; Blu-Tack®

Further practice

Photocopiable sheets
'Tens and units (1)'

Oral and mental starters for week 2

See bank of starters on pages 84 to 85. Oral and mental starters are also on the CD-ROM.

20 Number order

21 Wrong number order

22 Place value

Overview of progression

Children begin this week with making teen numbers using straws. They bundle ten straws and then represent the units as individual straws. They use arrow cards to make tens and units numbers, then represent these numbers on a two-spike abacus as well as plotting them on a number line. They compare two quantities, and use the vocabulary of more, fewer and equals, or the same amount. They repeat this for numbers, using more, less and equals, and find one more and one less than given numbers.

Watch out for

Check that children write tens and units numbers correctly, such as '19' for nineteen, not '91'. If children are unsure of 'which has more/ fewer?' of two sets, ask them to put their counters or cubes in a line, one set under the other to match them. Alternatively, ask them to use interlocking cubes, and compare the two sets by placing them together to see which has more/fewer.

Creative context

Consider using rhymes which count to 20 such as 'One, two, buckle my shoe'. Ask questions about the numbers such as: *For 17, how many tens and how many units?*

Vocabulary

add, altogether, answer, compare, count, explain, leaves, makes, minus (–), number sentence, operation, order, pattern, plus (+), read, record, show me, sign, subtract, sum, take away, total, write

Curriculum objectives
- To read and write numbers from 1 to 20 in numerals and words.
- When given a number, to identify one more and one less.

Success criteria
- I can make a ten and some units and say the number.

You will need
Equipment
Arrow cards; straws; elastic bands

Differentiation
Less confident learners
Decide whether to work with a group to complete this task. Encourage the children to express each number as a composite and a tens and units number.

More confident learners
Decide whether to extend the number range by including the 20 and 30 cards.

Lesson 1 Oral and mental starter 20

Main teaching activities

Whole-class work: Provide each child with some straws, elastic bands and a set of arrow cards. Explain that you will say a number, and you would like the children to count out that number of straws. Ask them to count out ten straws first and put an elastic band around them, then to count how many are left. So, for example, ask the children to count out 14 straws. Say: *How many straws did you count? So that is 1 ten and 4 ones.* Now explain how to show that number with their arrow cards. Repeat for other teen numbers, then 20.

Paired work: Ask the children to work in pairs with a set of arrow cards, using the 10 card and the 1–9 unit cards, straws and elastic bands. They take turns to show their partner a tens and units number and ask their partner to make this number with the straws and bands. Their partner then has to say this number in two ways: as how many tens and units, and as a whole number. For example, for 15, the child would say: *One ten and five units; the number is 15.*

Ask the children to continue the activity, but this time write each number they make as a tens and units numbers. For example, for 16 they write 1 ten and 6 units.

Progress check: Demonstrate a tens and units number, such as 18, and ask the children to say it with you: *1 ten and 8 units is the same as eighteen.* Repeat this for some more TU numbers up to 20. Now write on the board: 19. Ask:
- *How many tens is this?*
- *How many units?*
- *Say this number as a tens and units number.*

Say together: *19 is the same as 1 ten and 9 units.* Write on the board alongside 19: 1 ten and 9 units.

Review

On the board, write a TU number such as 17. Ask: *What is this number? How many tens are there? How many units?* Repeat for other numbers to 20, then extend the range into the twenties. Then extend into the range covered by the more confident learners, so that all of the class see and hear these numbers.

Now write 12 and 21 on the board. Point to 12 and ask: *What is this number?* Do the same for 21. Invite the children to explain how these numbers are different. Say: *But both numbers have a 2 and a 1. How can you tell which is which? Repeat this for 23 and 32.*

Curriculum objectives
● To read and write numbers from 1 to 20 in numerals and words.
● When given a number, to identify one more and one less.

Success criteria
● I can make tens and units numbers and say the number.
● I can say one more and one less than a number.

You will need
Equipment

Arrow cards; interlocking cubes

Differentiation
Less confident learners

Work with this group and check that the children can say the TU numbers and model them with the cubes.

More confident learners

Provide further tens cards, such as 20 and 30, and challenge the children to make numbers to 39. They should show each ten rod separately – for example, making 25 as two ten rods and five units.

Main teaching activities

Whole-class work: Provide each child with arrow cards to make the numbers to 20. Show the children how to make a TU number by placing the units arrow card on top of the tens card so that the arrows match. Explain that you will say some numbers. Ask the children to make these numbers with their arrow cards and hold up the cards to show you. Use numbers such as 12, 19, 20, 17....

Group work: Ask the children to work in pairs with the arrow cards for 10 and 1–9. They should take turns to choose a units card and place it onto the 10 card. The other child should say the number that has been made, then use the interlocking cubes to make that number as one ten and some units.

Ask the children to continue with the activity. Then, as well as saying the number, they write it down: 1 ten and 9 units is the same as 19. Ask them to do this eight times.

Progress check: Use the arrow cards to show '15' and ask the children to say the number with you. Use some interlocking cubes to make 1 ten and 5 units. Do this in front of the children. Invite a child to count each of the towers of cubes in front of the others. Now say:

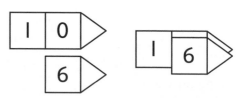

- *How many cubes are there in this tower (the tens tower)?*
- *How many cubes are there in this tower (the units tower)?*
- *So how many cubes are there altogether?*

Repeat this for another TU number, such as 19.

Review

Repeat the whole-class activity. Ask questions such as:

- *What number is this? How do you know?*
- *How many tens are there in this number? How many units? How can you tell?*

Now ask children to work in pairs. One of them makes 16 with their cards and the other 19. Ask: *Which is larger, 16 or 19? How do you know?* Repeat for another pair of cards, such as 13 and 18 but ask for the smaller number this time. Now invite individual children to make numbers 1, 2, 3... using their arrow cards and to stand in front of the class in line. Continue up to 30. Now invite children to say their number, and to say it as a tens and a units number (for example, 15, and one ten and five units), and then to say which numbers are either side of them.

Curriculum objectives

- To read and write numbers from 1 to 20 in digits and words.
- When a number, to identify one more and one less.

Success criteria

- I can say numbers on a two-spike abacus.

You will need

General resources

'Two-spike abacus'; interactive teaching resource 'Number line'

Equipment

Arrow cards; counters; Blu-Tack®

Differentiation

Less confident learners

Decide whether to limit the children to making just the numbers 10–15 with the arrow cards. Alternatively, an adult could work with this group to help them complete the task together, using just photocopiable page 'Two-spike abacus' and no recording page.

More confident learners

Decide whether to extend the range of numbers to up to 39.

Lesson 3   Oral and mental starter 21

Main teaching activities

Whole-class work: Each child will need a set of arrow cards. Reveal interactive teaching resource 'Number line' on the CD-ROM, with one end marked 0 and the other 30. Look at the enlarged photocopiable page 'Two-spike abacus' from the CD-ROM. Stick six counters onto the units spike. Ask: *What number does this represent? Show me that number with your arrow cards.* Stick one counter onto the tens spike and repeat the questions. Invite a child to point to the number made on the abacus on the number line. Repeat this for other numbers.

Group work: Ask the children to work in pairs. They should take turns: one child makes a number from 10 to 30 with the arrow cards, the other child makes the same number on photocopiable page 'Two-spike abacus' with counters. They should record each number and arrangement of counters in this form (see right):

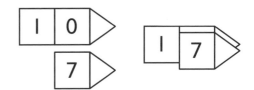

Leave the interactive teaching resource 'Number line' for the children to check the position of each number. If they need further help, provide them with a 0–30 printed number line.

Progress check: Ask a child to make a number with the arrow cards and show the class. Now ask another child to use the Blu-Tack® and counters and demonstrate this number on the enlarged version of 'Two-spike abacus'. Ask a third child to point to the number on the interactive resource 'Number line'. Say the number together. Ask questions such as:

- *(For 23) How do you know that this number has two tens?*
- *How many units does it have?*
- *How do you know that?*

Repeat for another example.

Review

Invite some children to demonstrate different numbers by placing counters onto the displayed abacus sheet. Include larger numbers for more confident children. Ask questions such as:

- *What number have you made?*
- *How many tens/units are there? How do you know?*
- *What if I put one more/one fewer counters on this spike? What number would it be then?*

Say: *What have you learned about tens and units? Tell your partner. What do you think you still need to learn?*

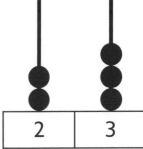

Curriculum objectives

● To identify and represent numbers using objects and pictorial representations including the number line, and use the language of: equal to, more than, less than (fewer), most, least.
● When given a number, to identify one more and one less.

Success criteria

● I can say the number that is one more and one less than a given number.

You will need

Equipment

Interlocking cubes; prepared labels – 'more', 'fewer', 'the same'

Differentiation

Less confident learners

Decide whether to limit the count to up to about 15.

More confident learners

Decide whether to extend the count to up to 30 counters.

Curriculum objectives

● To identify and represent numbers using objects and pictorial representations including the number line, and use the language of: equal to, more than, less than (fewer), most, least.
● When given a number, identify one more and one less.

Success criteria

● I can say the number that is one more and one less than a given number.

You will need

Photocopiable sheets

'One more and one less (2)'

Equipment

Interlocking cubes; prepared labels – 'more', 'fewer', 'the same'

Differentiation

Less confident learners

Work as a group, using the language of one more, one less as they find the answers.

More confident learners

Challenge the children to invent their own function machine with one less and one more numbers. They should use numbers in the range 20 to 30.

Lesson 4   Oral and mental starter 21

Main teaching activities

Whole-class work: Put a handful of cubes (between three and ten) on the table, between 3 and 10. Ask a child to make a tower from these, then to count aloud how many there are. Write the number on the board. Ask: *If I put one more on the table cube how many would there be then? If I took one cube away, so that there was one fewer, how many would there be then?* Repeat for another handful of cubes, but with two more cubes. Ask: *Which tower of cubes has more? So which tower of cubes has fewer?* Repeat for quantities between 10 and 15.

Paired work: Children use the 'More', 'Fewer' and 'The same' amount labels and up to 20 counters each. They each take a handful of counters, and count them. They decide who has more, who has fewer, or whether they have the same quantity and position them under each label.

Progress check: When the children have all completed at least one count, ask them to stop. Ask: *How many counters did you have? How many did your partner have? Who had more... fewer? How do you know? Who had the same amount?*

Review

Write '16' on the board. Ask the children to suggest a number less than 16, and write this up. Now say: *Which number is more? Which is less? How do you know that?* Repeat this for another number that the children suggest, this time asking for a number that is more than the suggested one.

Say: *Tell me the number that is one more/less than 14. How did you work that out? Tell me a number, and one more/less than that number. How did you work this out?*

Lesson 5   Oral and mental starter 22

Main teaching activities

Whole-class work: Repeat the whole-class work activity from lesson 4, choosing different quantities, such as 18 and 21; 19 and 25, and so on. Check that the children recognise 'more' and 'fewer' with numbers above 20.

Independent work: Provide photocopiable page 'One more and one less (2)' from the CD-ROM. This contains function machines. Check that the children understand where to write their answers.

Progress check: Discuss with the children the last two function machines on the photocopiable sheet. Say: *Look at number 5 and the number 7. What do you write in the next box? And the next box? Now look at number 6. What happens here? Who can explain this please?*

Independent work: Check that the children understand how to tackle questions 5 and 6 and then ask them to complete the photocopiable sheet.

Review

Use the enlarged version of 'One more and one less (2)'. Invite children to give the answers to question 1. Now move to question 5. Ask: *Look at the 7. What goes in the middle box? How do you know that? And what goes in the 1 more box? How did you work that out?*

Continue, completing question 5. Now review question 6:

The first box is empty. So is the second box. How shall we tackle this? So 1 more is 6. What would the number to go in the middle be? And what would the 1 less number be? How do you know?

Again, complete the questions.

Invite some of the more confident children to share their function machines. Then challenge the other children to state the number that is 1 less, then the number that is 1 more.

Developing mental strategies for addition

Expected prior learning

Children should be able to:

- count to and from 10 reliably
- read and write numerals to 10.

Topic	Curriculum objectives	Expected outcomes
Addition and subtraction	**Lesson 1**	
	To read, write and interpret mathematical statements involving addition (+), subtraction (−) and equals (=) signs. To represent and use number bonds and related subtraction facts within 20.	Use a number line to add to a total of 10. Count on or back using a mental number line for addition and subtraction.
	Lesson 2	
	To read, write and interpret mathematical statements involving addition (+), subtraction (−) and equals (=) signs. To represent and use number bonds and related subtraction facts within 20.	Use a number line to subtract to a total of 10. Count on or back using a mental number line for addition and subtraction.
	Lesson 3	
	To read, write and interpret mathematical statements involving addition (+), subtraction (−) and equals (=) signs. To represent and use number bonds and related subtraction facts within 20.	Count on or back using a mental number line for addition and subtraction. Count on or back using a mental number line for addition and subtraction.
	Lesson 4	
	To read, write and interpret mathematical statements involving addition (+), subtraction (−) and equals (=) signs. To represent and use number bonds and related subtraction facts within 20.	Count on or back using a mental number line for addition and subtraction. Count on or back using a mental number line for addition and subtraction.
	Lesson 5	
	To solve one-step problems that involve addition and subtraction, using concrete objects and pictorial representations, and missing number problems such as $7 = \square - 9$.	Use addition and subtraction skills to solve problems.

Preparation

Lesson 1: copy and enlarge 'Work mat' to A3

Lesson 2: copy and enlarge 'Work mat' to A3

Lesson 4: prepare dominoes from 'Double 9 dominoes', one set per group or laminate and copies of 'Double 9 dominoes'

You will need

Photocopiable sheets
'Dog show addition'

General resources
'Work mat'; 'Number line 0–20'; 'Double 9 dominoes'; interactive teaching resource 'Number line'

Equipment
Counters; Blu-Tack®; interlocking cubes

Further practice

Photocopiable sheets
'Addition to 6'; 'Subtraction to 6'

Oral and mental starters for week 3

See bank of starters on pages 84 to 85. Oral and mental starters are also on the CD-ROM.

25 Add and subtract to 5

22 Place value

23 Add and subtract to 10

26 Find the subtraction sentences

Overview of progression

The lessons this week concentrate on developing the use of mental number lines. In the first and second lessons, children use cubes, number lines and mental number lines to find the answers to addition and subtraction sentences. They develop this in lessons 3 to 5, using their growing skill with mental number lines, counting on and back, to find solutions to addition and subtraction sentences up to a total of 9. They begin to recognise that, for every addition sentence, there is another addition and two corresponding subtraction sentences that they can derive.

Watch out for

Some children may still count all. Check, especially where children are working slowly, or achieving wrong answers, how they are calculating. If necessary, provide a number line for them to use to find the answer.

Creative context

During finding and putting out equipment for other lessons across the curriculum, encourage the children to note how many things are needed, such as paint brushes for a group, how many they have already and how many more are needed. This will help them to see how addition and subtraction is useful in everyday activities.

Vocabulary

add, altogether, answer, calculate, calculation, difference, equals (=), explain, method, minus (−), number sentence, order, pattern, plus (+), problem, solution, subtract, sum, total

Curriculum objectives

● To read, write and interpret mathematical statements involving addition (+), subtraction (−) and equals (=) signs.
● To represent and use number bonds and related subtraction facts within 20.

Success criteria

● I can use a number line to help me to add.
● I can use a number line to help me to subtract.

You will need

General resources

'Work mat'; 'Number line 0-20'; interactive teaching resource 'Number line'

Equipment

Counters; Blu-Tack®; interlocking cubes

Differentiation

Less confident learners

Decide whether to limit the sum total to 4, then 5. Check that the children find the total by counting on in ones from the larger number, and demonstrate using your fingers.

More confident learners

Ask these children to make larger totals, such as 10 to 12.

Lesson 1   Oral and mental starter 25

Main teaching activities

Whole-class work: Use Blu-Tack® to stick five counters onto an enlarged copy of photocopiable page 'Work mat' from the CD-ROM. Say: *We are going to make some additions with these counters. Can anyone suggest an addition sentence we could make with this total?* The children may suggest 1 + 4 or 2 + 3. Ask them to check that each sum is correct by keeping the larger number in their heads and counting on in ones. Invite a child to demonstrate with the counters by separating the full set to show the two amounts, and by writing the addition sentence on the board.

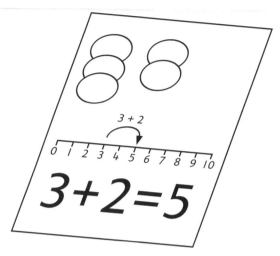

Open interactive teaching resource 'Number line' from the CD-ROM. Model the addition sentence on the board, counting on from the larger number to 5. Say together, for 3 + 2: *3 and 4, 5. So 3 add 2 equals 5.* Discuss how the answer is the same whether using cubes, a number line or counting on using a mental number line. Repeat this for another example, such as 3 + 6, asking the children to count on from the larger number.

Group work: Provide groups of three children with eight interlocking cubes. They should agree on a sum with a total of 8. While one child uses the cubes to make the sum, another child counts on using a number line and the third child works out the same sum by counting on mentally in ones from the larger number and states the total.

Repeat for other sums, taking turns to use the cubes, number line or mentally counting on, and all recording the sums.

Progress check: Invite a group to say one of their addition sentences. Ask the other children to count on mentally from the larger number to find the total. Say:
- *Do you agree with the total?*
- *Who 'knew' the answer?*
Repeat this for another addition sentence.

Review

Invite various children to write a sum from their recording on the board. Each time, ask:
- *What is the total?*
- *How did you work that out?*
Repeat this for other sums, checking that the children are confident with the strategy of 'keeping the larger number in their head and counting on in ones'.

Curriculum objectives

• To read, write and interpret mathematical statements involving addition (+), subtraction (−) and equals (=) signs.
• To represent and use number bonds and related subtraction facts within 20.

Success criteria

• I can use a number line to help me to add.
• I can use a number line to help me to subtract.

You will need

General resources

'Work mat'; 'Number line 0–20'; interactive teaching resource 'Number line'

Equipment

Interlocking cubes

Differentiation

Less confident learners

Ask these children to work with numbers 6 and 7.

More confident learners

These children could go on to work with numbers 12–15.

Lesson 2 Oral and mental starter 25

Main teaching activities

Whole-class work: Repeat the whole-class activity from lesson 1, choosing a starting number of 8 and providing children with cubes. This time, record these as subtractions, for example, for 8 partitioned into 5 and 3 record 8 − 5 = 3.

For each example, also use the interactive teaching resource 'Number line' on the CD-ROM. Model counting back using the number line. For example, for 8 − 2, say: *Begin with the larger number. Now count back along the number line: 8, 7, 6. So, 8 take away 2 equals 6.* Repeat for other starting numbers.

Group work: Repeat the group activity from lesson 1, but increase the quantity of the cubes for each threesome. Most of the class should be confident to partition a set of nine or ten cubes and make the corresponding subtraction sentences.

Progress check: Invite a group to say one of their subtraction sentences such as 9 − 5, but not to say their answer. Invite the other groups to count back mentally to find the answer. Say: *What is the answer? Do you all agree? Who 'knew' the answer? That is very good. Well done!*

Repeat this for another subtraction sentence.

Review

Encourage the children to explain their strategies for making the subtraction sentences.

Review how the children have recorded their calculations. Praise effective, efficient and neat recording.

Curriculum objectives

• To read, write and interpret mathematical statements.
• To represent and use number bonds and related subtraction facts within 20.

Success criteria

• I can count on or back using a mental number line.
• I can find the answers to addition and subtraction problems.

You will need

Photocopiable sheets

'Dog show additions'

General resources

'Work mat'; interactive teaching resource 'Number line'

Equipment

Interlocking cubes

Differentiation

Less confident learners

Provide individual number lines as additional support.

More confident learners

Ask children to write their own 'Dog show addition' using the blank on the sheet to test on a partner.

Lesson 3 Oral and mental starter 22

Main teaching activities

Whole-class work: Repeat the whole-class activity from lesson 1 to revise the strategy of counting on in ones from the larger number.

Independent work: Provide copies of photocopiable page 'Dog show additions' from the CD-ROM. This requires the child to match addition sentences to answers where the totals go up to 10.

Progress check: Invite a child to explain to the class how they calculated the answer to one of their addition sentences. Ask questions such as:

• *Who used this method?*
• *Who 'knew' the answer?*

Discuss with the children that they should use counting on mentally to find the answers.

Review

Choose some of the addition sentences from photocopiable page 'Dog show additions', making sure that there are questions for each group, and write them on the board without the answers. Ask:

• *What is the total of ___?*
• *How did you work it out?*
• *Who did this a different way? What did you do?*

▮ SCHOLASTIC

Lesson 4
Oral and mental starter 23

Main teaching activities

Whole-class work: Explain that you would like the children to solve a problem. Give each group a set of dominoes from photocopiable pages 'Double 9 dominoes' from the CD-ROM (or give out the laminated copies of 'Double 9 dominoes') and explain the problem: *Look at the set of dominoes. Your task is to find all the dominoes that have a total of 9 spots. Record what you find.*

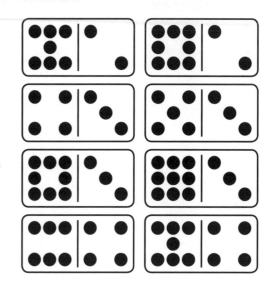

Group work: Encourage the children to decide for themselves how they will record their answers. When they have finished this ask them to write the subtraction sentences for domino totals of 9, such as 9 − 5 = 4, for the 4 and 5 domino.

Progress check: Invite individuals to explain their recording methods. Choose an efficient method and copy it onto the board. Ask:
- Why is this a good way of recording?
- What does it tell you?
- Who used this method?
- Who thinks they need to change their way of recording?

Review

Ask some children to explain how they solved the problem. On the board, write each domino as a number sentence (for example, 5 + 4 = 9). Ask the children to help you order the dominoes and number sentences, so that they can see a pattern: 9 + 0 = 9, 8 + 1 = 9 and so on. Discuss how, for example, 9 + 0 = 9 and 0 + 9 = 9 are the same domino. Model this with a domino, demonstrating both number sentences by turning the domino around. Discuss how the children recorded their results. Ask them which were the best ways of recording, and why. Some children may have ordered their responses and then checked whether any were missing: 0 + 9; 1 + 8; 2 + 7; 3 + 6; 4 + 5.

Oral and mental starter 26

Curriculum objectives
● To solve simple one-step problems that involve addition and subtraction, using concrete objects and pictorial representations, and missing number problems.

Success criteria
● I can solve problems using addition and subtraction.

You will need
General resources
'Number line 0–20'; interactive teaching resource 'Number line'
Equipment
Cubes; counters

Differentiation
Less confident learners
If the children struggle with 7, suggest that they start by using 5 as the answer.
More confident learners
Challenge these children to use 9 or above as the answer.

Lesson 5

Main teaching activities

Whole-class work: Explain that the children have a problem to solve. Write the number 8 on the board and say: *Tell me a number sentence that has 8 as the answer. How many different number sentences can you find? Talk to your neighbour for about a minute, and think of as many as you can.* Write the children's suggestions on the board. Point out that there is a pattern if the number sentences are written in order: 0 + 8 = 8; 1 + 7 = 8; 2 + 6 = 8, and so on. Repeat this for subtraction sentences. Remind the children that they can count up from the smaller to the larger number, keeping a tally with their fingers. So, for 8 − 6 they count 6 and 7, 8. So, 8 − 6 is 2. Demonstrate this using the interactive teaching resource 'Number line' on the CD-ROM and counting on from 6 to 8.

Group work: Ask the children to work in pairs, finding as many number sentences as they can with 7 as the answer. Suggest that they start with addition number sentences where the total is 7, and write these in order. Then they can find subtraction number sentences that begin 7 subtract.... Provide 0–20 number lines for the children to use as an aid to calculation, and cubes or counters. However, do also encourage those who are using mental methods!

Progress check: After a few minutes, ask a pair to say one of their addition sentences. Ask:
- *We have 4 + 3 = 7. What other addition sentence can we have using these numbers?*
- *So we also have 3 + 4 = 7. What subtraction sentences can we make with these numbers?*

Emphasise that for every addition sentence there is a corresponding subtraction sentence.

Review

Invite some children to write on the board an addition sentence where the total is 7. When they can find no more addition sentences, invite a child to rewrite them on the board in a logical order, so that the pattern of the numbers can be seen. For example:

7 + 0 = 7

6 + 1 = 7

5 + 2 = 7

Repeat this for subtraction, finishing with the number sentences in a logical order. Ask the children to look at the two sets of number sentences and tell you what they can see. Encourage them to notice that, for example, 6 + 1 = 7 and 7 − 1 = 6 contain the same numbers. Ask: *What can you tell me about the addition and subtraction number sentences? What patterns can you see in the numbers?* If the more confident children used 9 as their answer, review this so that all of the class can see and hear these number sentences.

Ask the children to work in pairs and to discuss what they have learned in this series of lessons, what they feel confident with and what they need to practise further. Invite children who you are targeting for assessment to feed back to the rest of the class.

Subtraction as difference

Expected prior learning

Children should be able to:

- use a number line to 10
- begin to know some addition facts to 10
- read and write numbers to 10 and signs and symbols.

Topic	Curriculum objectives	Expected outcomes
Addition and subtraction	**Lesson 1**	
	To read, write and interpret mathematical statements involving addition (+), subtraction (−) and equals (=) signs. To represent and use number bonds and related subtraction facts within 20. To add and subtract one-digit and two-digit numbers to 20, including zero.	Use mathematical signs and symbols when writing a number sentence. Find the difference between two quantities. Begin to know subtraction facts to 10.
	Lesson 2	
	To read, write and interpret mathematical statements involving addition (+), subtraction (−) and equals (=) signs. To represent and use number bonds and related subtraction facts within 20. To add and subtract one-digit and two-digit numbers to 20, including zero.	Use mathematical signs and symbols when writing a number sentence. Find the difference between two quantities. Begin to know subtraction facts to 10.
	Lesson 3	
	To read, write and interpret mathematical statements involving addition (+), subtraction (−) and equals (=) signs. To represent and use number bonds and related subtraction facts within 20. To add and subtract one-digit and two-digit numbers to 20, including zero.	Use mathematical signs and symbols when writing a number sentence. Find the difference between two quantities. Begin to know subtraction facts to 10.
	Lesson 4	
	To read, write and interpret mathematical statements involving addition (+), subtraction (−) and equals (=) signs. To represent and use number bonds and related subtraction facts within 20. To add and subtract one-digit and two-digit numbers to 20, including zero.	Use mathematical signs and symbols when writing a number sentence. Find the difference between two quantities. Begin to know subtraction facts to 10.
	Lesson 5	
	To solve one-step problems that involve addition and subtraction, using concrete objects and pictorial representations, and missing number problems such as $7 = \square - 9$.	Solves simple one-step subtraction problems about difference.

Preparation

Lesson 2: copy 'Difference', one per child; prepare 0–20 number cards, one set per pair; prepare 0–15 number cards, one set per pair for more confident children; provide number lines 0–20 for more confident children

Lesson 3: prepare 0–20 number cards, one set per pair

Lesson 4: copy 'Find the difference', one per child

Lesson 5: copy 'Solving difference problems', one per child; copy and enlarge 'Solving difference problems' to A3

You will need

Photocopiable sheets
'Difference'; 'Find the difference'; 'Solving difference problems'

General resources
'Number cards 0–20'; 'Number line 0-20'; interactive teaching resource 'Number line'

Equipment
1–6 dice; interlocking cubes

Further practice

Photocopiable sheets
'Difference problems'

Oral and mental starters for week 4

See bank of starters on pages 84 to 85. Oral and mental starters are also on the CD-ROM.

16 Counting to 50

27 Find the difference

Overview of progression

This week children learn about subtraction as difference. They use the vocabulary of difference, including more, fewer and less. They use cubes to compare two sets to find which has more or less and how many that difference is. They use number lines to plot two numbers and count up to find the difference. They use their developing mental skills to count up from the smaller to the larger number in order to find the difference. At this stage, when counting up mentally, encourage the children to keep a track of how many they counted by using their fingers.

Watch out for

Check that children, having ascertained the size of each tower, do not 'count all' when comparing towers of cubes, but count on to find the difference.

Creative context

The word 'difference' is used with other meanings in different contexts. Discuss, for example, how there can be a 'difference in the weather'; that Jan looks 'different' now she has had her hair cut, and so on. Explain that in maths we use the word 'difference' to mean how many more, fewer or less there are when comparing two numbers or sets.

Vocabulary

add, after, altogether, before, difference, equals (=), equal to, halfway, how many?, how many fewer is ___ than ___?, how many more is ___ than ___?, how many more to make ___?, how much less is ___?, how much more is ___?, leaves, less, makes, minus (−), more, nearly, plus (+), roughly, sign, subtract (−), sum, take away, total, what is the difference between ___?,

■SCHOLASTIC

Lesson 1   Oral and mental starter 16

Main teaching activities

Whole-class work: Explain that in this lesson, the children will learn about subtraction as difference. Show them a tower of five interlocking cubes, and another of three. Place these towers side by side and ask: *How many more is 5 than 3?* When children give the answer, ask how they worked it out. Say: *5 is 2 more than 3. Count on from 3 until you reach 5: 3, 4, 5. We need to count on 2.*

Write 5 − 2 = 3 on the board. Explain that this is how this type of number sentence is written. The children may find it helpful to keep a count with their fingers of how many they have counted on. Repeat this for other differences, such as: *How many more is 6 than 4? How many more is 6 than 2? How many more is 7 than 3?* Each time, say the counting-on sentence together.

Explain that another way of saying *How many more.___?* is to say *What is the difference between ___ and ___?* Ask some 'difference' questions, such as: *What is the difference between 7 and 4? What is the difference between 6 and 1?* Again, say the counting-on sentence together. For example: *The difference between 6 and 1 is 5. 2, 3, 4, 5, 6. We need to count on 5.*

Write 6 − 1 = 5 on the board. Explain that finding the difference is a way of subtracting. Again, the children may find it helpful to keep a count with their fingers of how many they have counted on.

Group work: Ask the children to work in pairs. They take turns to throw two 1–6 dice and find the difference between the scores, then write a subtraction sentence. They repeat this until they have written at least ten difference sentences.

Progress check: Ask questions, such as:
- *How do I find the difference between 6 and 4?*
- *Count up with me: 4 and 5, 6. So the difference between 6 and 4 is 2.*
- *How do I find the difference between 4 and 6?*

Review

Review some of the children's number sentences as a class, and write them on the board. Ask: *How did you work this out?* Say the number sentences together, for example: *The difference between 6 and 2 is 4. We count on 4 from 2: 3, 4, 5, 6.* Encourage the children to use their fingers to help them if necessary. Praise those who used a mental number line, and ask them to explain to the others how this helped them.

Curriculum objectives
● To read, write and interpret mathematical statements.
● To represent and use number bonds and related subtraction facts within 20.
● To subtract one-digit numbers to 10, including zero.

Success criteria
● I can write subtraction number sentences.
● I can find the difference between two quantities.
● I know some subtraction facts up to 10.

You will need
Photocopiable sheets
'Difference'

General resources
'Number cards 0–20';
'Number line 0–20';
interactive teaching resource
'Number line'

Differentiation
Less confident learners
Ask children to use cubes to make two towers, then count up to find the difference.

More confident learners
Use number cards 11–15 to increase the number range.

Curriculum objectives
● To read, write and interpret mathematical statements involving subtraction (−) and equals (=) signs.
● To represent and use number bonds and related subtraction facts within 20.
● Subtract one-digit numbers to 20, including zero.

Success criteria
● I can write subtraction number sentences.
● I can find the difference between two quantities.
● I know some subtraction facts up to 10.

You will need
General resources
'Number cards 0–20'

Equipment
1–6 dice per pair

Differentiation
Less confident learners
Limit the children to the number cards 0–6 and encourage them to count on in ones.

More confident learners
Use two shuffled sets of 0–9 cards instead of dice.

Lesson 2   Oral and mental starter 16

Main teaching activities

Whole-class work: Display interactive teaching resource 'Number line' on the CD-ROM. Circle 6 and 9. Ask: *What is the difference between 6 and 9? How do you work this out?* Invite a child to come to the front and to count on from 6 to 9. Say: *How many did we count? Yes, 3. So the difference between 6 and 9 is 3.* Discuss how 6 is 3 fewer than 9 and 9 is 3 more than 6. Repeat for 8 and 4.

Paired work: Provide photocopiable page 'Difference' from the CD-ROM. The children shuffle 0–10 cards, and take turns to turn over two cards. They mark the numbers on a number line, then count up to find the difference. They complete the number sentences.

Progress check: Ask questions such as:
● *Which is more, 7 or 3? So which is less?*
● *How did you work that out?*
● *What is the difference between 7 and 3? And the difference between 3 and 7?*
Repeat for other pairs of numbers to 10.

Review

On the board write 9 − 5 and ask: *What difference sentence can we make for these two numbers?* Agree that they could say, *What is the difference between 9 and 5?* Ask: *How shall we work this out?* Encourage the children to count up mentally this time to find the difference. Now ask:
● *How many more is 9 than 5?*
● *So how many less is 5 than 9?*
● *I have 9 sweets. Jake has 5 sweets. Who has more sweets? How many more?*
● *Who has fewer sweets? How many fewer?*
● *How did you work that out?*
Repeat for other, similar number sentences.

Lesson 3   Oral and mental starter 27

Main teaching activities

Whole-class work: Review the questions *How many more is ___ than ___?* and *What is the difference between ___ and ___?* Introduce the concept of 'less than'. Ask: *How many less than 5 is 3? How can I work this out?* Explain that we can count on from the lower to the higher number in order to find the difference. Write 5 − 3 = 2 on the board. Explain that this is how 'less than' sentences are written. Repeat for some more examples.

Group work: Provide each pair of children with a 1–6 dice and a set of 0–10 number cards. Ask them to take turns to throw the dice and take a card from the top of the shuffled pack. They write a subtraction number sentence for each difference.

Progress check: Allow the children a few minutes to begin, then ask of pairs:
● *What is the difference between 4 and 5?*
● *How did you work that out?*
● *So which is more, 4 or 5? How many more?*
● *Which is less, 4 or 5? How many fewer?*

Review

Review the number sentences that the children have written, asking individuals to say a 'more than', 'less than' or 'difference' number sentence (as requested by you) for each subtraction. If necessary, demonstrate this, so that all the children are clear about what vocabulary to use.

Curriculum objectives
- To read, write and interpret mathematical statements involving subtraction (−) and equals (=) signs.
- To represent and use number bonds and related subtraction facts within 20.
- To subtract one-digit numbers to 10, including zero.

Success criteria
- I can write subtraction number sentences.
- I can find the difference between two quantities.
- I know some subtraction facts up to 10.

You will need
Photocopiable sheets
'Find the difference'

Differentiation
Less confident learners
Ask the children to find up to a difference of 5.

More confident learners
Challenge the children to continue this to find differences for numbers up to 12.

Lesson 4   Oral and mental starter 27

Main teaching activities

Whole-class work: Explain that in this lesson children will be focusing upon which of a pair of numbers is more, or less, and what is the difference. Write on the board 9 and 2 and ask: *Which is more, 9 or 2? How do you know? So which is less? What is the difference between 9 and 2? In your heads count up from 2 to 9. You can keep track of how many you count using your fingers.* Agree that the difference is 7. Repeat for other pairs of numbers up to 10, such as 8 and 3, 1 and 10, and so on.

Paired work: Ask the children to work in pairs. They find all the pairs of numbers between 0 and 10 with a difference of 1, then with a difference of 2, and so on. They record this on photocopiable page 'Find the difference' from the CD-ROM.

Progress check: Ask:
- *How are you finding the differences?*
- *Who has begun at 0 and worked up to 10?*

Check that children are organising their number sentences in a way that shows whether any are missing, for example, for differences of 1: 0 and 1; 1 and 2, and so on up to 9 and 10.

Review

Review children's results, up to differences of 4 or 5. Ask questions such as:
- *Which pairs of numbers have a difference of 4?*
- *Tell me how to order these as I write them up.*
- *So, if 4 and 8 have a difference of 4, what is the difference between 8 and 4?*
- *How do you know that?*

Repeat for other differences.

Curriculum objectives
- To solve one-step problems that involve addition and subtraction, using concrete objects and pictorial representations, and missing number problems.

Success criteria
- I can find the answer to problems about difference.

You will need
Photocopiable sheets
'Solving difference problems'

Differentiation
Less confident learners
Work with this group, reading each question together and count up each time.

More confident learners
When they have finished ask them to work in pairs to write a difference problem for others to solve.

Lesson 5   Oral and mental starter 27

Main teaching activities

Whole-class work: Repeat the whole-class activity from lesson 4. Use pairs of numbers such as 5 and 9, 2 and 8, and so on, and encourage the children to work mentally, counting up to find the difference, and, if necessary, using their fingers to keep count. Now say: *Sam has 5 marbles and Jon has 3 marbles. Who has more? Who has fewer? How many more does Sam have than Jon? How many fewer marbles does Jon have than Sam?* Ask other, similar, questions, keeping the number range within 10.

Independent work: Provide photocopiable page 'Solving difference problems' from the CD-ROM. Ask the children to work individually. Read through questions 1 and 2 together.

Progress check: After a few minutes stop and review together the answer to the first question. Ask questions such as:
- *How did you work that out?*
- *Who 'knew' the answer?*

Now read the other questions together, to check that the children understand and can read the vocabulary.

Review

Pin up the A3 enlargement of 'Solving difference problems'. Read the first question together, then ask for the answer. Discuss how the children worked out the answer. Repeat for the other questions. Discuss how counting up in their heads, keeping a check of how many have been counted is a good strategy. Now ask: *What have you learned this week? How do you find the difference between two numbers?*

Measures

Expected prior learning

Children should be able to:

● sort items into recognisable groups
● begin to use the vocabulary of comparing by length, mass/weight and capacity.

Topic	Curriculum objectives	Expected outcomes
Measurement	**Lesson 1**	
	To compare, describe and solve practical problems for: ● lengths and heights [for example, long/short, longer/shorter, tall/short, double/half] ● mass or weight [for example, heavy/light, heavier than, lighter than] ● capacity and volume [for example, full/empty, more than, less than, quarter] ● time [for example, quicker, slower, earlier, later].	Compare two or more lengths, masses or capacity by direct comparison.
	Lesson 2	
	To compare, describe and solve practical problems for: ● lengths and heights [for example, long/short, longer/shorter, tall/short, double/half] ● mass or weight [for example, heavy/light, heavier than, lighter than] ● capacity and volume [full/empty, more than, less than, quarter] ● time [for example, quicker, slower, earlier, later].	Compare two or more lengths, masses or capacity by direct comparison.
	Lesson 3	
	To compare, describe and solve practical problems for: ● lengths and heights [for example, long/short, longer/shorter, tall/short, double/half] ● mass or weight [for example, heavy/light, heavier than, lighter than] ● capacity/volume [for example, full/empty, more than, less than, quarter] ● time [for example, quicker, slower, earlier, later].	Compare two or more lengths, masses or capacity by direct comparison.
	Lesson 4	
	To recognise and know the value of different denominations of coins and notes.	Name coins and notes for money.
	Lesson 5	
	To recognise and know the value of different denominations of coins and notes.	Begin to recognise the equivalence of, for example, two 1p coins for a 2p coin.

Preparation

Lesson 1: prepare the trays of equipment for each group

Lesson 2: prepare the trays of equipment for each group

Lesson 3: prepare the trays of equipment for each group; copy 'Filling', one per child

Lesson 5: prepare price labels 1p–10p

You will need

Photocopiable sheets

'Filling'

General resources

Interactive activity 'Estimating and measuring'; interactive teaching resource 'Money'

Equipment

Price labels 1p–10p; items to be compared such as scarves, gloves and shoes; tray for each group of items to be compared; classroom items for weighing; non-standard units of mass such as cubes or scoops of sand; bucket balances; a set of weighing scales; parcels for comparing; 100g weights; washing line; pegs; containers such as cups, egg cups, yogurt pots, margarine tubs; scoops or spoons; filling material such as sand, water, cubes; set of six 1-litre containers of various shapes and labelled A–F; interlocking cubes; pots to hold coins; coins: 1p, 2p, 5p, 10p, 20p, 50p, £1, £2; notes: £5, £10 and £20; Blu-Tack®

Further practice

Where possible, provide further practical experience of comparing and ordering items by length, mass and capacity. Also offer further experience of using non-standard units for length for estimating then measuring.

Oral and mental starters for week 5

See bank of starters on pages 84 to 85. Oral and mental starters are also on the CD-ROM.

23 Add and subtract to 10

24 Add and subtract: write

Overview of progression

Children begin the week with comparisons of length, then mass/weight and capacity. This includes the language of comparison, and also superlatives, such as most, least, longest, shortest, heaviest, lightest, and so on. In Lessons 4 and 5, they are introduced to money, learning the names of the coins, and find equivalents for coins up to 20p, and £1 coin, £5, £10 and £20 notes.

Watch out for

Check that children make direct comparisons, and that, for example for length, two ends are placed together. Similarly check that when using non-standard units children place the end of one unit adjacent to the next one, otherwise the measure is meaningless. Ensure that when children find equivalents for money that they do not, for example, count a 2p coin as '1', but recognise its value.

Creative context

Encourage the children to use their measuring skills in other contexts, such as in PE: Who takes the longer stride, Peter or Paul? Or in science, when comparing the sizes of materials.

Vocabulary

coins, comparatives such as longer/shorter, compare, deep, depth, different, guess, height, high, length, long, low, measure, money, narrow, notes, order, same, shallow, short, size, superlatives such as longest/shortest, tall, thick, thin, unit, wide, width, 1p, 2p, 5p, 10p, 20p, 50p, £1, £2 coins £5, £10 and £20 notes

Curriculum objectives
● To compare, describe and solve practical problems for: lengths and heights [for example, long/short, longer/shorter, tall/short, double/half].

Success criteria
● I can compare two lengths to find which is longer and which is shorter.

You will need
Equipment

Items to be compared such as scarves, gloves and shoes; tray for each group of items to be compared, such as pencils, rulers, cubes, books and so on

Differentiation
Less confident learners

Decide whether to ask the children just to make comparisons of two items, using the language of longer/shorter and wider/narrower.

More confident learners

When the children are confident with making comparisons (such as longest/widest), ask them to find their own sets of three objects and record them in the same way.

Lesson 1

Main teaching activities

Whole-class work: Explain to the children that this week they will be learning about measures. Show the children two scarves. Ask: *Are these the same length, or is one longer than the other? How can we find out?* Invite two children to hold the scarves with the end of each scarf just touching the floor, so that a direct comparison can be made. Point out that both scarves start at the same point so that we can compare them. Say for example: *The blue scarf is longer than the red scarf. So the red scarf is shorter than the blue scarf.* Repeat for other items, making comparisons of length and width. Agree which item is shorter or narrower, as well as which is longer or wider.

Longer	Shorter

When the children are confident with this, introduce a third item of different length, and ask: *Which is the longest? Which is the shortest? How can we find out? Can you help to put these in order, starting with the shortest?* Invite children to compare them. They should make sure that one end of each of the three items is level. Invite children to describe the comparisons, using sentences such as: *The yellow scarf is longest, the blue scarf is shortest. The yellow scarf is longer than the red scarf and shorter than the blue scarf.* Repeat for other items, making comparisons of length and width.

Group work: Provide each group of four to six children with a tray of items to compare. They should choose two items to compare and record the outcome in a table (see above). Then they compare three items for length which they can record by drawing them in order. If time allows, ask them to compare two sets of three items and draw these in order by length. Introduce the language of shortest and longest.

Progress check: Ask a child to show two items that they have compared to the other children. Ask:

- *Which is longer?*
- *How do you know that?*
- *So which is shorter?*
- *Here is another item. How can we tell which is longer/shorter now?*

Review

Ask some children to show the class what they have compared. Invite them to use comparative language, and for each pair of items to use sentences with both longer/shorter and wider/narrower. Then repeat for the superlatives longest/shortest and widest/narrowest. Ask:

- *Which is longer/shorter/wider/narrower? How can you tell?*
- *Which is the longest/shortest/widest/narrowest? How can you tell?*
- *What else is longer/shorter/wider/narrower than this?*
- *Look at these three things. Just by looking, estimate which is longest/shortest/widest/narrowest. Now let's check by comparing them side by side. Did you make a good guess?*

Curriculum objectives
● To compare, describe and solve practical problems for: mass or weight [for example, heavy/light, heavier than, lighter than].

Success criteria
● I can compare two weights to find which is heavier and which is lighter.

You will need
Equipment
Classroom items for weighing; non-standard units of mass such as cubes or scoops of sand; bucket balances; a set of weighing scales; parcels for comparing; 100g weights

Differentiation
Less confident learners
Work with this group and encourage the children to use the appropriate vocabulary.
More confident learners
Challenge these children to put all of their objects in order of weight, starting with the lightest.

Lesson 2   Oral and mental starter 23

Main teaching activities

Whole-class work: Show the children the parcels. Pass two parcels around the class; ask the children to hold one in one hand and one in the other and decide which is heavier. Then ask: *Which parcel is heavier/lighter?* Show the children a bucket balance and discuss how it is in balance when nothing is in the buckets. Now put one parcel in each bucket, and discuss what the children observe. *How can you tell from this which parcel is heavier?* Repeat for other pairs of parcels. The children will begin to realise that visible size does not determine weight. Extend this to comparing three parcels, using superlatives: *Which is the heaviest/lightest parcel?*

Group work: Provide each group of four children with a bucket balance and a set of objects to compare by weight. Ask them to take two items each time and compare how much they weigh by holding them, then check using the bucket balance. They should record their work as below:

My estimate	My check
The _____ was lighter than the _____	The _____ was lighter than the _____

Then ask the children to choose three objects from their list. They should estimate which is the heaviest and which is the lightest and use a balance to check. Challenge them to choose another three items to order by weight.

Progress check: Put a bucket balance is properly balanced where everyone can see it. Ask: *What do you notice about the buckets? What will happen when I put something in this/that bucket?* Discuss how the balance must be level before it is used.

Invite a child to demonstrate how they compared two objects for weight, using the balance. Ask:

- *How do you know which parcel is heavier/lighter?*
- *Now if I give you a third parcel how will you decide which is heaviest and which is lightest?*

Review

Invite some children to compare three objects by picking them up. Ask questions such as:

- *Which is the heaviest/lightest?*
- *How can you check this?*

Then invite children to demonstrate with a bucket balance. Ask questions such as: *How can you tell by looking at a bucket balance which side is heavier/lighter?*

Curriculum objectives
● To compare, describe and solve practical problems for: capacity and volume [for example, full/empty, more than, less than, quarter].

Success criteria
● I can compare two containers to find which holds more and which holds less.

You will need
Photocopiable sheets
'Filling'

General resources
Interactive activity 'Estimating and measuring'

Equipment
Containers such as cups, egg cups, yogurt pots, margarine tubs; scoops or spoons; filling material such as sand, water, cubes; set of six 1-litre containers of various shapes and labelled A–F

Differentiation
Less confident learners
Decide whether to ask children to compare just two containers. Extend to three over time.

More confident learners
Challenge the children to compare four containers and order these by their capacities.

Main teaching activities

Whole-class work: Show the children two containers, and ask: *Which container do you think holds more? Why do you think that? How could you check?* Explain that their estimate could be checked by filling. Ask a child to fill one container with sand, then pour the sand into another container. Ask:

- *Did all the sand from this container fit into that one? What does this tell you?*
- *Which container was full? Which container was nearly full?*
- *Which container held more? How can you tell? Which one held less?*

Repeat with two more containers. When the children are confident with this, extend to three containers. Encourage the children to use the superlatives *most* and *least*.

Group work: Provide each group of four children with a set of containers to compare for capacity, and some filling material, such as sand or water. Ask them to compare two containers each time by looking at them, then check by filling and pouring. They can record their work on photocopiable page 'Filling' from the CD-ROM. This also asks them to compare three containers, using appropriate vocabulary.

Children can then compare two lots of three containers, and to put them in order, starting with the one that held least.

Progress check: Invite two children to demonstrate how they compared two containers for capacity. Ask of all the children: *Which one held more/less? How do you know that?* Now ask another two children to demonstrate finding most and least using three containers. Ask:

- *Which container held most? How do you know?*
- *Which one held least? How do you know that?*
- *Tell me the order of these containers. Start with the one that held least.*

Review

Use the containers labelled A–F. Invite the children to compare three of these by looking at them. Ask: *Which holds the least/most? How can you check this?* Invite children to demonstrate this by pouring sand from the one they think holds the most to the next, then the one that holds the least. Ask: *Why do you think this container holds more than that one? Did you make a good guess/estimate? Which container holds the most/least? How do you know?*

Review all of the measures covered this week using the interactive activity 'Estimating and measuring' on the CD-ROM. (This activity can also be used as a half-term assessment activity. See page 83 for details.)

Curriculum objectives

● To recognise and know the value of different denominations of coins and notes.

Success criteria

● I can name coins and notes.
● I can find some equivalent values for coins.

You will need

Equipment

Pots to hold coins; coins: 1p, 2p, 5p, 10p, 20p, 50p, £1, £2; notes: £5, £10 and £20 Blu-Tack®

Differentiation

Less confident learners

Work with the children. It may be necessary to reinforce the equivalent values of the coins if they do not understand that a 2p coin is worth two 1p coins, and instead count it as 'one'.

More confident learners

Challenge the children to choose three coins each time, and to write out the sum with the answer.

Lesson 4
Oral and mental starter 23

Main teaching activities

Whole-class work: Remind the children of previous work that they have done with money. Set the context by discussing how we use money when we go shopping. Provide each group with some coins in a container. Ask the children to work together to sort the coins by their value. Check that they know the names of the different coins. Say to the children:

- *Hold up a penny.*
- *Now show me a 2... 5... 10... 20... 50 pence coin.*
- *Show me a £1... £2 coin.*
- *What is the name of the note?* (Show £5, then £10, then £20 notes.)

Discuss how every coin has a value. Concentrate on 1p, 2p, 5p and 10p coins. Explain that two 1p coins are worth the same as a 2p coin. Now consider the 5p coin: *How many penny coins are worth the same as a 5p coin?* Attach a 5p coin to the board with Blu-Tack®, and ask a child to attach sufficient pennies to make 5p. Now ask: *Which 2p and 1p coins are worth the same as a 5p coin?* Again, invite children to demonstrate their answers by attaching coins to the board. Their responses should include 2p + 2p + 1p and 2p + 1p + 1p + 1p. Write these as sums, as well as showing the coins. Explain that 'p' stands for pence. Repeat for the 10p coin.

Now put up a 2p and a 5p. *How much is this?* Encourage the children to count on in ones from the 5p: 5p and 6p and 7p. 5p and 2p is 7p. Repeat for other combinations of two coins, counting on from the larger number each time and keeping the totals to 10p or less.

Independent work: Provide each child with some 1p, 2p and 5p coins and paper. The children choose two coins and draw them, then add them and write the total.

Progress check: Invite a child to show which two coins they chose. Ask of everyone:

- *What are these coins called?*
- *How much is that altogether?*
- *How did you work that out?*

Encourage the children to count on from the larger coin, for the value of the smaller coin.

Independent work: Ask the children to make further choices of two coins each time, total the coins, and write the total.

Review

Invite various children to write a money sum on the board and challenge the others to work out the total mentally. Include examples suitable for each ability group. Ask questions such as:

- *How could you work this out? Why?*
- *How much is 5p and 2p?*
- *How did you work that out?*
- *What other way could we make 7p, using coins?*

Curriculum objectives
- To recognise and know the value of different denominations of coins and notes.

Success criteria
- I can name coins and notes.
- I can find some equivalent values for coins.

You will need

General resources

Interactive teaching resource 'Money'

Equipment

Price labels 1p–10p; pots to hold coins; coins: 1p, 2p, 5p, 10p, 20p, 50p, £1, £2 notes: £5, £10 and £20

Differentiation

Less confident learners

Check that the children understand that each coin has a specific value, and that they do not count every coin as being worth '1p'. Limit the range to up to 6p.

More confident learners

When the children have completed the group activity, challenge them to use coins to make the values 11p to 15p.

Lesson 5

Oral and mental starter 23

Main teaching activities

Whole-class work: Provide containers of coins for each pair of children to use. Show the children price labels 1p–10p. Explain that you will hold up a price label, and that the children should work with a partner to count out enough coins to make that amount. Begin with, say, 3p. Ask:

- *Which coins did you choose?*
- *Is there another way?*

Invite children to write number sentences on the board that show the coin sums:

2p + 1p = 3p and
1p + 1p + 1p = 3p.
Repeat for other values, until the children understand that coins can be combined to make a range of total values.

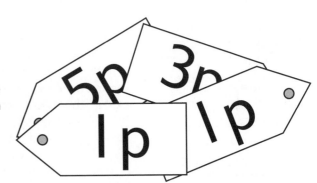

Paired work: The children work in pairs with some coins. They find different ways to make 5p. They total their coins, draw them, then write the total value alongside their drawings.

Children can then find different ways to make totals of 10p and to record by drawing the coins, then write the total.

Progress check: Review the equivalent coins that children have chosen. Ask the other children to place those coins in front of them and to total them to check the value. Ask, for example:

- *How did you find the total?*
- *What other coins could you choose to make that total?*

Review

Invite some children from each group to show the others the coins they used to make their specific values. Open interactive teaching resource 'Money' on the CD-ROM and use it to show the children's results on the whiteboard. Encourage the others to suggest alternative ways to make, for example, 6p, or 11p, and so on. Reintroduce the £1 and £2 coins, and the £5 and £10 notes, and invite children to come to the front to show how to make, for example £5 using just coins, £10 using coins and notes. Ask questions such as:

- *How did you work this out?*
- *Who has a different way to make the total?*

Ask the children to discuss with their partner what they have learned this week, about measures, and about money.

Addition and subtraction using money

Expected prior learning

Children should be able to:

- recognise coins to 10p
- add and subtract, using concrete materials, number lines or mental methods, to 10.

Topic	Curriculum objectives	Expected outcomes
Addition and subtraction	**Lesson 1**	
	To read, write and interpret mathematical statements involving addition (+), subtraction (−) and equals (=) signs.	Read and use signs when recording number sentences, and explain what the number sentence means.
	To represent and use number bonds and related subtraction facts within 20.	Use counting on to find totals and differences, and counting back to take away.
	To add and subtract one-digit and two-digit numbers to 20, including zero.	Begin to know addition and subtraction facts to 10.
	Lesson 2	
	To read, write and interpret mathematical statements involving addition (+), subtraction (−) and equals (=) signs.	Read and use signs when recording number sentences, and explain what the number sentence means.
	To represent and use number bonds and related subtraction facts within 20.	Use counting on to find totals and differences, and counting back to take away.
	To add and subtract one-digit and two-digit numbers to 20, including zero.	Begin to know addition and subtraction facts to 10.
	Lesson 3	
	To read, write and interpret mathematical statements involving addition (+), subtraction (−) and equals (=) signs.	Read and use signs when recording number sentences, and explain what the number sentence means.
	To represent and use number bonds and related subtraction facts within 20.	Use counting on to find totals and differences, and counting back to take away.
	To add and subtract one-digit and two-digit numbers to 20, including zero.	Begin to know addition and subtraction facts to 10.
	Lesson 4	
	To solve one-step problems that involve addition and subtraction, using concrete objects and pictorial representations, and missing number problems such as $7 = \square - 9$.	Use coins as an aid to solving problems for addition and subtraction.
	Lesson 5	
	To solve one-step problems that involve addition and subtraction, using concrete objects and pictorial representations, and missing number problems such as $7 = \square - 9$.	Use coins as an aid to solving problems for addition and subtraction.

Preparation

Lesson 1: prepare price labels 1p–10p: one large 'teaching' set and two small sets per pair

Lesson 2: prepare money word problem cards as described in lesson notes

Lesson 4: prepare price labels 1p–10p, one per group

Lesson 5: prepare price labels 1p–10p', one per pair

You will need

Equipment

Price labels 1p–10p; coins of values 1p, 2p, 5p and 10p; containers for coins

Further practice

Set up a class shop where children can buy items for up to 10p, depending on their level of confidence. At this stage they may count out just pennies to make their purchases.

Oral and mental starters for week 6

See bank of starters on pages 84 to 85. Oral and mental starters are also on the CD-ROM.

28 Missing number to make 10

27 Find the difference

26 Find the subtraction sentences

Overview of progression

Children use their growing knowledge of coins, finding totals up to 10p of two price tags. They find the answers to word problems that involve finding totals to 10p. They use coins to make amounts of money, up to 10p, using counting on methods to do this. They then begin to find the change from 10p, counting up from the total to 10p, using their understanding of difference developed in Autumn 1 Week 4.

Watch out for

Some children may count every coin as '1p'. Check that they can, for example, count 2p as 2 and so on.

Creative context

Choose stories about going to the shops, and ask children to tell others about their shopping experiences.

Vocabulary

add, answer, change, coins, cost, count, count on, count up, method, number sentence, problem, record, sign, 1p, 2p, 5p, 10p

Curriculum objectives

- To read, write and interpret mathematical statements involving addition (+), subtraction (–) and equals (=) signs.
- To represent and use number bonds and related subtraction facts within 10.
- To add and subtract one-digit numbers to 10, including zero.

Success criteria

- I can write number sentences.
- I can say some add and take away facts to 10.

You will need

Equipment

Price labels 1p–10p; coins of values 1p, 2p, 5p and 10p; containers for coins

Differentiation

Less confident learners

Decide whether to limit the activity to using the labels for 1p to 3p.

More confident learners

These children can combine the price labels for 1p to 7p.

Lesson 1 — Oral and mental starter 28

Main teaching activities

Whole-class work: Explain that you would like the children to combine two price labels to make a new total, then show this amount in coins. Hold up pairs from the teaching set of price labels, using the labels 1p to 5p. Encourage the children to 'put the larger number in your head and count on in ones' to find the total, then put out coins to represent the total. To begin with children may use just the 1p coins. Encourage them to exchange 1p coins for others of equivalent value. Say, for example, for 3p and 5p: *What is 3p add 5p? How many 1p coins is 8p? What other coins could we choose to make 8p?* Ask the children to work in pairs for a short while to find solutions. Agree that they could have chosen four 2p coins, or a selection of 1p and 2p coins to make 8p, or 1p, 2p and 5p coins. Repeat for 4p and 6p.

Group work: Each pair will need two sets of 1p to 5p price label cards. The children should combine pairs of price labels to make as many different totals as possible. Ask them to write each sum on paper, then draw coins to make the same total. Encourage them to use the smallest possible number of coins.

Progress check: Ask a pair to say one of their pairs of price labels such as 4p and 2p. Ask:

- *What is 4p add 2p?*
- *What coins could we use to show 6p?*

Invite the children to suggest different ways, such as six 1p coins, three 3p coins, or 5p and 1p coins.

Review

Review the children's work, asking questions such as:

- *How did you work that out?*
- *Is there another way of making that amount?*
- *How could you do that using fewer coins?*

Curriculum objectives
- To read, write and interpret mathematical statements involving addition, subtraction and equals signs.
- To represent and use number bonds and related subtraction facts within 10.
- To add and subtract one-digit numbers to 10, including zero.

Success criteria
- I can write and explain number sentences.
- I can say some add and take away facts to 10.

You will need
Equipment
Money word problems: three different ones, each written on a separate piece of card

Differentiation
Less confident learners
Provide simpler money problems with calculations to 5p. Provide coins for support.

More confident learners
Provide harder problems, which involve calculating totals to 15p. Children should work mentally to find solutions.

Curriculum objectives
- To read, write and interpret mathematical statements involving addition (+), subtraction (–) and equals (=) signs.
- To represent and use number bonds and related subtraction facts within 10.
- To add and subtract one-digit numbers to 10, including zero.

Success criteria
- I can write and explain number sentences.
- I can say some add and take away facts to 10.

Differentiation
Less confident learners
These children may benefit from working as a group, with an adult to help them write out their word problems.

More confident learners
Children invent word problems for totals up to 15p.

Lesson 2
Oral and mental starter 29

Main teaching activities

Whole-class work: Explain that the children will be asked to solve some problems involving money. Ask them to solve the following problem, working mentally: *James paid exactly 4p for some sweets. Which coins could he have used?* Encourage the children to explain how they worked out the answer. Write their solutions on the board, and demonstrate with coins that each solution is correct. Repeat the problem, using a different amount, such as 5p.

Group work: Provide the children with three cards, each containing a money word problem. For example:
- *John buys an apple for 3p and an orange for 4p. How much does he spend altogether?*
- *I pay 6p for some chews. Write three ways of making 6p.*
- *Jill bought a lolly for 4p and a cone for 6p. How much did she spend?*
The children should write the problems and answers as addition sentences.

Progress check: Ask questions of the children such as:
- (For 5p add 3p) *What total did you make?*
- *What coins would you choose to pay this amount?*
- *How could you pay using fewer coins?*

Review
Choose one problem from the cards for each group and invite some children to explain how they solved it. Ask questions such as:
- *How did you work that out?*
- *Who found a different solution?*
- *What if the total was ___ instead? Can you solve that too? How did you work it out?*

Lesson 3
Oral and mental starter 28

Main teaching activities

Whole-class work: Set the children some more money word problems. Ask individuals to answer and to explain how they worked it out. For example:
- *Anna buys a toffee for 3p and a chew for 2p. How much does she pay? Which coins would you use to pay this?*
- *Tom buys two mystery bags at the fair. He pays 4p for each them. How much does he pay in total? What coins would you use to pay this amount? What other ways could you use?*
- *The shopkeeper sells Sam a marble for 6p and a marble bag for 3p. How much does Sam pay altogether? Which coins do you think he used to pay that amount? How else could he pay it?*

Paired work: Ask pairs to invent at least three word problems involving money up to 10p. After ten minutes, ask each pair to work with another pair. They take turns to read out a problem for the other pair to solve.

Progress check: Ask a pair to read one of their problems aloud. Ask: *How can we work out the answer? Is there another way? What coins would you use to pay this?*

Review
Invite pairs of children to read out a problem for the others to solve. Ask: *How did you solve this problem? What strategy did you use?* Talk about the vocabulary the children have used, such as 'total' and 'altogether'. Ask children to suggest how each problem could be reworded using a different word for 'total'. Discuss the range of calculation strategies that they can use.

Curriculum objectives

● To solve one-step problems that involve addition and subtraction, using concrete objects and pictorial representations, and missing number problems.

Success criteria

● I can use coins to help me to solve money problems.

You will need

Equipment

Price labels 1p–10p; coins of values 1p, 2p, 5p and 10p; containers for coins; large sheets of paper

Differentiation

Less confident learners

Decide whether to limit this to find two ways of making each price.

More confident learners

Decide whether to extend this to prices up to 15p.

Lesson 4   Oral and mental starter 27

Main teaching activities

Whole-class work: Explain that in this, and the next, lesson, children will be solving money problems. Ask: *How many different ways can we find to make 5p?* Write the responses onto the board and ask a child to find the relevant coins. For example, for 2p, 2p and 1p coins say *2p and 2p is 4p and 1p is 5p*. Repeat for another way to make 5p.

Group work: Ask the children to work in groups of four with a set of price labels 1p–10p, some coins, and a large sheet of paper on which to make a group recording. They take turns to choose a price label, then all of them find ways to make the price. The children take turns to record on their large sheet of paper, drawing around the coins and writing its value inside, and the total at the end.

Progress check: As the children work, ask each group in turn to explain how they found their solutions. Say:

- *How many different ways did you find to make ___ p?*
- *Look again. Is there another way?*

Review

Explain that you will say a money problem. Ask the children to use their coins to solve the problem. Say, for example:

- *I buy an orange for 6p. I use three coins to pay. What coins did I use?*
- *I buy an apple for 4p. I use two coins. What coins did I use?*
- *I buy a banana for 9p. I give a 5p coin, and three more coins. What are these coins?*

Each time ask questions such as:

- *How did you work this out?*
- *Does anyone think that there is another way?*

Curriculum objectives

● To solve one-step problems that involve addition and subtraction, using concrete objects and pictorial representations, and missing number problems.

Success criteria

● I can use coins to help me to solve money problems.

You will need

Equipment

Price labels 1p–10p; coins of values 1p, 2p, 5p and 10p; containers for coins

Differentiation

Less confident learners

Decide whether to work as a group to find the totals. At this stage children, may not yet be confident to begin to find change.

More confident learners

Decide whether to include labels to 7p, and to find change from 15p.

Lesson 5   Oral and mental starter 26

Main teaching activities

Whole-class work: Choose two price labels, between 1p and 5p and show the children. Ask: *How much is this altogether? Yes, 6p. If I give the shop keeper 10p, how much money would he give me? Find the difference between 6p and 10p.* Encourage the children to use coins to find the solution, counting up from 6p to 10p in ones. Repeat for another example, such as 4p and 3p.

For change of 3p ask the children to find the fewest number of coins needed, that is a 2p and 1p. Repeat for a total of 6p, and change from 10p.

Paired work: Take turns to choose two labels from a set of 1p–5p labels. They total the pair of labels, then using coins to count up, they find the change from 10p. Ask children to record the two prices, what the change is, then draw the coins they chose. They should use the fewest number of coins each time.

Progress check: Invite a pair to give their first total, the change, and the coins that they chose. Ask of everyone:

- *How else could we give the change?*
- *Which way uses the fewest number of coins?*

Check that the children understand that fewer coins does not mean less money, and that they count the coins by value, not by the number of coins.

Review

Ask pairs to give examples of their totals, change and coins used. Ask:

- *Is there another way to give this change?*
- *How many ways can we think of?*
- *Which way is best? Why do you think that?*

You will need
1. Check
Oral and mental starter
17 Counting pictures

2. Assess
Counters

3. Further practice
Oral and mental starter
18 Counting by pointing

Photocopiable sheets
'Counting pictures'

Counting objects and pictures

Most children should be able to count pictures up to at least 10 by pointing.

Some children will not have made such progress and will require further experience of counting by coordinating pointing and saying the counting number.

1. Check

17 Counting pictures

Encourage the children to count carefully to find the totals. Observe which children are confident and which need further practice. Encourage the children to check their count by counting starting from a different point in the picture.

● *What was the last number you said in the count? So how many are there?*
● *What if you count them in a different order? How many are there then?*

2. Assess

Ask the children to work in pairs. They take turns to put out a handful of counters for their partner to count. Ask the children to place them spread out in a line. Their partner counts using the touch, count and move method. They record the count on paper. Their partner checks the count. Ask the children to do this ten times each. Record the outcomes.

3. Further practice

Use the suggested OMS to provide further reinforcement of counting by pointing. The photocopiable sheet 'Counting pictures' on page 87 will give further experience of counting pictures, then drawing a given number of pictures.

You will need
1. Check
Oral and mental starter:
23 Add and subtract to 10

2. Assess
'Add and subtract to 10'

3. Further practice
Oral and mental starters
24 Add and subtract: write
27 Find the difference

Photocopiable sheets
'Addition to 6'; 'Subtraction to 6'; 'Animal problems' (page 88)

Read and write addition and subtraction sentences

Most children should be able to read and write addition sentences to 10.

Some children will not have made such progress and will require further experience of reading and writing number sentences to 5 before moving on.

1. Check

23 Add and subtract to 10

Check which children read aloud the card as you hold it up. Note who is able to answer correctly and who needs further practice. Extend the more confident children, asking individuals to read aloud the question and say the answer quickly.

● *How did you work that out?*
● *Who used a different way?*

2. Assess

Provide photocopiable sheet 'Add and subtract to 10 (1)' on page 86. Ask the children to work individually to complete the page. For less confident children, provide number lines. For more confident children, challenge them to work quickly and accurately to complete the sheet, and to put a dot against those answers which they 'knew'. Record the outcomes.

3. Further practice

Use the suggested starters to provide further reinforcement for developing recall of addition and subtraction facts to 10. The photocopiables listed offer further opportunities to read and write number sentences.

Curriculum objectives
● To recognise and know the value of different denominations of coins and notes.

You will need
1. Check
Oral and mental starter
32 Coin recognition

2. Assess
Set of 1p, 2p, 5p and 10p coins for each pair; price labels 1p–10p

3. Further practice
General resources
Interactive teaching resource 'Money'

Coin recognition

Most children should be able to recognise and name the coins.

Some children will not have made such progress and will require further experience of naming coins and finding named coins.

1. Check

32 Coin recognition

Encourage the children to look carefully at the coins to check that they have found the one that you say. Note which children are confident and which need further practice. Extend by asking for, for example, two coins that together are worth 6p. Then extend again to include notes as well as coins.

- *Which coins are bronze?*
- *Which coins are silver?*
- *Which coins are gold?*
- *Which coins have a circle for a face/have straight edges?*

2. Assess

Ask the children to work in pairs. They need a pot of coins. Ask the children to take a price label 1p–10p and find coins that are worth that amount of money. Decide whether to limit the less confident children to prices up to 5p. Once they are confident with that, extend to 10p. Challenge the more confident children to find, where possible, two ways of making each price. Record the outcomes.

3. Further practice

Provide children with target amounts and ask them to record the combinations of coins they used to make up these amounts. They can record these on paper or using the interactive teaching resource 'Money' on the CD-ROM.

Curriculum objectives
● To compare, describe and solve practical problems for: lengths and heights; capacity and volume.

You will need
1. Check
Oral and mental starter
31 Longer or shorter

2. Assess
Pairs of different weights of parcels labelled A and B; pairs of different capacities of containers labelled C and D

3. Further practice
Two parcels, one small and heavy and the other one larger and lighter; two transparent containers, one short and wide and the other one tall and thin.

Comparing lengths, weights and capacities

Most children should be able to compare two items for length, weight and capacity.

Some children will not have made such progress and will require further support in making comparisons before moving on to comparing more than three items.

1. Check

31 Longer or shorter

Observe which children can make direct comparisons of length, by lining up one end of each item. Extend to comparing more than two strips for those who are confident.

- *Which is longer/shorter? How do you know that?*
- *Here is a third strip. Which is longest/shortest now?*

2. Assess

Ask the children to compare the weight of parcels by estimating first, and then using the bucket balance to find the heavier and lighter. Similarly provide two containers so that children can make estimates then compare by pouring to find which holds more and less. They can record by writing a sentence such as 'A weighs more than B', and so on. Record the outcomes.

3. Further practice

At this stage, provide further practical experience of comparing and ordering items by length, weight and capacity. Use the suggested resources to provide further reinforcement for developing understanding of how to make comparisons of weight and capacity.

Oral and mental starters

Number and place value

16 Counting to 50

Ask the children to count from 0 to 50. Count with them, so that if they falter they will hear the numbers in order. Repeat this several times, keeping a good pace. Now count back from 50 to 0, again, keeping the pace sharp and saying the numbers yourself in a firm voice to keep the count going.

17 Counting pictures

Ask the children to look carefully at the picture from the big book or poster. Ask questions such as: *How many ___ can you see? Are there more/fewer ___ than ___? How many more/fewer?* Where children find it difficult to count the pictures, encourage them to point to each one in turn. Remind them that they need to remember which items they have counted and which they still need to count.

18 Counting by pointing

Put out six cubes where all the children can see them. Invite the children to point and count how many. Now ask a child to count by touching and saying the number name. Repeat this for larger quantities up to about 20. Ask: *How many are there? How did you count them? How do you know you have only counted each one once?*

19 Write that number

Explain that when you say a number, you would like the children to write it on their whiteboards. When you say *Show me*, the children should hold up their boards to show you their written number. Say: *Write 3... 8... 10... 15... Show me. Write the number that is one more than ___ . Show me. Write the number that is one less than ___ . Show me. Repeat this for other teen numbers to 20.*

20 Number order

Put up the washing line. Tell the children that you have a set of 0 to 10 cards which need to be pegged on the line in order. Hold up the 0 and ask: *What number is this? Where do you think this card should go?* Invite a child to peg it to the line. Discuss whether the others agree with this position. Repeat for the 10 card. Taking the other cards in random order, ask children to peg each one to the line, repeating the questions above. Now invite some children to take a given card from the line, saying, for example: *Take the 6 card.... Take the card that is between 3 and 5....*

Extension: Over time extend the number range to up to 20.

21 Wrong number order

Before the lesson, peg 0 to 10 numeral cards onto the washing line in the wrong order. Encourage the children to discuss which number should go where, and why, before you ask individuals to move each numeral to its agreed new position.

Extension: Over time extend the number range to up to 20.

22 Place value

Provide each child with a set of arrow cards, with a 10 card and cards 0 to 9. Explain that when you say a number they should make the number with their cards. When you say *Show me*, they hold up their cards for you to see. Keep the number range from 10 to 19 at this stage.

Extension: Over time include the 20 card, and say the number 20.

Addition and subtraction

23 Add and subtract to 10

You will need a teaching set of cards from these photocopiable pages from the CD-ROM: 'Add facts to 5', 'Take away facts to 5', 'Add facts 6 to 10' and 'Take away facts 6 to 10'. Shuffle the cards. Ask the children to read each card aloud together as you show it. Then when you raise your hand, altogether the children say the answer. Keep the pace of this sharp and look to see who is answering and who is not yet sure. Ask questions such as: *How did you work out the answer? Who 'knows' the answer? Well done!*

24 Add and subtract: write

Use the same cards as in OMS 23 'Add and subtract to 10'. Provide individual whiteboards and pens. Hold up a card and ask the children to read the card, then write the answer. When you say *Show me*, the children turn their whiteboards for you to see. Keep the pace of this sharp.

25 Add and subtract to 5

Tell the children that you will say some additions, and you would like them to show you the answer each time by holding up fingers. Say: *What is 1 add 1? Show me! What is 2 add 1? Show me! What is 3 add 2? What is 4 added to 1? And 2 added to 3? How many is 1 and 3? And 2 and 2?*

Allow time between the questions for the children to work out the answers. At this stage, some of them may have rapid recall of some addition facts. Ask: *How did you work that out?* where a child has worked very quickly. Also praise those who take longer and have the correct answer. Repeat for subtraction facts such as 5 − 2, 4 − 2, and so on.

26 Find the subtraction sentences

Ask, for example, *What is 3 + 6? How did you work that out? Tell me a subtraction sentence that has 3, 6 and 9 in it.* (9 − 3 = 6 or 9 − 6 = 3). *Now tell me another one.* Repeat this for other number sentences up to a total of 10.

27 Find the difference

Show the interactive teaching resource 'Number line' on the CD-ROM and ask: *What is the difference between 6 and 10? How did you work that out?* Together count up from 6 to 10, pointing to the numbers on the number line as you count. Repeat this for other difference pairs, such as 9 and 6, 10 and 5, and so on.

28 Missing number to make 10

Ask the children to say what number is missing to make a total of 10. Say: *What number must I add to 6 to make 10? How many more do I need to add to 5 to make 10? What number goes with 3 to total 10?* Children can use their fingers to show you their answer when you say *Show me.*

29 Number stories

Explain that you will say a number story. Ask the children to put up their hands to answer the question. Say: *There are 5 dogs in the park. Another 2 dogs come into the park. How many dogs is that in total? 7 swans swim on the lake. 2 swans fly away. How many swans are on the lake now? 10 geese sit on the grass. 4 geese walk away. How many geese are still sitting on the grass?*

Ask other, similar number story questions, both addition and subtraction, to 10. Ask: *How did you work out the answer? Who did it a different way? Who 'knew' the answer? Well done!*

Oral and mental starters 30–32 continue on the CD-ROM.

Add and subtract to 10 (1)

■ Write the answers.

1. $3 + 5 =$ ☐

2. $4 + 4 =$ ☐

3. $3 + 3 =$ ☐

4. $9 - 5 =$ ☐

5. $7 - 2 =$ ☐

6. $10 - 10 =$ ☐

7. $8 + 2 =$ ☐

8. $4 + 3 =$ ☐

9. $8 - 4 =$ ☐

10. $9 - 6 =$ ☐

11. $9 - 0 =$ ☐

12. $7 - 2 =$ ☐

13. $6 + 4 =$ ☐

14. $3 + 7 =$ ☐

15. $8 - 7 =$ ☐

16. $10 - 5 =$ ☐

17. $4 + 6 =$ ☐

18. $9 - 8 =$ ☐

19. $4 + 5 =$ ☐

20. $10 + 0 =$ ☐

I can add and subtract to 10.

How did you do?

Name: _____   Date: _____

Counting pictures

■ Write how many.

1.

2.

3.

4.

■ Draw some marbles to match the number in the box.

5. 8

6. 9

7. 6

8. 10

I can count objects and pictures to 20.

How did you do?

Animal problems

■ Write the answers to the questions.

I.

6 elephants like buns.
3 elephants like carrots.
How many more elephants like buns than carrots?

2.

3 monkeys sit on the swing.
4 monkeys climb ropes.
How many monkeys are there altogether?

3.

5 penguins swim.
5 penguins sit on a rock.
How many penguins are there in total?

4.

9 seals swim.
I seal gets out of the water.
How many seals are swimming now?

5.

7 snakes are asleep.
2 snakes have spotty skins.
How many snakes do not have spotty skins?

I can solve problems using addition and subtraction.

How did you do?

SCHOLASTIC
www.scholastic.co.uk

Counting, reading and writing number patterns

Expected prior learning

Children should be able to:

- count in ones to and from at least 30
- find one more and one less of numbers to 20
- read and write numerals to 20
- count quantities to at least 10.

Topic	Curriculum objectives	Expected outcomes
Number and place value	**Lesson 1**	
	To count to and across 100, forwards and backwards, beginning with 0 or 1, or from any given number.	Count to 50, then 100, forwards and backwards.
	To count, read and write numbers to 100 in numerals, count in multiples of twos, fives and tens.	Count in twos to 20 and back again.
	Lesson 2	
	To count to and across 100, forwards and backwards, beginning with 0 or 1, or from any given number.	Count to 50, then 100, forwards and backwards.
	To count, read and write numbers to 100 in numerals, count in multiples of twos, fives and tens.	Count in twos to 20 and back again.
		Begin to recognise odd and even numbers to 20.
	Lesson 3	
	To count to and across 100, forwards and backwards, beginning with 0 or 1, or from any given number.	Count to 50, then 100, forwards and backwards.
	To count, read and write numbers to 100 in numerals, count in multiples of twos, fives and tens.	Count in twos to 20 and back again.
		Begin to recognise odd and even numbers to 20.
	Lesson 4	
	When given a number, to identify one more and one less.	Find the number that is one more or one less than numbers up to about 30, then 50.
	To read and write numbers from 1 to 20 in numerals and words.	Begin to read and write numbers in words.
	Lesson 5	
	When given a number, to identify one more and one less.	Find one more and one less numbers up to about 30, then 50.
	To read and write numbers from 1 to 20 in numerals and words.	Begin to read numbers in words.

Preparation

Lesson 1: copy 'Counting in 2s (1)', one per child; prepare number line to 20 on interactive teaching resource 'Number line'

Lesson 3: prepare number cards 0–20, one set per pair; prepare a teaching set of number cards. 0–20

Lesson 4: prepare number tracks from 'Blank number tracks' by putting a small spot on the sixth square of each track before copying, one page per pair; prepare enlarged versions of number tracks from 'Blank number tracks' by putting a small spot on the sixth square of each track before copying; prepare 'Number cards 11–20'

Lesson 5: prepare number word cards zero to twenty, one set per pair

You will need

Photocopiable sheets
'Counting in 2s (1)'

General resources
Number word cards zero to twenty; 'Number cards 0–20'; 'Blank number tracks'; interactive teaching resource 'Number line'; interactive teaching resource 'Number square'

Equipment
Interlocking cubes; washing line and pegs; number cards 21–30

Further practice

Photocopiable sheets
'Numbers to 30'; 'I more and I less to 50'

Ask the children to play 'Snap', with a shuffled set of number cards 0–20 and number cards 0–20. They can play in pairs, or groups of four.

Oral and mental starters for week 1
See bank of starters on pages 122 to 123. Oral and mental starters are also on the CD-ROM.

33 Count pictures

34 Counting to 100

37 Odds and evens

Overview of progression
This week children extend their counting forwards and back in ones to and from 0 up to 100. They count in twos to 20 and beyond, forwards and back again. They begin to recognise the repeating patterns of odd and even numbers to 20, through practical tasks using cubes, and through observation of the units (0, 2, 4, 6, 8 repeat in each decade, for example, as part of even numbers). They find 1 more and 1 less of numbers up to 30 and beyond. They begin to read numbers in words to 20.

Watch out for
Some children may not know how to count across a decade, saying instead, for example, 'twenty-eleven', 'twenty-twelve', and so on. Provide more experience of listening to the counting numbers.

Creative context
Encourage children to recognise numbers in the environment. You could make a classroom collection of numbers that children have seen, such as the door number for where they live, their postcode number, and so on.

Vocabulary
counting numbers to 100, even, odd, one less than, one more than, **tens**, **units**

Curriculum objectives

- To count to and across 100, forwards and backwards, beginning with 0 or 1, or from any given number.
- To count, read and write numbers to 100 in numerals, count in twos.

Success criteria

- I can count to 100 and back again.
- I can count in twos to 20 and back again.

You will need

Photocopiable sheets

'Counting in 2s (1)'

General resources

Number word cards zero to twenty; 'Number cards 0–20'; interactive teaching resource 'Number line'

Differentiation

Less confident learners

Decide whether to work with the group to complete photocopiable page 'Counting in 2s (1)'. Encourage the children to count aloud each time to find the missing numbers.

More confident learners

Challenge the children to write their own missing number patterns, counting in twos from 20, then 21.

Lesson 1   Oral and mental starter 33

Main teaching activities

Whole-class work: Ask the children to count with you, from 0 to 50 and back again. Repeat this several times, extending the count each time to 60, then 70, and so on up to 100. Repeat counting to and from 100 several times.

Now ask the children to count with you, from 0 to 20, but explain that this time you will be saying every other number. Ask the children to think the missing number but not say it. They can tap their knees in time with the count, as they think the missing numbers. Say: *Zero, two, four,... twenty*. Repeat this several times. Then include counting back from twenty: *Twenty, eighteen... zero*.

Reveal interactive teaching resource 'Number line' on the CD-ROM, showing a number line to 20. Ask the children to repeat their count, and to follow as you point to the numbers they say. Do this forwards and back again. Now ask questions such as:

- *Which numbers up to 10... 20 did we say in our count in twos?*
- *Which numbers between 5 and 10... did we not say in our count of twos?*

Independent work: Provide photocopiable page 'Counting in 2s (1)' from the CD-ROM. Explain that there is a number line at the top of the sheet to help them if they are not sure. They write in the missing 'counting in twos' numbers.

Progress check: Ask the children to look at the number line to 20 on interactive teaching resource 'Number line'. Say, for example:

- *If I start counting in twos from 8, what number do I say next... and next?*
- *If I count back in twos from 20, 18, what number do I say next... and next?*
- *If I count on in twos from 9 what number do I say next... and next?*
- *If I count back in twos from 17, what number do I say next... and next?*

Review

Ask the children to count in twos from 0, this time to 30, or beyond. Keep the pace sharp. Ask questions such as:

- *If we count in twos from 10 to 20, which numbers do we say?* (Write these on the board: 10, 12, 14...)
- *If we count in 2s from 20, which numbers do we say?* (Write these on the board.)
- *What do you notice about these numbers? Look carefully at the units.*

Discuss how, if we count in twos from 0, we always have the same unit numbers, that is 0, 2, 4, 6, 8.

Repeat the counting in twos, this time to 50, and back again.

Curriculum objectives
● To count, read and write numbers to 100 in numerals, count in twos.

Success criteria
● I can find odd and even numbers to 20.

You will need
Equipment
Interlocking cubes

Differentiation
Less confident learners
Decide whether to limit the children to numbers to 10 to begin with.

More confident learners
Challenge the children to find all odd and even numbers to 30, and beyond.

Lesson 2   Oral and mental starter 34

Main teaching activities

Whole-class work: Make a tower of six cubes and invite a child to count them. Now ask a child to make two equal towers from the six-cube tower. Explain that if the tower will break into two equal towers, then the starting number is even. Repeat this for an eight-cube tower. Now ask a child to come out and make a nine-cube tower. Ask the child to try to break the tower into two equal towers. Discuss how, if this is impossible, then the starting number is odd. Repeat for a tower of 11 cubes.

Paired work: Ask the children to work in pairs. They make towers of cubes from 1 to 20 and check to see if the total number of cubes is odd or even by trying to break the tower into two equal towers. They record their results in a table like this.

Odd numbers from 0 to 20	Even numbers from 0 to 20

Progress check: Invite children to say whether a number such as 4 is odd or even, then 5. Ask questions such as:

- *How can you tell whether the next number is going to be odd or even?*
- *So, 4 is even. What is 3?*

Review

Invite children to demonstrate, by making towers then trying to break them into two equal towers, whether a number is odd or even. Begin with 1 and work up to 10, to begin with. Now say:

- *What patterns do you see?*
- *If you count in twos from 0 to 10, are these odd or even numbers?*
- *If you count in twos from 1 to 19, are these odd or even numbers?*

Ask children then to say whether 11 is odd or even, and how they could work this out. Continue with numbers up to 20.

Invite the more confident learners to say whether 21, 22 and so on is odd or even, and write these into the table. Invite the children to predict whether 31, 32 and so on is odd or even and how they worked that out. Invite the children to look for patterns in the units numbers.

■ SCHOLASTIC

Curriculum objectives

● To count to and across 100, forwards and backwards, beginning with 0 or 1, or from any given number.
● To count, read and write numbers to 100 in numerals, count in multiples of twos, fives and tens.

Success criteria

● I can find odd and even numbers to 20.

You will need

General resources

'Number cards 0–20'

Equipment

Interlocking cubes

Differentiation

Less confident learners

Ask a more confident child to explain why the number is odd or even after each selection.

More confident learners

Challenge the children to work mentally. They will need to reason with their partner to explain why a number is odd or even.

Lesson 3

Oral and mental starter 34

Main teaching activities

Whole-class work: Repeat the whole-class activity from lesson 2, this time focussing on the numbers 11 to 20.

Group work: Ask the children to work in pairs, with a set of number cards 0–20 and a set of 20 interlocking cubes. They take turns to turn over a card. They say whether they think the number is odd or even. If their partner agrees, they place the card face up on the table. If their partner disagrees, the partner counts out the relevant number of cubes to make a tower, and tries to make two equal towers from the original tower. If the partner is correct, they place the card on the table in front of them, face up. At the end of the game they count how many cards they each have and the winner is the player with more.

Progress check: Ask questions such as:

● *How do you know that 11 is odd... 14 is even?*
● *Which numeral helps you more, the tens numeral or the units numeral? Tell me why?*

Review

Play 'Is it odd?' You will need a shuffled teaching set of number cards 0–20. Ask the children to read the number on the card that you hold up. If it is odd, they sit up straight with arms folded in front of them. If it is even ,they put their hands on their heads. Keep the pace of this sharp, and note which children need further practice at recalling the odd and even numbers. Play the game again, this time without the cards to act as an aid. Say the numbers, randomly, from 0 to 20. Now ask:

● *How did you work out whether a number was odd or even?*
● *Why is the units number important to help you to work out if it is odd or even?*
● *Is 19 odd or even?*
● *So what do you think 29 will be?*
● *And 39...?*

Repeat this for even numbers, extending the range as above.

Curriculum objectives

● When given a number, to identify one more and one less.
● To read and write numbers from 1 to 20 in numerals.

Success criteria

● I can find one more and one less numbers to about 30.

You will need

General resources

Interactive teaching resource 'Number square'; 'Number cards 0–20'

Equipment

Number cards 21–30

Differentiation

Less confident learners

Decide whether to limit the number range to 10–15 in order to increase the children's confidence with these numbers.

More confident learners

If the children are confident with numbers to 40, include the cards for 31–40 in their pack.

Lesson 4   Oral and mental starter 37

Main teaching activities

Whole-class work: Ask the children to look at the interactive activity 'Number square'. Say: *Look at the number 15. What is one more/less than that? How do you know?* Discuss with the children how the number one more or less is next to a given number in the counting order. Repeat this for other numbers, up to about 30. Ask similar questions while hiding numbers on the 100 square, so that the children rely on their memory.

Group work: Give each pair of children a prepared number track from photocopiable page 'Blank number tracks' from the CD-ROM. Ask them to choose a number card at random from 11–20. They write this number in the sixth box on the track (marked with a spot). One child writes the numbers that are one more/less than the starting number on the track. The other child writes the number that is one more than the largest number and the number that is one less than the smallest number. They continue until the track is complete, then they start again with another random number card. Children continue the game, but this time with numbers to 30, beginning with 26.

Progress check: Ask: *What is 1 more/less than 16... 19... ? How did you work that out?*

Review

Play the game with the children, using enlarged blank number tracks. Ask: *How do you know which number is one more/one less? How can you work it out?* Some children will 'know' the answer. Many will say the given number and count on or back one. Some may still need to say all of the counting numbers, which is an inefficient method. Encourage these children to count on or back from the given number.

Curriculum objectives

● When given a number, to identify one more and one less.
● To read numbers from 1 to 20 in words.

Success criteria

● I can find one more and one less numbers to about 30.
● I can read numbers in words to about 20.

You will need

General resources

Number word cards zero to twenty

Equipment

Washing line and pegs

Differentiation

Less confident learners

Children establish the link between numerals and words.

More confident learners

These children to lead Review session, identifying the position of numbers on the line without using the number names.

Lesson 5   Oral and mental starter 37

Main teaching activities

Whole-class work: Explain that today the children will be learning the number names as words. Begin by pinning up the number words from zero to ten onto the washing line. Read aloud the words together. Now ask the children to take turns to collect a card by saying for example: *Jon, take the card that is 1 more than 6.... 1 less than ....* When all the cards have gone, invite the children holding the cards to put them back on the line. Say, for example: *Who has the card that reads 5?* The children peg their cards back onto the line. Repeat this so that everyone has a turn at taking and replacing a card. Now extend this to the cards up to 20.

Paired work: Ask the children to work in pairs with the card words to ten. They shuffle the cards, then take turns to draw a card, read it together, then place it on the table. They place the cards in number order.

Progress check: Ask pairs to explain why they have placed cards in a particular sequence in front of them. Say, for example: *Which cards will fit either side of 15? How did you work that out?*

Review

With all twenty number word cards on the washing line, invite children to take the card that you indicate. Say, for example: *Take the number word card that is 1 more/less than 5... 15.*

Repeat this until all the cards have been removed. Now say: *Who has the card that has the number 1 less/more than 10? Peg it onto the washing line.*

Repeat this until all the cards are back, in place, on the line.

Doubles and near doubles

Expected prior learning

Children should be able to:

- add and subtract to 10.

Topic	Curriculum objectives	Expected outcomes
Addition and subtraction	**Lesson 1**	
	To represent and use number bonds and related subtraction facts within 20.	Begin to use double facts to add to 20.
	To add and subtract one-digit and two-digit numbers to 20, including zero.	
	Lesson 2	
	To represent and use number bonds and related subtraction facts within 20.	Begin to use double facts to add to 20.
	To add and subtract one-digit and two-digit numbers to 20, including zero.	
	Lesson 3	
	To represent and use number bonds and related subtraction facts within 20.	Begin to use double facts to add to 20.
	To add and subtract one-digit and two-digit numbers to 20, including zero.	
	Lesson 4	
	To represent and use number bonds and related subtraction facts within 20.	Begin to use near double facts to add and subtract, to 20.
	To add and subtract one-digit and two-digit numbers to 20, including zero.	
	Lesson 5	
	To represent and use number bonds and related subtraction facts within 20.	Begin to use near double facts to add and subtract, to 20.
	To add and subtract one-digit and two-digit numbers to 20, including zero.	
	To solve one-step problems that involve addition and subtraction, using concrete objects and pictorial representations, and missing number problems such as $7 = \square - 9$.	Solve simple problems using double and near double facts.

Preparation

Lesson 1: prepare teaching set of cards from 'Double facts to 5 + 5'

Lesson 2: prepare teaching set of cards from 'Double facts 5 + 5'; prepare 'Number cards 0–20', one set per pair

Lesson 3: prepare spinners from 'Double and double add 1', one spinner per pair

You will need

Photocopiable sheets
'Doubles and near doubles'; 'Double facts to 5 + 5'; 'Double and double add 1'

General resources
'Number cards 0–20'

Equipment
Interlocking cubes; 1–6 dice; paper clips

Further practice

Photocopiable sheets
'Double facts to 12'; 'Near doubles'

Oral and mental starters for week 2

See bank of starters on pages 122 to 123. Oral and mental starters are also on the CD-ROM.

40 Add and subtract facts to 10

41 Double facts to 5 + 5

Overview of progression

Children begin the week by generating double facts to 20, using cubes and counting on methods. They find the corresponding subtraction facts, so that for 6 + 6 = 12 they can find 12 − 6 = 6. They begin to find near doubles, such as 5 + 4 and 9 + 10, using both the methods 'double, add 1' and 'double, subtract 1'. The week finishes with some double and near-double number sentences. Some of these are of the missing number type.

Watch out for

Some children may still want to count all when finding doubles. Consider using a number line. Ask them to, for say double 6, find 6 on the number line, then count on in ones for another 6 to find the answer.

Creative context

Ask the children to look for examples of doubles, for example when shopping. They might see '2 for the price of 1' examples.

Vocabulary

add, altogether, double, equals, leaves, makes, minus (−), near double, plus (+), subtract, sum, take away, total

Curriculum objectives
- To represent and use number bonds within 20.
- To add and subtract one-digit numbers to 20.

Success criteria
- I can use cubes to find double facts.

You will need

Photocopiable sheets
'Double facts to 5 + 5'

Equipment
Interlocking cubes

Differentiation

Less confident learners
Decide whether to work as a group to make the doubles.

More confident learners
Challenge these children to find the double of 11 without using cubes.

Lesson 1
Oral and mental starter 40

Main teaching activities

Whole-class work: Explain that the children will be finding doubles. Show a card from photocopiable page 'Double facts to 5 + 5' from the CD-ROM. Ask the children to read the question, then respond by showing the double fact on their fingers. Ask individual children: *What is double ___? What is ___ add ___?* Extend to doubles to 10, by showing a tower of six cubes. Say: *How can we find double 6?* The children may suggest making another tower and counting on from 6: 7, 8... or counting on from 6 using the tower you already have. Praise this as a good way of working. Make another tower of 6 and count from the first tower: 6, 7, 8...12. Say: *So double 6 is 12. 6 + 6 = 12.*

Group work: Ask the children to find doubles for 7, 8, 9 and 10. They can use cubes and record as an addition sentence. Ask them to look for a pattern in their answers.

Progress check: Ask: What is double 2... 3 ...7? How can we find out that answer?

Check that children are using efficient methods, such as counting on mentally, or using towers of cubes. Encourage them to count on with towers of cubes, too, not to count all.

Review

Write the number sentences on the board: double 1, 2, 3 and so on to double 10. Invite the more confident learners to give the answer to double 11. Ask: *What pattern can you see?* Agree that all the 'answers' to the addition sentences are even. Also agree that each double is 2 more than the previous double.

Curriculum objectives
- To represent and use number bonds and related subtraction facts within 20.
- To add and subtract one-digit numbers to 20.

Success criteria
- I can find doubles of numbers to 20.
- I can use a double fact to find a take away fact.

You will need

Photocopiable sheets
'Double facts to 5 + 5'

General resources
'Number cards 0–20'

Differentiation

Less confident learners
Decide whether to provide interlocking cubes so that children can model each double fact with these.

More confident learners
Decide whether to include cards up to 15, as a challenge.

Lesson 2
Oral and mental starter 40

Main teaching activities

Whole-class work: Repeat the whole-class activity from lesson 1. Ask: *How did you work these out?* Remind children that if they are counting on mentally, then they can use their fingers to keep track of how many they have counted.

Group work: Provide a pack of 1–10 cards for each pair. Ask the children to shuffle the cards and take turns to take a card. They say the double fact. If their partner agrees, they can keep the card. The winner is the player with more cards at the end of the game. They reshuffle the cards and play again. Encourage them to recall facts, and to work out new facts from those they already know, for example, if 6 + 6 is 12, then 7 + 7 is 2 more, or 14.

Progress check: Ask questions such as: *What is double 5? How did you work that out? So what is double 6? How do you know that?* Encourage the children to use a double fact they know to find an unknown one.

Review

Ask double facts to 10 + 10 of the class. Discuss how the children worked out the facts if they do not yet have recall. Now ask: *If I know that double 3 is 6, what subtract fact can I work out?* Write 3 + 3 = 6 and 6 – 3 = 3 onto the board. Repeat this for double 4, 5... to double 10, in order. Ask the children to see if they can spot a pattern for the subtraction facts.

Curriculum objectives
● To represent and use number bonds and related subtraction facts within 20.
● To add and subtract one-digit numbers to 20.

Success criteria
● I can use doubles to find a near double fact.

You will need

Photocopiable sheets
'Double and double add I'

Equipment
Interlocking cubes; I–6 dice; paper clips

Differentiation

Less confident learners
Ask these children just to throw the dice and to write a 'double, add I' fact for the score. So if they throw 5, they should write
$5 + 5 + 1 = 5 + 6 = 11$.

More confident learners
When the children have completed about eight addition sentences, suggest that they write some 'double, take away I' number sentences. So for a dice score of 5, they would write
$5 + 5 - 1 = 5 + 4 = 9$.

Lesson 3

Main teaching activities

Whole-class work: Hold up a tower of four cubes and ask a child to count them. Agree that there are four. Now hold up a tower of five cubes and ask a child to count them. Ask: *What is 4 + 5? How did you work that out?* Discuss strategies; the children may have counted on in 1s from 5. Explain that you will teach them a new strategy. Say: *What is 4 + 4? Yes, double 4 is 8. So 4 + 5 is double 4 and 1 more.* Ask the children to use this strategy to work out some other near doubles: *What is 3 + 4? What is 5 + 4? What is 5 + 6?* Some children may notice that it is also possible to double the larger number and subtract 1. Praise this, and explain that it is also a good strategy.

Group work: Provide each pair of children with a spinner from photocopiable page 'Double and double add I' from the CD-ROM, a paper clip, pencil and a I–6 dice. Ask the children to take turns to spin the paper clip on the spinner and to throw the dice. They should write an addition sentence, using the outcomes. For example, for 'double add I' and a dice score of 5, they should write $5 + 5 + 1 = 5 + 6 = 11$.

Ask children to find the double subtract I number sentence and answer for each dice throw. They write the number sentence, for 'double 4 subtract I': $4 + 4 - 1 = 7$.

Progress check: Invite a child to say one of their addition sentences for the class to find the answer, for example, 'double 4 add I'. Ask questions such as: *What is the answer? How did you work that out?*

Review

Review what the children have done. Invite some children to write one of their 'double, add I' sums on the board for the others to solve. Ask: *How did you work that out? How does knowing double facts help you?* Ask some more confident children to demonstrate their 'double, take away I' number statements for the others to try. Repeat that this is also a good strategy to use. Now review some of the 'double, subtract I' number sentences. Invite a child to say one of theirs. Write this onto the board, for example: $5 + 5 - 1 = $. Ask: *How did you work out the answer?* Repeat for other 'double, subtract I' sentences.

Curriculum objectives
● To represent and use number bonds and related subtraction facts within 20.
● To add and subtract one-digit numbers to 20.

Success criteria
● I can use doubles to find a near double fact.

Differentiation

Less confident learners
Decide whether to ask the children to find 'double 3, subtract 1', 'double 4, subtract 1', 'double 5, subtract 1'.

More confident learners
Challenge the children to find the solutions to 'double 11, subtract 1' and 'double 12, subtract 1'.

Lesson 4
Oral and mental starter 41

Main teaching activities

Whole-class work: Write onto the board: 6 + 5 and ask: *How could we find the answer to this?* Children may suggest 6 + 6 − 1 or 5 + 5 + 1. Explain that both of these are good strategies. Invite the children to calculate 6 + 6 − 1 and write up 11. Repeat this for 5 + 5 + 1 = 11. Explain that either way of finding the answer is good. Repeat for 6 + 7.

Paired work: Ask the children to find the solutions to 'double 7, subtract 1', 'double 8, subtract 1', 'double 9, subtract 1' and 'double 10, subtract 1'. Ask them to double the number and then subtract 1 each time. They write a number sentence: $7 + 7 - 1 = \square$.

Progress check: When children have completed at least one of these number sentences, ask them to explain how they found the answer. Ask questions such as: *What is double 7 subtract 1? So what is 7 + 6? And what is 6 + 7?*

Review

Write up each number sentence that the children found as follows:

'double 8, subtract 1' is the same as 8 + 8 − 1 = 15 and 8 − 7 = 15.

Use the children's answers to each 'double, subtract 1' to complete the other number sentences. Discuss how useful the strategy of 'double, subtract 1' is, and that this is called 'near doubles'.

Curriculum objectives
● To add and subtract one-digit numbers to 20.
● To solve one-step missing number problems.

Success criteria
● I can use doubles to find a near double fact.
● I can solve a problem using double and near double facts.

You will need

Photocopiable sheets
'Doubles and near doubles'

Differentiation

Less confident learners
Provide blank number lines to support children's calculations.

More confident learners
Ask children to prepare some word problems using similar number sentences for children to solve during the Review section.

Lesson 5
Oral and mental starter 40

Main teaching activities

Whole-class work: Review the 'double add 1' and 'double subtract 1' strategies for adding near doubles. Ask questions such as:

- *What is 5 + 6? How did you work that out?*
- *What is 3 more than 4? How could you work it out?*
- *What is 7 + 6? How did you find the answer?*
- *What is 9 + 10?*
- *How did you find the answer? Who used a different method?*

Independent work: Check that the children are confident with at least one of the two strategies, then ask them to complete photocopiable page 'Doubles and near doubles' from the CD-ROM.

Progress check: When the children have completed the first two questions ask them all to stop and say: *What is 5 + 5? So what would 4 + 5 be? How did you work that out?* Check that children are confident with what they are doing. Refer to the third question in the second column and ask: *How would you work out the answer? What do we add to 4 to make 9?*

Review

Ask the children more 'double, add 1' questions. Choose individuals to answer, checking that they are using this strategy. Ask: *What is double 5? What is 5 + 6? How did you work that out? What is 4 + 5... 7 + 8... 9 + 10...? What do we add to 5 to make 11? How did you work that out?*

Grouping and sharing

Expected prior learning

Children should be able to:

- count out at least 10 objects.

Topic	Curriculum objectives	Expected outcomes
Multiplication and division	**Lesson 1**	
	To solve one-step problems involving multiplication and division, calculating the answer using concrete objects, pictorial representations and arrays with the support of the teacher.	Use grouping into equal quantities to begin to understand repeated addition and then multiplication.
	Lesson 2	
	To solve one-step problems involving multiplication and division, calculating the answer using concrete objects, pictorial representations and arrays with the support of the teacher.	Use sharing into equal quantities to begin to understand repeated subtraction and then division.
	Lesson 3	
	To solve one-step problems involving multiplication and division, calculating the answer using concrete objects, pictorial representations and arrays with the support of the teacher.	Use grouping into equal quantities to begin to understand repeated addition and then multiplication. Use sharing into equal quantities to begin to understand repeated subtraction and then division.
	Lesson 4	
	To solve one-step problems involving multiplication and division, calculating the answer using concrete objects, pictorial representations and arrays with the support of the teacher.	Use grouping into equal quantities to begin to understand repeated addition and then multiplication. Use sharing into equal quantities to begin to understand repeated subtraction and then division.
	Lesson 5	
	To solve one-step problems involving multiplication and division, calculating the answer using concrete objects, pictorial representations and arrays with the support of the teacher.	Use grouping into equal quantities to begin to understand repeated addition and then multiplication. Use sharing into equal quantities to begin to understand repeated subtraction and then division.

Preparation

Lessons 3 to 5: prepare the dice (showing 1, 1, 2, 2, 3, 3), one per group; 1–6 dice; copy 'Track jump', one per pair as appropriate

You will need

Photocopiable sheets

'Track jump'

Equipment

Interlocking cubes; PE or sorting hoops; shape tiles; 5 paper plates per pair; counters; dice showing 1, 1, 2, 2, 3, 3; straws; elastic bands; 1–6 dice

Further practice

Photocopiable sheets

'Grouping'; 'Sharing (1)'

Oral and mental starters for week 3

See bank of starters on pages 122 to 123. Oral and mental starters are also on the CD-ROM.

33 Count pictures

37 Odds and evens

42 Double facts to 10 + 10

Overview of progression

This week, children begin to learn about grouping and sharing. They count out a number of items, make equal groups from them and count how many groups they have, saying for example: There are four groups of 3 in 12. They share out items equally, again saying a sentence such as '15 shared between 3 is 5'. For the last three lessons, there is a circus of practical activities, with some very simple investigations recommended for lesson 5.

> ### Watch out for
> Check that children make equal groups or share equally. Some may not understand the importance of each set having the same quantity.

Creative context

Children can write simple stories about sharing, such as sharing out raisins between friends. Encourage them to think about making the sharing fair by giving everyone the same amount.

Vocabulary

count, equal groups, group, share, share equally

Curriculum objectives
● To solve one-step problems involving division, calculating the answer using concrete objects with the support of the teacher.

Success criteria
● I can make equal groups.

You will need
Equipment
Interlocking cubes

Differentiation
Less confident learners
Decide whether to work as a group to reinforce the need to make equal groups.

More confident learners
Challenge the children to try towers using 18 cubes. Ask them to put the cubes into equal groups. Challenge them to try this in different ways.

Lesson 1 — Oral and mental starter 33

Main teaching activities

Whole-class work: Explain to the children that this week they will be learning about grouping and sharing. Begin with six interlocking cubes. Invite a child to help you to make the cubes into towers of two. Ask: *How many towers do you think we can make?* When the cubes are made into three towers of two, say: *So we can make three towers of two from six.* Break the towers up and ask another child to use the cubes to make towers of three. Again ask: *How many towers do you think we can make?* Say together: *We can make two towers of three from six.* Repeat this for eight cubes, making four towers of two and two towers of four.

Paired work: Ask the children to work in pairs. They will need some interlocking cubes. Ask them to take ten cubes and to make towers of two. They count the towers they have made.

Progress check: Ask the children: *How many towers did you make? So we can make five towers of two from ten cubes. Now make towers of five. How many did you make?*

Paired work: Children repeat the activity, this time using 12 cubes. They make towers of two and count the towers they have made.

Progress check: Ask the children: *How many towers did you make? So we can make six towers of two from 12. Now make towers of six. How many did you make?*

Paired work: Ask the children to use the 12 cubes and to make towers of three and count how many towers they made. Then they repeat this for towers of four.

Review

Review the towers of three, and then the towers of four. Ask questions such as:
- *How many towers of three/four did you make?*
- *So how many towers of three can we make from 12?*

Invite the more confident children to show how they grouped their 18 cubes in different ways. Invite them to say a sentence about each grouping.

Curriculum objectives
● To solve one-step problems involving division, calculating the answer using concrete objects with the support of the teacher.

Success criteria
● I can share into equal groups.

You will need
Equipment
PE or sorting hoops; shape tiles; 5 paper plates per pair; counters

Differentiation
Less confident learners
Decide whether to work as a group to carry out the activity.
More confident learners
Encourage the children to estimate how many for each plate before each sharing.

Lesson 2

Oral and mental starter 37

Main teaching activities

Whole-class work: Ask the children to sit in a circle so that they can see what you do. Put out three hoops on the floor. Now ask a child to count out six square tiles from the shape tiles. Ask: *How shall we share these tiles into the hoops? Each hoop must have an equal share?* Invite suggestions. Children may suggest putting one in each hoop and repeat this until all the tiles are shared. At this stage, this is a helpful suggestion. Invite a child to share out the tiles. Ask: *Are the tiles shared equally? How many are in each hoop? So six shared between three hoops is two. Each hoop has two tiles.* Repeat this for another sharing, this time between two hoops, and with ten tiles.

Paired work: Ask the children to work in pairs. They need five paper plates and 12 counters. Ask them to put out three plates and to share the counters equally between the plates. Ask them to count how many counters are on each plate.

Progress check: Ask: *How many counters are on each plate? So 12 shared between three plates is four.* Say this sentence together.

Paired work: Repeat the activity, this time with two plates and 12 counters.

Progress check: Ask: *How many counters are on each plate? So 12 shared between two plates is six.* Say this sentence together.

Paired work: Repeat the activity, this time with ten counters and five plates, then ten counters and two plates. Stop the children each time and ask them to say their 'sharing' number sentence as above.

Review

Repeat the main activity, this time with eight shapes and two hoops, then eight shapes and four hoops. Ask questions such as:

- *If I share eight shapes equally between two hoops how many are there in each hoop?*
- *So if I share eight shapes equally between 4 hoops how many are there in each hoop?*
- *Now see if you can work this out. If I share ten counters equally between two plates how many counters will there be on each plate?*
- *And if I share ten counters equally between five plates how many counters will there be on each plate?*
- *What pattern can you see?*

Curriculum objectives
● To solve simple one-step problems involving division, calculating the answer using concrete objects with the support of the teacher.

Success criteria
● I can make equal groups.
● I can share into equal groups.

You will need
Photocopiable sheets

'Track jump'

Equipment

PE or sorting hoops; shape tiles; straws; elastic bands; interlocking cubes; paper plates; 1, 1, 2, 2, 3, 3 dice; 1–6 dice

Differentiation
Less confident learners

Decide whether to make the totals smaller for this group. For example, for activities 3 and 4, children could share out 12.

More confident learners

Challenge the children to try larger quantities. For activity 1 they could place 5, then 6 counters on each plate.

Lessons 3 to 5   Oral and mental starter 37 42

Main teaching activities

Whole-class work: Share out six shape tiles between two hoops. Say: *three add three is six.* Now pick up the shape tiles and put down another hoop. Ask a child to share out the tiles equally. Say together: *There are three groups of two in six.* Repeat this for two hoops and ten shape tiles.

For each of these lessons, choose one of the following activities to discuss with the children. Then, for each group of children, choose which activity you would like them to try. The next lesson children swap round so that they try a different activity. Activities 1 and 2 would be best for lessons 3 and 4. During lesson 5, all the children can try activity 3, and activity 5 is recommended for the more confident learners.

Group and paired work: Choose from these activities.

1 Collections

Ask the children to work in groups of four with four paper plates each, a dice (showing 1, 1, 2, 2, 3, 3) and a pot of counters. First, each child counts out 12 counters and puts them in a pile beside them. The children take it in turns to roll the dice and take that number of counters from their pile. The object of the game is to place three counters on each plate. The first child to do this and say a sentence such as 'There are four groups of three in 12', wins. The game can be repeated for, say, 15 counters and three plates with five counters on each.

2 Straw bundles

Ask the children to work in pairs. Provide straws and elastic bands so that children can make bundles. They count out 15 straws, then make bundles of five. Ask: *How many bundles can you make?* They say: 'There are three bundles of five in 15'. Repeat this, for five bundles of three. Then 16 straws make four, two, eight bundles, and say an appropriate sentence each time.

3 Share out 18

Children work in pairs with 18 counters and some paper plates. They share equally the counters between two, three, six plates. Each time, they say a sentence, such as '18 shared between two plates is 9'.

4 24

The children work in groups of four with 24 interlocking cubes each. They find different ways of sharing these equally. Provide some paper plates so that they can first share them between two plates and write a sentence such as '24 shared between two is six'. They then try three plates and so on. Ask them to record which equal sharings are not possible (5, 7, 9, 11, and so on).

5 Track jump

More confident learners: Ask the children to work in pairs with photocopiable page 'Track jump' from the CD-ROM. They roll a 1–6 dice, then try equal jumps along the track to see how many jumps will take them from 'Start' to 30. Remind them that not all jumps will take them exactly to 30. One of them makes the jumps while the other one counts and writes how many jumps are made. *We can make five jumps of six to get to 30.*

Progress check: Ask questions such as: *How many groups did you make? How did you find the answer?*

Check that children can say a sentence to show what they have done, such as: *I made five groups of two. I shared ten between five plates. There were two on each plate.*

Review

Review one of the activities each lesson. At the end of the lesson 5, ask questions such as: *What have you learned this week? Tell me what we mean by making equal groups. Here are six cubes. Make me two equal groups. Tell me what we mean by sharing equally. Here are two plates. Share these eight counters between the plates.*

Fractions

Expected prior learning

Children should be able to:

- know the names of 2D shapes
- compare lengths, weights and capacities
- count quantities to at least 16.

Topic	Curriculum objectives	Expected outcomes
Fractions	**Lesson 1**	
	To recognise, find and name a half as one of two equal parts of an object, shape or quantity.	Find halves of shapes.
	Lesson 2	
	To recognise, find and name a half as one of two equal parts of an object, shape or quantity.	Find halves of measures.
	Lesson 3	
	To recognise, find and name a half as one of two equal parts of an object, shape or quantity.	Find halves of measures.
	Lesson 4	
	To recognise, find and name a half as one of two equal parts of an object, shape or quantity.	Find halves of quantities.
	Lesson 5	
	To recognise, find and name a half as one of two equal parts of an object, shape or quantity.	Find halves of quantities.

Preparation

- Enlarge a copy of 'Half the cubes' to A3.
- Select starter and required resources.

Lesson 1: cut a large rectangle and a large circle from paper

Lesson 3: prepare the coloured water

Lessons 4 and 5: prepare sets of the even number cards, one set per pair; prepare sets of the doubles dominoes from 'Double 9 dominoes', one set per pair; copy 'Half the cubes', one per child

You will need

Photocopiable sheets

'Half the cubes'; 'Double 9 dominoes'

General resources

'Number cards 0–20'; interactive activity 'Finding half'

Equipment

Paper; A3 sheets of sugar paper; scissors; glue sticks; 2D shape tiles (of symmetrical shapes); scarf; ribbon, string; metre sticks; rulers; bucket balances; sand and dried peas; pairs of identical transparent containers; jugs of water, coloured with food colouring; interlocking cubes; counters; paper plates

Further practice

Photocopiable sheets

'Halves (1)'

Use the activities in lessons 4 and 5 for further experience of finding halves of quantities.

Oral and mental starters for week 4

See bank of starters on pages 122 to 123. Oral and mental starters are also on the CD-ROM.

34 Counting to 100

43 Totals to 10

44 Near doubles

Overview of progression

During this week, children use the vocabulary of fractions in practical activities involving measures and quantities. This week brings together the work already done on odd and even numbers, and finding doubles, and now uses them in the context of fractions. In particular, children find halves of measures and quantities. For lesson 5, there is a simple investigation available.

> ## Watch out for
> Check that the children understand that finding halves involves two equal parts. Encourage children to use the word equal when talking about two halves of objects or quantities.

Creative context

Use the language of fractions when, for example, children compare the length of their stride. Ask a child to take a step half as long as another child, and so on.

Vocabulary

equal, even number, half, odd number, share, whole

Curriculum objectives
● To recognise, find and name a half as one of two equal parts of a shape.
Success criteria
● I can find halves of shapes.

You will need
Equipment
Paper; A3 sheets of sugar paper; scissors; glue sticks; 2D shape tiles (of symmetrical shapes)

Differentiation
Less confident learners
Check that the children fold as carefully and exactly as they can to show 'half'.
More confident learners
Ask the children to cut several squares. Now challenge them to find different ways of folding each square exactly in half.

Lesson 1
Oral and mental starter 34

Main teaching activities

Whole-class work: Explain to the children that this week they will be finding out about 'half'. Hold up a rectangle of paper and say: *This is a whole rectangle. I am going to fold this in half.* Make the fold and show the children the result. Open out the paper again and say: *This is the whole. Now watch as I fold the paper. This is the half. How many halves are there?* Agree that there are two halves to make a whole. Repeat this for the circular piece of paper.

Group work: Provide each group with some 2D shape tiles, paper, pencils and scissors. Ask the children to draw around the shape tiles and cut them out. They fold the paper shapes carefully to show 'half'.

Provide large sheets of sugar paper. As a group, the children choose one of their squares, and stick that onto the paper. Next to it they stick a square folded in half. Ask them to label these. They repeat this for their other paper shapes.

Progress check: Ask the children to hold up their square, unfolded. Now ask them to fold it in half and hold it up. Repeat this for the other shapes that they have cut out. Write the names of the shapes onto the board, and also 'half'. Read these together.

Review

Ask each group to show their work. Ask: *Which shape is this?* Point to it folded in half. Now invite the more confident learners to show their work. Discuss how a square can be folded in different ways. Ask the children to name the shapes that are made when folding a square in half.

Curriculum objectives
● To recognise, find and name a half as one of two equal parts of a length.
Success criteria
● I can find halves of lengths.

You will need
Equipment
Scarf; ribbon; string; metre sticks; rulers

Differentiation
Less confident learners
Check that the children understand how to find half of their string for each of the measurements they make.
More confident learners
Challenge the children to compare the string to shorter lengths, such as an eraser, crayon, and so on, and to cut the string to match and then find half.

Lesson 2
Oral and mental starter 43

Main teaching activities

Whole-class work: Explain that in today's lesson the children will be finding halves of lengths. Hold out the scarf and ask: *How can we find half the length of the scarf?* Say: *This is half of the scarf.* Repeat this with a piece of string, and then a ribbon. Open out the ribbon again. Say: *Now we can see the whole ribbon.*

Paired work: Ask the children to cut a piece of string the same length as a metre stick. They halve the length of the string by folding. They repeat this for the length of a ruler, length of a book, height of a bookcase, width of a table, and so on.

Progress check: Ask the children to hold up their metre length of string. Say: *That is the whole length. Now fold this in half.* Check that the children understand how to do this.

Review

Invite children from each group to show the pieces of string they cut. Ask them to say what they used to measure out the string against, and then to show half. Now invite a confident child, of average height, to come to the front of the class. Match a piece of string to the height of the child, and cut it. Hold the string up and invite a child to fold the string to show half, and hold it against the child again. Ask: *How have we found half of the height of ...? Where should we hold the string to show half of the height?* Discuss how it could be held, halved, from the floor up, or from the head down. Both would show half.

Curriculum objectives
● To recognise, find and name a half as one of two equal parts of weights and capacities.

Success criteria
● I can find halves of weights.
● I can find halves of capacities.

You will need
Equipment
Bucket balances; sand and dried peas; pairs of identical transparent containers; jugs of water, coloured with food colouring

Differentiation
Less confident learners
All of the children should be confident enough to carry out these tasks. Check that they can use the vocabulary of fractions to describe what they have done.

More confident learners
Invite the children to try finding half of a pouring medium, using two non-identical containers. Discuss with them why this is so difficult to do with reasonable accuracy.

Lesson 3   Oral and mental starter 43

Main teaching activities

Whole-class work: Show the bucket balance. Explain that you have some sand in a container. Ask: *How can we use the bucket balance to find half of the sand?* Discuss how the sand can be poured between the two buckets until the buckets are balanced. Say: *Each bucket has half of the sand in it.*

Demonstrate with a transparent container with some water in it. Ask: *How can we find half of the water?* Show another, identical, container. Demonstrate that by pouring until both containers have the same level of water, it is possible to find half of the water. Ask a child to pour the water from one of the containers into the other. Now ask: *How much water is in this container? Yes, it is full.*

Paired work: It is suggested that both activities are provided, and that the children swap activities halfway through the available time.

1 Fill and pour

Explain that there are two containers that are identical. Ask the children to fill one of them, then pour half into the other. Ask them all to check that it is half full. They can use coloured water, sand, dried peas, so that they experience this with different pouring media. When they have determined that both containers contain half, they then pour one back into the other, to check that one container is then full, and the other empty.

2 Balance the buckets

Provide some sand in a container and cubes, dried peas and so on. Ask the children to work in pairs to pour out the contents into both buckets until they have balance. They draw a picture of the balance level and write a sentence underneath, for example: *There is half of the sand in each bucket.* They can repeat this with a different pouring medium such as cubes.

Progress check: When the children have had half of their allotted time, ask them to stop what they are doing. Say:
- *How do you know when you have half of the sand in each bucket? What does the bucket balance look like?*
- *How can you tell when you have half of the water in each container?*

Review

Ask pairs of children to show their recording when using the bucket balance. Discuss how the balance must be level in order to show that half of the sand is in one bucket and the other half is in the other bucket. Repeat this for pouring out half from one container to another. Encourage the more confident learners to explain why it is important to use two identical containers when pouring out half. Say:
- *What have you learned today?*
- *Why is it important to use two containers that are the same when pouring out half of the sand or water?*
- *Why is it important to make sure that the bucket balance balances when finding half of the sand?*

Curriculum objectives
● To recognise, find and name a half as one of two equal parts of a quantity.

Success criteria
● I can find halves of quantities.

You will need

Photocopiable sheets

'Double 9 dominoes'; 'Half the cubes'

General resources

'Number cards 0–20'; interactive activity 'Finding half'

Equipment

Interlocking cubes; counters; paper plates

Differentiation

Less confident learners

For lesson 4, decide whether to reduce the quantities in activity 1, to 8, 10 and 12 cubes or counters.
For lesson 5, decide whether to use activity 3, where children can use the domino spots to help them to find the double, then say the half fact.

More confident learners

For lesson 4, decide whether to increase the number of cubes, even numbers, to 30.
For lesson 5, ask the children to undertake activity 4. Instead of cubes ask them to use counters, so that the number of counters picked up each time is larger.

Lessons 4 and 5   Oral and mental starter 44

Main teaching activities

Whole-class work: Invite a child to make 12 cubes into a tower. Ask: *How many cubes are there? How can we find half of them?* Snap the tower to show two equal halves and invite children to count each tower to check. Say: *Half of 12 is six.* Now put out 14 counters and two plates. Explain that another way to find half is to share the counters equally between the plates. Invite a child to do this and count how many are on each plate. Say: *Half of 14 is seven.*

Explain that children can use the double facts they know to find half. Write on the board: 8 + 8 = ☐ and ask for the answer. Now write 16 − 8 = ☐. Say: *Think about what the answer is.* Put out some cubes and ask a child to count out 16, make a tower, and then snap it into two equal towers. Ask the child to count both towers to check. Say together: *Half of 16 is eight. 16 take away eight is eight.*

Paired work: Here are some activities about finding half of quantities. Activity 4 is a simple investigation, to help the children to realise that only an even number of items can be halved exactly. You may prefer to ask all the children to do activity 4 in lesson 5 as it is a simple investigation.

1. Children find half of 16, 18 then 20. One of them makes a tower of cubes then breaks it in half to find how many. The other child shares the required number of counters between two paper plates in order to find half. They record their results by writing: Half of ☐ is ☐.

2. Children need a shuffled set of number cards with 0 and the odd numbers removed. They take turns to turn over a card. They use their knowledge of doubles to find half of the number. If their partner disagrees with their answer, then they can use cubes to make a tower, snap it and check the answer. They can play this game several times.

3. Ask children to use a set of the doubles dominoes from photocopiable pages 'Double 9 dominoes' from the CD-ROM. They place the dominoes face down on the table, then take turns to choose one of them. They say the double, such as 'double 9', the total, and then what half is.

4. Ask the children to take turns to take a handful of cubes. They count how many, and then make a tower. They break the tower to see if they can make two equal halves. Ask them to record this on photocopiable page 'Half the cubes' from the CD-ROM. They will find that only even quantities of cubes can be made into two equal halves.

Progress check: Ask questions such as: *How did you find half? You know some doubles. How does that help you to find half?*

Review

Say a number and ask the children to find the half. Begin with numbers to ten, so that children can, if needed, use their fingers to help them. Say, for example: *What is half of four? How did you work that out? What is half of eight? What is half of ten? How can we find half of 12? 16? 20?*

Invite the children to explain their methods. Some may realise that they can use double facts that they know to find the half.

Review activity 4. Put up photocopiable page 'Half the cubes'. Invite children to say how many cubes they picked up, whether this was an odd or even number, and whether they could make two equal halves. Fill in the chart so that everyone can see. Now say: *What do you notice about the odd numbers? Is it possible to make two equal groups from an odd number of cubes? So what is special about even numbers?* Remind the children that double numbers are always even.

To assess their understanding of 'half', give each child the interactive activity 'Finding half' on the CD-ROM in lesson 5 or as a half-term assessment activity.

Measures, including time

Expected prior learning

Children should be able to:

● compare at least two items for length, weight and capacity.

Topic	Curriculum objectives	Expected outcomes
Measurement	**Lesson 1**	
	To sequence events in chronological order using language such as: before and after, next, first, today, yesterday, tomorrow, morning, afternoon and evening.	Re-tell a story in an order that is sensible. Use the vocabulary of time to sequence events.
	Lesson 2	
	To tell the time to the hour and half past the hour and draw the hands on a clock face to show these times.	Set a clock face to hour and half hour times with reasonable accuracy. Read the o'clock and half past times.
	Lesson 3	
	To measure and begin to record the following: ● lengths and heights ● mass/weight ● capacity and volume ● time (hours, minutes, seconds).	Use uniform non-standard units of length.
	Lesson 4	
	To measure and begin to record the following: ● lengths and heights ● mass/weight ● capacity and volume ● time (hours, minutes, seconds).	Use uniform non-standard units of weight.
	Lesson 5	
	To measure and begin to record the following: ● lengths and heights ● mass/weight ● capacity and volume ● time (hours, minutes, seconds).	Use uniform non-standard units of capacity.

Preparation

Lesson 1: copy 'David's birthday' for yourself; copy 'Jack and Jill', one per child

Lesson 2: ; copy 'Times of the day', one per child

Lesson 3: copy 'How long?', one per child

Lesson 4: prepare parcels of different weights; prepare sets of cards from 'Measures vocabulary' for yourself and one set per group

Lesson 5: prepare sets of cards from 'Measures vocabulary', one set per group

You will need

Photocopiable sheets
'David's birthday'; 'Jack and Jill'; 'Times of the day'; 'How long?'

General resources
'Measures vocabulary'; interactive teaching resource 'Clocks'

Equipment
Teaching clock; string; about ten straws; scissors; interlocking cubes; parcels and reading books of different sizes and weights 100g weights and balances; containers for filling and pouring; scoops and spoons; sand or water; two jugs, cups; egg cups

Further practice

Use oral and mental starter 47 'Tell the time' to encourage the children to set o'clock then half past times. Provide further experience of estimating and measuring using uniform non-standard units such as: straws to measure the length and width of tables; spoonfuls of sand to estimate, then weigh, items in the classroom by using a bucket balance cupfuls of sand or water to estimate, then measure the capacity of jugs, bottles, margarine tubs.

Oral and mental starters for week 5

See bank of starters on pages 122 to 123. Oral and mental starters are also on the CD-ROM.

43 Totals to 10

45 Days of the week

47 Tell the time

Overview of progression

The week begins with the children learning some vocabulary associated with time, and then they begin to tell o'clock and half-past times. Children are encouraged to set the clock faces as accurately as they can. Then children use uniform non-standard units to estimate and measure length, weight and capacity.

Watch out for
Check that the children understand which way the hands of the clock turn. Also ensure that children understand where the minute and the hour hands are placed for o'clock and half-past times. Demonstrate this with a geared teaching clock so that the children see the movement of both clock hands from o'clock to half past to o'clock again.

Creative context

Encourage children to re-tell stories, in the chronological order of what occurred. Encourage them to use vocabulary such as 'first', 'next', 'then', 'before', 'last'.

Vocabulary

afternoon, balance, before, capacity, centimetre (cm), **clock**, container, day, days of the week, deep, depth, evening, first, hands, heavier/ heaviest, height, high, holds more/holds most, hour, last unit, length, long, longer/ longest, low, measuring jug, metre (m), metre stick, midnight, morning, narrow, next, night, ruler, scales, shallow, short, size, tall, tape measure, then, thick, thin, time, today, tomorrow, week, weekend, weight, wide, width, yesterday

Curriculum objectives
● To sequence events in chronological order using language such as: before and after, next, first, today, yesterday, tomorrow, morning, afternoon and evening.

Success criteria
● I can say the names of the days of the week in order.

You will need
Photocopiable sheets
'Jack and Jill'; 'David's birthday'

Differentiation
Less confident learners
Say both verses of the 'Jack and Jill' rhyme again, asking children to point to the corresponding picture as you say each line. Repeat asking them to move the pictures into the correct sequence.

More confident learners
Children to choose another nursery rhyme and draw some pictures for it. They can swap with each other, cut out the pictures and put them into the correct time sequence.

Lesson 1
Oral and mental starter 43

Main teaching activities
Whole-class work: Say the days of the week together. Ask: *What day is it today? What day will it be tomorrow? What day was it yesterday?* On the board, write the days of the week, starting with Monday, and ask the children to say together the next day as you write. Ask: *Which days do we come to school? Which days do we not come to school?* Explain that Saturday and Sunday are the weekend days. Read the children the story on photocopiable page 'David's birthday' from the CD-ROM. Ask: *What happened first? Who can remember what happened next? What happened at the end of the story? Who would like to tell the story in their own words?*

Discuss how the events in the story took place in a particular order. Ask: *What do you do when you get up in the morning? What do you do next?* Encourage the children to use the vocabulary of ordering time.

Paired work: Recite both verses of the nursery rhyme 'Jack and Jill' together. Ask the children to cut out the pictures on photocopiable page 'Jack and Jill' from the CD-ROM, then sequence them to tell the story. When they are sure their sequence is correct, they should glue the pictures onto paper.

Progress check: Hold up a picture. Invite children to explain which picture comes next and why.

Review
Ask questions such as: *What did we do first? And next? What did we do before/after...? What do you think we will do next?*

Say together the days of the week in order. Point to the names of the days of the week out of order and ask the children to read them together.

Curriculum objectives
● To tell the time to the hour and half past the hour and draw the hands on a clock face to show these times.

Success criteria
● I can read and find o'clock times on a clock face.
● I can read and find half-past times on a clock face.

You will need
Photocopiable sheets
'Times of the day'
General resources
Interactive teaching resource 'Clocks'
Equipment
Teaching clock; clocks

Differentiation
Less confident learners
Decide whether to limit the children to o'clock times.

More confident learners
Decide whether to introduce 'quarter past' times as well.

Lesson 2
Oral and mental starter 45

Main teaching activities
Whole-class work: Talk about how the hands on the clock turn. Set the hands on the teaching clock to 9 o'clock. Ask: *What time is this?* Repeat this for other o'clock times, until the children are confident with reading these. Now set the hands to half past two. Ask the children to describe where the minute hand is, and explain that when it is 'straight down' or pointing to the 6, this means it is a 'half past' time. Encourage the children to say that the minute hand has moved halfway round the clock, and demonstrate this by moving the hands to show 3 o'clock and then half past three. Set the clock to various o'clock and half past times for the children to read. Use the interactive teaching resource 'Clocks' on the CD-ROM for this, using the random time generator set to o'clock and half past times.

Paired and Independent work: Provide the children with clocks. They take turns to say an o'clock or half past time. Their partner sets the clock to show each time. Tell the children that they will have only about ten minutes for this activity. Then provide copies of photocopiable page 'Times of the day' for children to complete individually.

Progress check: Set the 'Clock' to an o'clock time and ask: *What time is this?* Repeat this for more o'clock times, then for half past times.

Review
Go over the individual activity and ask: *What do you do at 7 o'clock in the evening? What time is your bedtime/dinnertime/playtime?* Encourage the children to answer with a sentence, and to use the vocabulary of time appropriately.

 SCHOLASTIC

Curriculum objectives
● To measure and begin to record lengths.
Success criteria
● I can use straws or cubes to find how long a book is.

You will need
Photocopiable sheets
'How long'
Equipment
String; about ten straws; scissors; cubes and interlocking cubes

Differentiation
Less confident learners
Ask an adult to work with this group. The children may need help with matching the string along the line, then matching the length cut off to cubes.

More confident learners
Challenge the children to draw lines for each other and to use this method of measuring and estimating first.

Lesson 3
Oral and mental starter 47

Main teaching activities

Whole-class work: Remind the children of the work they did previously on measuring the lengths of things. Draw a straight line on the board. Invite the children to look carefully at this line and estimate how long it is in straws. Ask them how they could measure this line. The children may suggest putting straws against the line until they have gone along its length, then counting the straws.

Explain that another way to do this would be to use a line of straws on the table. Ask a child to make this. Now show the children how to measure the line on the board with a piece of string, then measure the string against the straws. Emphasise that you are matching the end of the string to the end of the line of straws. Compare the measured length with the children's estimates.

Draw a curved line on the board. Ask the children to estimate how long this is. Then invite two children to take some string and match the string along the line. They can cut off the extra string if this helps. Now ask them to match the length of string against the line of straws. Can they say how long the line on the board was? Compare the measure with the children's estimates.

Paired work: Ask the children to work in pairs. Each pair will need a long piece of string, scissors, cubes and each child will need a copy of photocopiable page 'How long?' from the CD-ROM. They should estimate and measure the length of each line on the sheet, using string and matching it to a line of cubes, and record their estimates and measures on the sheet.

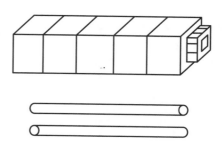

Progress check: Ask pairs to demonstrate to the class how they measure. Check that they place the string carefully and as accurately as they can, then match it against the line of cubes. Discuss how important it is to have the cubes touching each other to make the measure as accurate as they can.

Review

Discuss how well the children managed this method of measuring. Invite them to talk about what was easy about it, and what they found more difficult. Ask: *Was your measure about the same as ___ cubes? Was your estimate just over what you measured? Was it just under?*

Curriculum objectives
● To measure and begin to record mass/weight.
Success criteria
● I can use cubes to find how heavy a pencil is.

You will need
Photocopiable sheets
'Measures vocabulary'
Equipment
Parcels and reading books of different sizes and weights 100g weights and balances; interlocking cubes

Differentiation
Less confident learners
Work with an adult to carry out the estimation and measuring task, discussing the accuracy of the measuring using appropriate language.
More confident learners
Challenge the children to choose a book that they estimate to be heavier than the other book they have used. Ask them to weigh it and write a sentence about how it compares with the of the first book.

Lesson 4   Oral and mental starter 47

Main teaching activities

Whole-class work: Explain to the children that they will be making estimates and measures of mass. Pass one of the parcels around the class for the children to weigh in their hands. Then ask: *How many cubes do you think will balance the parcel?* Write some suggestions on the board. Invite a child to balance the parcel with some cubes. As they do this, ask the children to count together for each cube put into the pan. Say: *Describe how it was balanced.* For example, they might say:
● *We used ten cubes to balance the parcel.*
● *Ten cubes nearly balanced the parcel. Eleven cubes were too many.*
● *The parcel needed nearly/close to ten cubes to balance it.*
● *It weighed just over ten cubes.*
● *It weighed just under eleven cubes.*
Write some of these sentences on the board. Read out the appropriate vocabulary from photocopiable page 'Measures vocabulary'.

Group work: Ask the children to work in groups of about four. Each group chooses four different reading books. They estimate the masses and then balance with cubes. They use the cards from 'Measures vocabulary' to help them write sentences about their estimates and measures.

Progress check: Ask questions of each group such as:
● *Did you make a good guess about how many cubes balanced each book?*
● *What helped you to make a good guess?*

Review

Invite pairs of children to report their results. Discuss how close their estimates were. Ask: *How many cubes did you need to balance the parcel? So the parcel weighed just over how many cubes? And it weighed just under how many cubes?*

Curriculum objectives
● To measure and begin to record capacity.
Success criteria
● I can use spoons of sand to find how many a margarine tub will hold.

You will need
General resources
'Measures vocabulary'
Equipment
Containers for filling and pouring; scoops and spoons Sand or water; two jugs, cups, egg cups

Differentiation
Less confident learners
Work with an adult to carry out the estimation and measuring task, discussing the accuracy of the measuring using appropriate language.
More confident learners
Challenge the children to select different containers and compare them to those used in the lesson.

Lesson 5   Oral and mental starter 43

Main teaching activities

Whole-class work: Explain that the children will be estimating and measuring capacity (how much something holds). Show the children a container (such as a jug) and ask them to estimate how many cups of water it will hold. Write some of their estimates on the board. Ask a child to check by filling the container and (all together) count the number of cupfuls used. Ask: *Did the container hold all of the last cup of water? Is it full to the top? How many cups of water did it hold?* Encourage the children to talk about 'just over four cups', 'nearly five cups', and so on.

Group work: Ask the children to work in groups of four. Each group chooses four different containers. They estimate the capacity of each, then measure by filling with scoops or spoonfuls of water. They make a group record of their estimates and measures. They use the cards from photocopiable page 'Measures vocabulary' help them write some sentences about their estimates and measures.

Progress check: Observe the children as they work. Ask: *How did you make your estimate? Was it a good estimate?*

Review

Invite pairs of children to report their results. Discuss how close their estimates were, and how accurately they could measure with the scoops or spoonfuls of water. Ask questions such as: *How many scoops of water did you need to fill the container? So the jug contained just over how many scoops of water? And it contained just under how many scoops of water?*

Now ask the children to work in pairs and discuss what they have learned about estimating and measuring length, weight and capacity.

Addition and subtraction to 15

Expected prior learning

Children should be able to:

- Recall some addition and subtraction facts to 10.

Topic	Curriculum objectives	Expected outcomes
Addition and subtraction	**Lesson 1**	
	To add and subtract one-digit and two-digit numbers to 20, including zero.	Add and subtract mentally to 10.
	Lesson 2	
	To add and subtract one-digit and two-digit numbers to 20, including zero.	Use known facts to find addition facts to 15.
	Lesson 3	
	To add and subtract one-digit and two-digit numbers to 20, including zero.	Use known facts to find addition facts to 15.
	Lesson 4	
	To add and subtract one-digit and two-digit numbers to 20, including zero.	Use known facts to find addition facts to 15. Derive subtraction facts to 15.
	Lesson 5	
	To solve one-step problems that involve addition and subtraction, using concrete objects and pictorial representations, and missing number problems $7 = \square - 9$.	Solve simple one-step problems for addition and subtraction to 15.

Preparation

Lesson 1: prepare a teaching set of cards from 'Add facts to 5', 'Take away facts to 5', 'Add facts 6 to 10' and 'Take away facts 6 to 10', per group

Lesson 2: prepare spinners from '6, 7, 8 and 9 spinner', one spinner per pair

Lesson 3: prepare spinners from '6, 7, 8 and 9 spinner', one spinner per pair

Lesson 4: copy 'Number trios', one per child

You will need

Photocopiable sheets

'Add facts to 5'; 'Take away facts to 5'; 'Add facts 6 to 10'; 'Take away facts 6 to 10';'Number trios'; '6, 7, 8 and 9 spinner'

Equipment

Individual whiteboard and pens; interlocking cubes; tubs of 5p and penny coins for each group; tubs of 10p, 5p, 2p and 1p coins for each group

Further practice

Photocopiable sheets

'Money'; 'Number trios (1)'; 'Number trios (2)'

Provide practical experience of buying and totalling two items in the class shop.

Oral and mental starters for week 6

See bank of starters on pages 122 to 123. Oral and mental starters are also on the CD-ROM.

34 Counting to 100

36 Counting in 2s

47 Tell the time

45 Days of the week

Overview of progression

Children begin the week by revising addition and subtraction facts to 10, because these will be helpful to them in subsequent lessons.

In lesson 2, they learn a new strategy for adding some numbers by adding 5s. For example, for 5 + 8, show the children a tower of five cubes, and another of eight. Explain that the eight tower can be broken into a five and a 'bit'. Invite a child to do this, making towers of five and three. Invite the children to check by counting the cubes in each tower. Now say: 5 add 8 is the same as 5 add 5 add 3. So 5 and 5 is 10 and 3 more: 11, 12, 13. Write on the board: 5 + 8 = 5 + 5 + 3. Ask: *What is 5 add 5? Yes, 10. And 10 add 3 is? 13. So 5 add 8 is 13. Write on the board: 5 + 8 = 5 + 5 + 3, 10 + 3 = 13. So 5 + 8 = 13.* If the children do not recognise that, for example, 10 + 3 is 13, ask them to count on in ones from 10.

They use this method to find addition of 5 to 6, 7, 8, 9 and 10. They find the corresponding subtraction facts. In lesson 5, they use coins to find totals, using the adding 5s strategy to find the total of two prices, then find the fewest number of coins needed to make that total.

Watch out for

Check that children understand that numbers larger than 5 can be broken down into 5 add something: 6 = 5 + 1, 7 = 5 + 2 and so on.

Creative context

Children can use the class shop to purchase two items, one of which costs 5p and the other between 6p and 10p, and find the total cost.

Vocabulary

add, altogether, and, equals, subtract, take away, total

Curriculum objectives
- To add and subtract one-digit numbers to 10.

Success criteria
- I can add and subtract to 10.

You will need
Photocopiable sheets
'Add facts to 5'; 'Take away facts to 5'; 'Add facts 6 to 10'; 'Take away facts 6 to 10'

Differentiation
Less confident learners
Decide whether to provide cubes or a number line to support children's recall.

More confident learners
Encourage the children to recall the facts where possible, and to put a dot against those that they think that they 'know'.

Lesson 1   Oral and mental starter 34

Main teaching activities

Whole-class work: In this lesson children will revise some addition and subtraction facts to 10, in preparation for the next four lessons. Explain that you will say an addition or subtraction with totals to 10. Ask the children to find the answer as quickly as possible. Use shuffled cards from photocopiable pages 'Add facts to 5', 'Take away facts to 5', 'Add facts 6 to 10' and 'Take away facts 6 to 10' from the CD-ROM. Keep the pace of this sharp. Now ask: *If 5 + 4 equals 9, what other addition sentence can you make from 5, 4 and 9? Tell me a subtraction sentence that uses 5, 4 and 9. Tell me another one.* Write the answers onto the board. Repeat for, say, 3 + 6.

Paired work: Ask the children, in pairs, to write addition and subtraction sentences on their individual whiteboards for their partner to complete. If necessary, prompt with example (such as 4 + 5, 7 − 2 and so on) and check both partners understand the questions and answers.

Progress check: Check children's rapid recall of number facts by asking: *How did you find the answer? Which questions could you answer straight away? Which questions did you need to work out the answer?*

Review

Write a number trio onto the board, such as 3, 4 and 7. Ask the children for two addition and two subtraction facts for these numbers. Write their number sentences. Ask questions such as: *How did you work that out? Who did this another way? Who 'knows' these facts? Well done!*

Repeat for another trio such as 6, 2 and 8.

Curriculum objectives
- To add one-digit numbers to 20.

Success criteria
- I can work out addition facts to 15.

You will need
Photocopiable sheets
'6, 7, 8 and 9 spinner'

Equipment
Interlocking cubes

Differentiation
Less confident learners
The children will benefit from working in a group, with an adult, to carry out the activity. The adult should check that the children can partition and then add. If necessary, they can add by counting on in ones from 10.

More confident learners
Challenge the children to use their knowledge of tens and units numbers to find totals such as 10 + 3 rapidly.

Lesson 2   Oral and mental starter 36

Main teaching activity

Whole-class work: Explain that today, the children will learn a new strategy to help them add. On the board, write the addition sentence 5 + 8 = and use the process described in 'Overview of progression' to explain how children can use the method 'five and a bit' for adding. Repeat this for another example of adding 6, 7, 8 or 9 to 5.

Paired work: Ask the children to work in pairs. They take turns to spin a paper clip around a pencil on the spinners made from photocopiable page '6, 7, 8 and 9 spinner' from the CD-ROM, then add the number to 5. Provide interlocking cubes at this stage so that the children can model the strategy. They record on paper as an addition sentence: 5 + 7 = 5 + 5 + 2. 10 + 2 = 12. So 5 + 7 = 12

Progress check: Invite two confident children to say one of their solutions. Write up their recording onto the board so that everyone can see. Ask questions such as:
- *How did the cubes help you?*

Discuss how breaking (partitioning) the larger number into a 5 and some more to make a 10 is a helpful strategy as all that has to be added then is a few more.

Review

Invite children to work mentally to find some addition answers. Say, for example:
- *What is 5 add 7?*
- *How did you work that out?*
- *So how many did you add to 10 to find the answer?*

Repeat for 5 + 8 and 5 + 9, 7 + 5, 8 + 5, 9 + 5.

Curriculum objectives
● To add 1-digit numbers to 20.

Success criteria
● I can work out addition facts to 15.

You will need
Photocopiable sheets
'6, 7, 8 and 9 spinner'

Equipment
Tubs of 5p and 1p coins for each group

Differentiation
Less confident learners
Decide whether to ask the children to work as a group with an adult to help them. Ask the adult to encourage them to say the counting on sentence each time.

More confident learners
Provide 2p coins as well. The children can then put out the amounts such as 5p and 8p as 5p and 5p and 2p and 1p and total them.

Lesson 3

Main teaching activities

Whole-class work: Provide each group with some 5p and 1p coins. Explain that children will total amounts, using the method that they learned in lesson 2. Ask: *What is 5p add 7p? How could we work this out?* If children need a prompt, remind them that in lesson 2 they added 5 + 7 as
5 + 5 + 2. Ask the children to put out a 5p coin, and the 7p as a 5p coin and two 1p coins. Say together: *5p and 5p is 10p and 1p is 11p and 1p is 12p. So 5p and 7p is 12p.* Repeat this for another amount, such as 5p and 8p.

Paired work: Ask the children to work in pairs. They will need some 5p and 1p coins. They use the spinners from photocopiable page '6, 7, 8 and 9 spinner' from the CD-ROM and add the spinner number in pence to a 5p coin each time. They say aloud the 'addition by counting on' sentences to their partner.

Progress check: Ask the children to explain how they would total 5p and 9p. Say the number sentence together: *5p and 5p is 10p and 4p is 11p, 12p, 13p, 14p. So 5p and 9p is 14p.* Check that children join in with this, and those that do not, work with them for a little while as they use the coins to help them.

Review
Ask the children to use their coins to help them to total amounts that you say. Say, for example:
- *What is 5p and 7p?*
- *How did you work that out?*
- *How would you total 5p and 8p?*
- *Now how would you total 6p and 7p?*

Curriculum objectives
● To add and subtract 1-digit numbers to 20.

Success criteria
● I can work out addition facts to 15.
● I can work out subtraction facts to 15.

You will need
Photocopiable sheets
'Number trios'

Equipment
Interlocking cubes

Differentiation
Less confident learners
Provide interlocking cubes if necessary to help the children to find the solutions.

More confident learners
Encourage the children to recall the number sentences and to work accurately and quickly.

Lesson 4

Main teaching activities

Whole-class work: Write onto the board: 5, 6, 11 and ask: *What addition sentence can you say for these three numbers?* Write up 5 + 6 = 11 and 6 + 5 = 11. Now ask the children to find the corresponding subtraction sentences and write those up: 11 − 5 = 6 and 11 − 6 = 5. Repeat this for 5, 8, 13.

Independent work: Provide photocopiable page 'Number trios' from the CD-ROM. Ask the children to write the two addition and two subtraction sentences for each number trio.

Progress check: When the children have completed the first number trio ask them to stop work and to review this with you. Ask, for example:
- *How did you work out the answers?*
- *Did anyone find a different way to do this?*
- *Who knew the answer? Well done!*

Review
Write up the final number trio onto the board: 5, 10, 15. Say:
- *Who can tell me an add sentence with these numbers?*
- *How did you work that out?*
- *Now tell me another add sentence for these numbers?*
- *How did you work that out?*
- *So tell me a subtraction sentence with these numbers. And another subtraction sentence.*

Discuss how, when adding a units number to 10, the unit number changes: *5 + 10 is 15. So 10 + 5 is 15. And 15 − 5 is 10 and 15 − 10 is 5.* Repeat this for 10 + 6.

 SCHOLASTIC

Lesson 5 Oral and mental starter 34

Main teaching activities

Whole-class work: Explain that in this lesson the children will use what they have learned this week to solve some problems. Say: *I buy a pencil for 5p and a notepad for 8p. How much do I spend?* Invite children to suggest how this could be calculated such as: 5p and 5p is 10p and 3p is 13p. Provide some 10p, 5p, 2p and 1p coins for each group and ask the children to work the answer using the fewest number of coins. Demonstrate that 5p and 5p is 10p, so a 10p coin can be used. Then show them that the 3p can be a 2p and a 1p coin. So just three coins are needed to make 13p. Repeat this for another total, such as 5p and 6p.

Paired work: Ask the children to work in pairs, with some 10p, 5p, 2p and 1p coins. Display a school 'shop' with a number of small items- for example, ball, pencil - with price labels up to 10p. Ask the children to select two items, total the cost, then write an addition sentence to show the coins that they will use to pay for them. Encourage them to shown their workings and to write out the number sentences in full.

Progress check: When the children have had time to complete the first addition, ask:

● *Which coins did you decide you needed?*
● *How did you work out the answer?*

Check that the children understand that they can show their workings, and that they should show completed number sentences.

Review

Work through the different totals and how children worked them out. For example, for 5p + 7p, say: *That is the same as 5p add 5p add 2p. So 5p and 5p is 10p and 2p is 12p.* Invite the children to use the coins to count on with you. Repeat this for other totals. Now say:

● *What have you learned this week?*
● *Tell your partner what you think you know well, and where you will need further practice.*

You will need:

1. Check

Oral and mental starter

38 Washing line numbers

2. Assess

Teaching set of number word cards; washing line and pegs

3. Further practice

Oral and mental starters

39 Number and word match

Photocopiable sheets

'Numbers and word match'

Numerals and number words to 20

Most children should be able to read the number words and read and write the numerals to 20.

Some children will not have made such progress, and will require further support and practice of reading and writing number words to 20 before moving on to reading number words to 10 then 20.

1. Check

38 Washing line numbers

Observe which children are confident about reading the numerals and placing them correctly. Encourage less confident children to place the numerals to 10. Extend the more confident children to concentrate on numerals to 20.

- *Which number comes next?*
- *Which number comes before ...?*
- *How did you work that out?*

2. Assess

Use the washing line, pegs and number word cards and use these in the same way as oral and mental starter 38 'Washing line numbers'. Check that children can read the number words and recognise which number it represents. Challenge the more confident children by concentrating on number words 'eleven' to 'twenty'. Record the outcomes.

3. Further practice

Use the suggested oral and mental starters to provide further reinforcement for developing the skills of reading both numerals and numeral words to 20. The photocopiable sheet 'Numbers and word match' on page 124 is a game for two players, which provides similar reinforcement.

You will need:

1. Check

Oral and mental starter

34 Counting to 100

2. Assess

Interactive teaching resource 'Number square'

3. Further practice

Oral and mental starters

35 Count from any number to 100

Counting in ones to and from 100

Most children should be able to count to and from 100 in ones.

Some children will not have made such progress and will require further practice in counting to and from 20, then 40 and so on.

1. Check

34 Counting to 100

Note which children count with confidence and which are unsure, especially at, for example, 29 then 30, 39 then 40 and so on. Provide further practice where necessary. Extend the more confident children by asking them to count from any number to 100, back to 0 then on to the start number.

- *What number comes next after 79?*
- *What number comes just before 90?*

2. Assess

Ask the children to use the interactive teaching resource 'Number Square' They take turns to point to a number on the hundred square, as their start number, then turn the whole page over. They count together from that number to 100 and back again. Decide whether to limit the count to 50 for those who are less confident. Challenge the more confident children to count up to 100, back to zero then on to stop at the start number. Record the outcomes.

3. Further practice

Use the suggested oral and mental starters to provide further practice in counting to and from 100, starting from any number. Provide blank number lines with start and finish numbers to give children further experience in identifying sequences of counting numbers.

 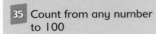

Curriculum objectives
- To represent and use number bonds and related subtraction facts within 20.

You will need
1. Check

Oral and mental starter

`40` Add and subtract facts to 10

2. Assess
'Add and subtract (1)'

3. Further practice

Oral and mental starters

`41` Double facts to 5 + 5

`42` Double facts to 10 + 10

`43` Totals to 10

Photocopiable sheets
'Double facts to 12';
'Number trios (1)'

Addition and subtraction facts to 10

Most children should be able to calculate addition facts to 10 and derive related subtraction facts to 10.

Some children will not have made such progress and will require further practice of addition and subtraction bonds to 5, before moving on to number bonds to 10.

1. Check

`40` Add and subtract facts to 10

Keep the pace sharp and note which children answer confidently and which need further practice. Those who need further practice encourage them to use their fingers or provide a number line.

- *How did you work that out? Who did this another way?*
- *Tell me two numbers that total 8. Tell me two more numbers that total 8.*

2. Assess

Provide photocopiable sheet 'Add and subtract (1)' from page 125 and ask children to complete it individually. Ask individual children how they found the answers. Note who is using fingers for counting on or back. Provide further opportunities to practise using a mental number line approach to finding answers. Challenge the more confident to respond to questions such as: *If 4 + 5 = 9, what is 9 − 5?* Record the outcomes.

3. Further practice

The suggested oral and mental starters give practice in using specific mental skills. The photocopiables also help children to practise specific mental skills to help with rapid recall of these facts such as doubles and using an addition fact to derive a subtraction fact.

Curriculum objectives
- To sequence events in chronological order using language such as: before and after, next, first, today, yesterday, tomorrow, morning, afternoon and evening.

You will need
1. Check

Oral and mental starter

`45` Days of the week

2. Assess
'My day'; scissors; glue sticks; paper

3. Further practice

Oral and mental starters

`46` Sequencing time vocabulary

`45` Days of the week

Sequencing time and events

Most children should be able to recite the days of the week in order and use sequencing time vocabulary.

Some children will not have made such progress and require practice of recognising the days of the week, and talking about their day, in order.

1. Check

`45` Days of the week

Encourage the children to say the days of the week in order, and check who knows which day it is today, what tomorrow will be and what day it was yesterday. For those who are less confident provide regular practice of saying the days in order and answering questions about the days.

- *Which is the first day/last day of our school week?*
- *What day will it be tomorrow?*

2. Assess

Ask the children to complete photocopiable sheet 'My day' from page 126 individually. Ask the children questions about the day, such as: *What do you do next? What happens after you have breakfast...?* Challenge the more confident children to draw another picture to put into their sequence, of something else they do during the day. Record the outcomes.

3. Further practice

Use the suggested oral and mental starters to provide further opportunities for the children to use the vocabulary of time passing. Encourage them to talk in sentences, rather than a one word answer, about things they have done, and the order in which they did them.

Oral and mental starters

Number and place value

33 Count pictures

Prepare the interactive teaching resource 'Money' with up to 20 5p coins positioned around the drop area. Ask the children to look carefully at the screen then say: *How many coins can you see? How did you count them?* Discuss with the children how they need to count and estimate, and if necessary, support them with this task by pointing to sections of the screen. Now ask the children to point in a different order. Ask: *Did you find the same number of coins? What would happen if you counted them again. Would there still be the same number?*

Repeat this with other coins and/or collect pictures containing a number of objects, animals etc. to use for the same purpose.

34 Counting to 100

Ask the children to count together from zero to 100. If they falter, say the numbers loudly and keep the counting rhythm going so that the children hear the correct sequence of numbers. Repeat this several times. Now count back from 100 to zero.

Extension

Count with a good pace and rhythm from zero to 100, and back again several times. Ask questions such as: *What is the next number after 28... 39...? When we count back what is the next number we say after 70... 60?*

35 Count from any number to 100

Ask the children to start their count on the number that you say. Ask them to count up to 100, keeping a good pace. They count back to their start number. If they started counting on 45, ask questions about the number range they just counted, such as: *What number comes after 56...? Before 93...? If you counted back to 45 and kept going what would the next number be?* Repeat this for other starting numbers.

36 Counting in 2s

Ask the children to count with you in twos, from 0 to 20 and back again. Keep the pace sharp. Repeat this, but this time start from 1 to 19 and back again.

Extension

Repeat the count in twos from 0 and extend the count to and from 30, then 40 and so on so that over time children count to 100 in twos and back again.

Repeat this for odd numbers, counting in twos, to and from 19, 29, 39, and so on to 99.

37 Odds and evens

Explain that you will say a number from 0 to 20. Ask the children to tell you whether they think it is odd or even. Write the numbers onto the board into a table, headed 'Odd numbers' and 'Even numbers'. Now ask, for example: *How do you know that 5 is odd? So what is 15? What do you think 25 will be? Is 8 odd or even? How do you know? What is 18... 20? How did you work that out?*

38 Washing line numbers

You will need a washing line, pegs and a teaching set of number cards 0–20. Peg up 0 at the left-hand side of the line, and 20 at the right-hand side. Shuffle the cards and then invite a child to take the top card and decide where to peg it onto the line. Repeat this until all the cards are pegged up. Some cards may have to be adjusted if insufficient room has been left. Now say: *Take the card that reads 9... 12....15.... Take the card that shows 1 more than 14... 1 less than 18....* Repeat this until all the cards have been removed. Now say *Who has the zero? Peg it back where it belongs please. What is the next number? Who has that card? Please peg it back...* and so on until all the cards are back on the line.

39 Numbers and word match

You will need a washing line, pegs, and a teaching set of number cards 0–20. Give out numeral cards 0 to 20. Shuffle the number words cards 0 to 20 and ask a child without a numeral card to read the word aloud. Ask the children with the numeral card that matches the word card to hold up their card. Repeat this until all the cards are given out. Some children may have two cards. Now starting from zero, ask the children with number word and numeral to peg these to the washing line until all are pegged on. Repeat this so that the children see the number word and numeral matched twice.

Addition and subtraction

40 Add and subtract facts to 10

You will need a teaching set of cards from photocopiable pages from the CD-ROM: 'Add facts to 5', 'Take away facts to 5', 'Add facts 6 to 10' and 'Take away facts 6 to 10'. Explain that you will show the children a fact. Ask them to show you the answer on their number fan when you say *Show me*. Keep the pace sharp, but give enough time for children to count up or back to find the answer if they do not have recall of it yet. Ask questions such as: *How did you work that out? Is there another way? Who 'knows' the answer? Well done!*

41 Double facts to 5 + 5

Ask the children to read each card, then to put up their hands when they have an answer. Ask questions such as: *How did you work out the answer? So if 5 + 5 is 10, what would 6 + 6 be? How did you work that out?*

Over time, children should have rapid recall of these facts.

42 Double facts to 10 + 10

Say a double such as 6 + 6 and ask the children to hold up their hands when they have the answer. Ask, for example: *How did you work that out?* Discuss how, if they do not 'know' the fact, they can count on from 6 for another 6, keeping a check of their counting on their fingers. Repeat this for other doubles up to 10 + 10.

43 Totals to 10

Explain to the children that you will say a number between 5 and 10. Ask them to suggest an addition fact that totals this number. For example, if you say 8, they might say 5 + 3 or 4 + 4.... Write up the addition sentences onto the board and encourage the children to think of as many different possibilities as they can. If they are unsure, ask them to hold up, say, eight fingers. Now ask them to think about the different combinations of fingers that make eight and to count those.

44 Near doubles

Ask the children to calculate the answer to a near double, such as 4 + 5, or 5 + 6, and so on. Encourage them to use the 'double, add 1' or 'double, subtract 1' methods to find the solution. Ask, for example: *What is 6 + 5? How did you work that out? What about 7 + 6? What is the total of 8 + 7? What is 9 and 10 altogether?*

Measurement

45 Days of the week

Say the days of the week together in order. Now ask questions such as: *What day is it today? Which day was it yesterday? Which day will it be tomorrow? Which day comes after Tuesday...? Which day comes before Tuesday...? Which days do we come to school? And which days do we not come to school? What do we call Saturday and Sunday?*

Oral and mental starters 46–47 continue on the CD-ROM.

Numbers and word match

- ■ Play this game with a partner.
- ■ You need a shuffled set of 0 to 20 numeral cards.
- ■ You need a shuffled set of 0 to 20 number word cards.
- ■ Take turns to turn over a card from the top of both sets.
- ■ Say each of the numbers.
- ■ If they match, you keep the cards.
- ■ Write how many cards you have each collected.
- ■ Shuffle the cards and play the game again.

Name	Number of cards

Name	Number of cards

Name	Number of cards

I can read and write numbers to 20.

How did you do?

Name: _____ Date: _____

Add and subtract (1)

- Read the number sentence.
- Draw a line to the answer.

9 + 1   9

8 − 5   5

3 + 5

2

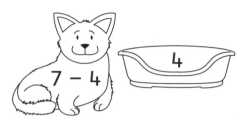
7 − 4   4

2 + 2   7

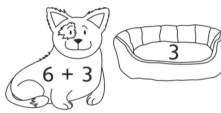
6 + 3   3

8 − 6

3

6 − 6

10

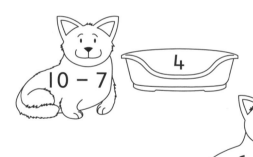
10 − 7   4

6 − 1   3

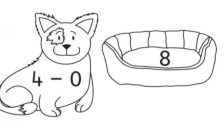
4 − 0   8

5 + 2   0

I know addition and subtraction.

How did you do?

My day

- ■ Look carefully at the pictures.
- ■ They are not in the right order.
- ■ Cut out the pictures.
- ■ Glue them onto paper in the correct order of events in a day.

Counting and place value

Expected prior learning

Children should be able to:

- count to at least 30 in ones
- count to 20 in twos.

Topic	Curriculum objectives	Expected outcomes
Number and place value	**Lesson 1**	
	To identify and represent numbers using objects and pictorial representations including the number line, and use the language of: equal to, more than, less than (fewer), most, least. When given a number, to identify one more and one less.	Compare and order numbers to 30. Identify one more and one less of numbers to 30.
	Lesson 2	
	To identify and represent numbers using objects and pictorial representations including the number line, and use the language of: equal to, more than, less than (fewer), most, least.	Say what the tens digit and unit digit stand for.
	Lesson 3	
	To count, read and write numbers to 100 in numerals, count in multiples of twos, fives and tens.	Count in twos, and recognise odd and even numbers.
	Lesson 4	
	To count, read and write numbers to 100 in numerals, count in multiples of twos, fives and tens.	Count in fives and recognise the pattern, when starting from zero of the units number: 0 or 5.
	Lesson 5	
	To count, read and write numbers to 100 in numerals, count in multiples of twos, fives and tens.	Count in twos, and recognise odd and even numbers. Count in fives and recognise the pattern, when starting from zero of the units number: 0 or 5.

Preparation

Lesson 1: prepare sets of cards from number, one set per pair

Lesson 2: prepare a teaching set of arrow cards; prepare sets of cards from arrow cards, one set per child; copy 'Tens and units (2)'

Lesson 3: prepare sets of number cards 0–40, one set per pair; copy and 41–50 for more confident learners

Lesson 4: prepare sets of number cards 0–40 and 31–40 for more confident learners

Lesson 5: copy 'Hops and jumps', one per pair; copy and enlarge 'Hops and jumps' to A3

You will need

Photocopiable sheets

'Tens and units (2)'; 'Hops and jumps'

General resources

'Number cards 0–20'

Equipment

Number cards 21-50; arrow cards; counting stick (an unnumbered stick about 1m long, divided into ten sections); rulers; counters

Further practice

Photocopiable sheets

'Missing numbers (2)'; 'Counting in 2s and 5s'

Oral and mental starters for week 1

See bank of starters on pages 160 to 161. Oral and mental starters are also on the CD-ROM.

53 Add numbers to 5

52 Show me complements of 10

49 Count the cubes

Overview of progression

Children begin the week by comparing numbers to 30, identifying which numbers fit between two given numbers, such as 21 and 25, and also identifying the number that is one more or one less than any given number to 30. They use arrow cards to make tens and units numbers to 30, and say how many tens and how many units there are. The children count in 2s, and find odd and even numbers to 20, then 30. They count in 5s, and recognise which numbers they say when counting from 0. They also recognise that multiples of 5 have either a 0 or 5 as their unit digit. They complete a simple investigation about counts of 2s and 5s.

Watch out for

Check that children understand that the order of digits is what determines place value, so that 13 is not the same number as 31.

Creative context

Encourage children to collect numbers to 40 in their environment at home and at school. These could be from house numbers, car numbers, page numbers in a book and so on. If found around the school, suggest that the children use the school's digital camera to photograph the number in place, then make a display of the photographs to show the numbers.

Vocabulary

count, count in ones, twos, fives, tens, count on from, count on to, count up to, digit, ones, teens, **tens**, **units**

Curriculum objectives
- When given a number, to identify one more and one less.
- To use the language of: more than, less than (fewer).

Success criteria
- I can compare numbers to 30.
- I can find one more and one less numbers to 30.

You will need
General resources
'Number cards 0–20'
Equipment
Number cards 21–40

Differentiation
Less confident learners
Limit the number range to 10 or 15, then increase the range over time.
More confident learners
Provide number cards 0–40. Ask them to write two intermediate numbers for each pair of numbers chosen.

Lesson 1
Oral and mental starter 53

Main teaching activities

Whole-class work: Remind the children of their previous work on ordering numbers. Write 15 and 20 on the board, leaving a space between them. Say: *Tell me a number that is between 15 and 20. What other numbers go between 15 and 20?* Repeat this for other pairs of numbers from 0 to about 20, then extend to 30. Ask, for each pair of numbers: *How did you work out which numbers go in between?*

Ask: *What is 1 more than 25? How did you work that out? What is 1 less than 25?* Repeat for other numbers between 20 and 30.

Paired work: Ask the children to shuffle the number cards 0–30. They take turns to take the top two cards. If these are consecutive numbers, they put them back and shuffle again. If not, they write down the pair of numbers in order, smaller and then larger, and a number that goes between them. They record their number sets on paper.

Progress check: Ask for example: *What numbers go between 24 and 27? What is one less than 24...? What is one more than 27...?*

Review

Invite children from each group to say pairs of numbers, challenging the other children to suggest numbers that go in between. Start with some less confident learners, then extend the number range to suit the average and then the more confident learners. Ask: *What numbers go between ___ and ___? How do you know this? How did you work it out? Tell me all the numbers that go between 13 and 16... between 18 and 23....*

Curriculum objectives
- To identify and represent numbers using objects and pictorial representations.

Success criteria
- I know what the tens digit stands for.
- I know what the unit digit stands for.

You will need
Photocopiable sheets
'Ten and units (2)'
Equipment
Arrow cards, teaching set

Differentiation
Less confident learners
Support children in their understanding of place value using the arrow cards or 100 square.
More confident learners
Give children sets of arrow cards to construct numbers over 30. Ask them to record the numbers identifying the tens and units

Lesson 2
Oral and mental starter 53

Main teaching activities

Whole-class work: Using the teaching set of arrow cards, hold up the 10 card and ask: *What number is this? How many tens does it have? How many units?* Show the children how to place a unit card onto a tens card by placing the 8 over the 0 of 10.

Ask: *What number is this? How many units are there? How many tens?* Repeat this for other 'teen' numbers. Now show the 20 card and repeat the process to produce numbers up to 29. Ask questions such as: *What does the 2 stand for? Which is the tens number? Which is the unit? What if I changed the tens number to 1 ten, what number would it be then?*

Independent work: Ask the children to complete photocopiable page 'Tens and units (2)' from the CD-ROM.

Progress check: Ask individual children to explain how they worked out which tens and units join to which number. Check that they can say the number both as tens and units, and as a number.

Review

Give each child a set of arrow cards. Ask them to make the numbers that you say, then hold up the cards when you say *Show me*. Say, for example:
- *Show me the number 15... 18... 21... 29... 30....*
- *Show me the number that has 1 ten and 4 units... 2 tens and 3 units... 2 tens and 6 units....*
- *How many tens/units does this number have?*

Curriculum objectives
● To count, read and write numbers to 100 in numerals, count in multiples including twos.

Success criteria
● I can count in twos.

You will need
Equipment
Number cards 0–50; counting stick (an unnumbered stick about 1m long, divided into ten sections); rulers

Differentiation
Less confident learners
Provide a number track, such as a ruler marked in centimetres only up to 20cm. The children can count along this to check whether their number is odd or even.

More confident learners
When the children are confident with the group activity, decide whether to give them a set of number cards 41–50 as well.

Lesson 3

Main teaching activities

Whole-class work: Ask the children to count around the class in twos, from 0 to about 20 and back. Repeat this, starting from 1. Ask: *Which are the odd numbers? Which are the even numbers? Tell me an odd/even number less/more than 7... 8... 12...*. Now ask the children to count individually around the class in 2s from 0 to 20 and back, then from 1 to 19 and back. Keep the pace sharp.

Show the children the counting stick, and explain that one end shows 0. Count together in twos, and point to each section as you count. Explain that you will point to a section, and you would like the children to say which number it represents. Wipe the stick and pretend to empty the 'numbers' onto the floor. Now repeat the process with odd numbers (starting from 1).

Paired work: Ask the children to work in pairs with a set of number cards 0–20. They take turns to take a card and say whether it shows an odd or an even number. They can record this on a sheet of paper with the headings 'Odd numbers' and 'Even numbers'.

Odd numbers	Even numbers

Progress check: Ask the children to say some odd numbers. Invite them to say if they notice a pattern, that is that the odd numbers always have a 1, 3, 5, 7 or 9 in their units.

Paired work: Provide each pair with number cards 31–40. Ask pairs to add these cards to those they already have, shuffle them all together, and repeat the activity above. This time they place the cards into two sets, odd numbers in one pile and even numbers in the other.

Review
Write the headings 'Odd numbers' and 'Even numbers' on the board. Explain that you will say a number. Ask the children to say together 'odd' or 'even' for each number. Invite a child to write the odd numbers, and another child to write the even numbers, on the board. Ask questions such as:

● *Is this number odd or even?*
● *How can you tell?*

Discuss how the odd or even numbers in a counting sequence are 'every other number'.

If the numeral cards 41–50 were used, invite the more confident children to state which are odd and which are even.

Curriculum objectives
● To count, read and write numbers to 100 in numerals, count in multiples including fives.

Success criteria
● I can count in fives.

You will need
General resources
'Number cards 0–20'
Equipment
Counters; number cards 21–40

Differentiation
Less confident learners
The children can play in a group with an adult, using four sets of number cards. The adult checks that the children recognise the multiples of five, using supporting resources such as 100 squares to assist where necessary

More confident learners
Decide whether to add the 31–40 cards.

Lesson 4
Oral and mental starter 52

Main teaching activities

Whole-class work: Tell the children that today they will start to count in fives. Say the counting pattern for fives loudly from 0 to 20, inviting the children to join in. Repeat this, counting forwards and back. Write 'Counting in fives' on the board. Ask the children which numbers they say when counting in fives from 0. Write up 0, 5, 10, 15, 20. The children should notice that the units number is either 5 or 0. *How does this help you to say the pattern of fives? What would the next number be after 20?*

Paired work: The children play 'Snap' with two sets of number cards 0–20. They take matching cards if they say 'Snap' first. If the matching numbers are multiples of five, they say 'Fives snap' and take a counter too. The child with the most counters at the end wins.

Provide each pair with two sets of number cards 21–30. Ask the children to shuffle all their cards together, then play 'Snap' again.

Progress check: Ask, for example:
● *Which numbers do you say when you count in 5s from 0?*
● *Tell me some numbers that are not in that count.*

Review

Invite the children to count with you. This time, instead of saying the multiples of five, they should nod: *One, two, three, four,* (nod), *six....* Repeat this several times, counting up to 20 and back again. Ask: *Which numbers come in the pattern of fives?* Say some numbers that do not come in the pattern of fives. Repeat this count, counting to 30 and back, then extend to 40, then 50 and back again.

Curriculum objectives
● To count, read and write numbers to 100 in numerals, count in multiples of twos, fives and tens.

Success criteria
● I can count in twos.
● I can count in fives.

You will need
General resources
'Number cards 0–20'
Photocopiable sheets
'Hops and jumps'
Equipment
Counting stick (a plain, unmarked stick about a metre in length); number cards 21-50; counters

Differentiation
Less confident learners
Simplify the problem so that the children go from the Start line to 10.

More confident learners
Challenge the children to consider a third child, Josh, who leaps in threes, and extend the number track to 30. They need to find the numbers all three children land on.

Lesson 5
Oral and mental starter 49

Main teaching activities

Whole-class work: Tell the children that they will be solving a problem. Show them the A3 version of the photocopiable page 'Hops and jumps' from the CD-ROM. Say: *Tom and Sara are playing 'hops and jumps'. Tom hops along the track in twos from 'start'. Sara jumps along the track in fives from 'start'. Which numbers do they both land on?* Give each pair photocopiable page 'Hops and jumps' and a pot of counters. Ask them to talk in pairs about how they will solve the problem and decide how to record their work.

Paired work: The children solve the problem and record their work. Allow them about 15–20 minutes.

Progress check: After about 5 minutes, ask questions such as:
● *Have you found a number that both children land on? What is it?*
● *How did you find that number?*
● *What other number do you think they will both land on? Why do you think that?*

Review

Using the A3 version of photocopiable page 'Hops and jumps', invite some children to say which numbers Tom and Sara land on. Mark the hops in twos in one colour and the jumps in fives in another. Ask: *Which numbers does Tom visit? Which numbers does Sara visit? Which numbers do both children visit? Who visited just even numbers? Who visited odd and even numbers?* Ask the more confident children to explain how they extended the problem, and to say which numbers were visited. Discuss these facts: the only number visited by all three children is 30; Tom and Sara both visited 10 and 20; Sara and Josh both visited 15. Ask children to describe the problem-solving strategies they used.

Addition and subtraction beyond totals of 10

Expected prior learning

Children should be able to:

- recall some addition and subtraction facts to 10
- use the strategy of 'making 5 and a bit more' to total 5 and 6, 7, 8 or 9.

Topic	Curriculum objectives	Expected outcomes
Addition and subtraction	**Lesson 1**	
	To add and subtract one-digit and two-digit numbers to 20, including zero.	Add two unit numbers with a total of more than 10.
	Lesson 2	
	To add and subtract one-digit and two-digit numbers to 20, including zero.	Add two unit numbers with a total of more than 10.
	Lesson 3	
	To add and subtract one-digit and two-digit numbers to 20, including zero.	Derive subtraction sentences from addition with totals of more than 10.
	Lesson 4	
	To add and subtract one-digit and two-digit numbers to 20, including zero.	Derive subtraction sentences from addition with totals of more than 10.
	Lesson 5	
	To solve one-step problems that involve addition and subtraction, using concrete objects and pictorial representations, and missing number problems.	Solve simple one-step problems using addition and subtraction strategies.

Preparation
● Make an A3 version of 'Number trios (3)'.
● Enlarge Number trios 4 to A3 onto card if possible and cut out to make a teaching set.

Lesson 1: copy 'Number line 0–20', one per group

Lesson 2: copy 'Find the answer', one per child; copy 'Number line 0–20', one per child

Lesson 3: copy 'Number trios (3)', one per child; copy and enlarge 'Number trios (3)' to A3; copy 'Number line 0–20' for less confident children as appropriate

Lesson 4: copy '6, 7, 8 and 9 spinner', one per pair; copy 'Number line 0–20' for less confident learners as appropriate

Lesson 5: copy 'Number trios (4)', one per child; prepare a teaching set of cards from 'Number trios (4)'; copy 'Number line 0–20' for less confident learners as appropriate

You will need
Photocopiable sheets
'Find the answer'; 'Number trios (3)'; 'Number trios (4)'; '6, 7, 8 and 9 spinner'

General resources
'Number line 0–20'; interactive activity 'Number pairs'

Equipment
Scissors; interlocking cubes

Further practice
General resources
Interactive activity 'Number pairs'

Photocopiable sheets
'Dice roll add'; 'Number trios (4)'; 'Addition'

Oral and mental starters for week 2
See bank of starters on pages 85 and 160. Oral and mental starters are also on the CD-ROM.

53 Add numbers to 5

25 Add and subtract to 5

23 Add and subtract to 10

Overview of progression
At the beginning of the week, children review the strategy of adding a unit number larger than 5 by making 'a 5 and a bit'. This is extended to adding two unit numbers larger than 5, such as 6 + 7, 6 + 8 and so on. They use cubes, number lines and count on mentally to find solutions. Children explore number trios such as 6, 8 and 14 to derive the two related addition sentences and the two related subtraction sentences.

Watch out for
If children are unsure about how to make 'a 5 and a bit more' from any number from 6 to 9, write missing number addition sentences for them such as: $5 + \square = 6$, $5 + \square = 7$, and so on. Encourage them to work mentally to find the solutions. If necessary, provide a number line for counting on from 5.

Creative context
Use opportunities in the classroom environment to count and total. For example, for an art lesson, ask a child to count how many paint brushes there are and how many more are needed for a given number of children. Encourage mental counting on or back strategies to solve such practical problems.

Vocabulary
add, altogether, and, equals, leaves, minus, subtract, take away, total

Curriculum objective
● To add one-digit numbers to 20.

Success criteria
● I can add two numbers to make a total of more than 10.

You will need
General resources
'Number line 0–20'

Differentiation
Less confident learners
Decide whether to work as a group. If children find the new strategy too difficult, use cubes and number lines to model the strategy and solutions.

More confident learners
Challenge the children to solve 9 + 8, using only the new strategy.

Lesson 1

Main teaching activities

Whole-class work: Remind the children of the strategy 'make a 5 and a bit more' when adding numbers 6, 7, 8 and 9 to 5: add the two 5s to make 10, then count on for the rest. Explain that in this lesson children will be adding two numbers up to 10, but each greater than 5. Write '6 + 7' on the board and say: *Use the strategy of making '5 and a bit more'. So what does 6 become?* Underneath the 6 on the board, write: 5 + 1. Repeat this for 7, and write 5 + 2 so that the new number sentence is 5 + 1 + 5 + 2. Say: *Let's move the 5s to be together like this: 5 + 5 + 1 + 2. Now say with me: 5 add 5 is 10 and 1 is 11 and 2 more is 12, 13. So 6 + 7 equals 13.* Onto the board write up 10 + 1 + 2 = 13.

Repeat this for another addition such as 6 + 8: 5 + 1 + 5 + 3 = 10 + 1 + 3 = 14.

Group work: Write these additions on the board: 9 + 6, 8 + 7, 9 + 7, 8 + 8. Ask the children to work in groups of four. Provide photocopiable page 'Number line 0–20'. They take turns in pairs to use either: the new strategy for addition and write out the number sentence or a number line to count on from the larger number to find the solution. They compare their answers, and if these differ, swap over strategies to try again. They swap strategies for each addition sentence.

Progress check: After about 5 minutes, ask the children to stop work. Invite a group to explain how they worked out the answer. Write up the jottings onto the board, like this:

9 + 6 = 5 + 4 + 5 + 1

5 + 5 + 4 + 1 = 10 + 1 + 4

10 + 5 = 15

Now ask the pair who counted on along the number line:
- *Which number did you count on from?*
- *Did you get the same answer?*

Ask if any group needs help with the new strategy and target those children for a few minutes.

Review

On the board work through each addition with the children. Invite individuals to explain how to total. For example, for 8 + 7:

8 + 7 = 5 + 3 + 5 + 2

5 + 5 + 3 + 2 = 10 + 3 + 2

10 + 5 = 15

Repeat this for the other addition sentences. If the more confident have also solved 9 + 8, invite them to explain how they work this out.

Curriculum objectives
- To add one-digit numbers to 20.

Success criteria
- I can add two numbers to make a total of more than 10.

You will need

Photocopiable sheets
'Find the answer'

General resources
'Number line 0–20'

Equipment
Interlocking cubes

Differentiation

Less confident learners
Decide whether to provide cubes as well as number lines as aids for finding answers.

More confident learners
Challenge the children to work mentally, without number lines.

Lesson 2   Oral and mental starter 53

Main teaching activities

Whole-class work: Explain that children will be adding two numbers in different ways. Write onto the board: 6 + 6 and say: *We can do this by doubling, and counting on. Or we can work out the answer by making '5s and a bit more'. Now choose a method and try this in your head. Use your fingers if that helps.* Give the children a few moments to find an answer and ask:

- *How did you work this out?*
- *Who found the answer a different way?*

Invite a child who used 'doubling by counting on' to explain the method, and invite everyone to try this: 6 and 7, 8, 9, 10, 11, 12. So 6 and 6 is 12. Now invite a child who made '5s and a bit more' to explain, and invite everyone to try this. Write it onto the board:

6 + 6 = 5 + 1 + 5 + 1

5 + 5 + 1 + 1 = 10 + 2 = 12

Explain that both methods work. Ask:

- *Which is easier do you think?*
- *Why do you think that?*

Paired work: Ask children to work in pairs with a copy each of photocopiable page 'Find the answer' from the CD-ROM. Provide copies of photocopiable page 'Number line 0–20' from the CD-ROM for children to choose to use if they need further support.

Progress check: After a few minutes of working, invite a pair to explain which numbers they chose for their first addition sentence and how they worked out the answer. Invite the other children to respond to questions such as:

- *Who used a different way?*
- *Tell us how you did this.*

Review

Explain that you will say a double. Ask the children to find the answer. Say, for example: *What is 4 + 4? So 4 + 4, or double 4, is 8. What is double 5? How do you know that? What about double 6.... 10?* Discuss how the children worked out the answers each time. Now say: *How would you use a double fact, like double 6 to work out 6 + 7? Who did this another way?* Discuss how, if you know a double fact you can then work out the near double. Ask: *What about 9 + 8? How would you work that out?* Some children may know 9 + 9 and subtract 1; some may know 8 + 8 and add 1; others may use 5 + 4 + 5 + 3 = 10 + 7 = 17, which is also a good strategy.

Curriculum objectives
- To add and subtract one-digit numbers to 20.

Success criteria
- I can add two numbers to make a total of more than 10.
- I can find subtraction answers using addition totals.

You will need
Photocopiable sheets
'Number trios (3)'
General resources
'Number line 0–20'
Equipment
Interlocking cubes

Differentiation
Less confident learners
Provide cubes and photocopiable page 'Number line 0–20' from the CD-ROM as a support.

More confident learners
Challenge the children to work mentally to solve these problems.

Curriculum objectives
- To add and subtract one-digit to 20.

Success criteria
- I can add two numbers to make a total of more than 10.
- I can find subtraction answers using addition totals.

You will need
General resources
'Number line 0–20'; '6, 7, 8 and 9 spinner'; interactive activity 'Number pairs'
Equipment
Interlocking cubes

Differentiation
Less confident learners
Provide cubes and photocopiable 'Number line 0–20'.

More confident learners
Give early finishers, the interactive activity 'Number pairs' to check whether they can apply their knowledge to find pairs of numbers that make 20

Lesson 3
Oral and mental starter 25

Main teaching activities

Whole-class work: Write onto the board 6 + 8 = ☐ and ask the children to work out the answer. Write 14 onto the board to complete the number sentence. Now ask the children to tell you another addition fact that uses these numbers. Write up 8 + 6 = 14. Ask: *Which subtraction sentence uses these numbers? Tell me another subtraction sentence.* Write up both 14 − 8 = 6 and 14 − 6 = 8. Discuss how by using an addition fact, three other facts can be found.

Independent work: Provide photocopiable page 'Number trios (3)' from the CD-ROM and ask the children to write two addition and two subtraction sentences for each number trio.

Progress check: Ask the children to discuss with you as a class the first number trio. Ask questions such as: *How did you work out the addition sentences? How did you use that to work out the subtraction sentences?*

Remind the children that if they can find an addition sentence, then they can find another addition and two subtraction sentences that use the same number trio.

Review

Stick the A3 version of 'Number trios 3' on the board. Review each of the trios with the children, writing in answers. Discuss each time how if one number sentence is found, then the children can write three others. Ask questions such as: *How did you work this out? Who did it a different way?*

Now ask the children to work mentally using the number trio 9, 7 and 16. Write onto the board the addition and subtraction sentences that the children suggest.

Lesson 4
Oral and mental starter 23

Main teaching activities

Whole-class work: Explain that in this lesson the children will use addition facts to find corresponding subtraction facts. Write onto the board: 7 + 8 and ask: *How can we find the answer?* Children may suggest either 'double and add/subtract 1' or 'make 5 and a bit and add'. Write the addition sentence with its answer: 7 + 8 = 15. Now ask the children to suggest another addition sentence, then two subtraction sentences using these three numbers.

Paired work: Ask children to use photocopiable page '6, 7, 8 and 9 spinner' from the CD-ROM to generate a number, then spin again for a second. They write two addition and two subtraction sentences using these two numbers and their total. Ask them to repeat this four more times.

Progress check: Invite a pair to give one of their number pairs to the rest of the class. Ask the children to total those two numbers, and to find the other addition and both subtraction sentences using those three numbers. Ask questions such as: *How did you find the total? Which method did you use? Who did this a different way?*

Review

Explain that you will say two numbers. Ask the children, in groups of four, to total the two numbers, then between them work out all four number sentences – two addition and two subtraction. Encourage them to work quickly. Include some pairs of numbers for those who are less confident so that they can answer confidently. When the first pair of numbers have been used ask: *What addition sentence did you make? Tell me another one. What about subtraction sentences? How did you work these out?*

Curriculum objectives
● To solve one-step missing number problems that involve addition and subtraction.

Success criteria
● I can solve simple problems using addition and subtraction strategies.

You will need
Photocopiable sheets
'Number trios (4)'
General resources
'Number line 0–20'
Equipment
Scissors; interlocking cubes

Differentiation
Less confident learners
Ask an adult to work with these children. Ask the children to use photocopiable page 'Number line 0–20' to help them.
More confident learners
Challenge the children to work mentally, counting on or back in their heads as necessary.

Lesson 5
Oral and mental starter 23

Main teaching activities

Whole-class work: Explain that in this lesson the children will be solving missing number problems. On the board write 6, 8, ☐ and say: *This is a number trio but there is a number missing. What is the missing number?* Give the children a brief time to find the answer. Ask: *What is the answer? How did you work out that it is 14?* Now tell me two addition sentences for this number trio. Write up 6 + 8 = 14 and 8 + 6 = 14. *Tell me two subtraction sentences for this number trio.* Write up 14 − 6 = 8 and 14 − 8 = 6. Ask: *How did you work that out?*

Independent work: Provide photocopiable page 'Number trios (4)' from the CD-ROM. Explain that two of the three numbers for each number trio are there. The children write the missing number onto the space on the triangle. Provide photocopiable page 'Number line 0–20' on the CD-ROM as an aid if needed.

Progress check: Give the children about 10 minutes to complete the first part of photocopiable page 'Number trios 4'. Ask them to say the answer to the first number trio. Write onto the board 6 + 7 = 13. Repeat this for the other trios and ask children to correct any mistakes.

Paired activity: Ask the children to work in pairs and to cut out their number trios. They use one set of number trios and take turns to hold a number trio, covering just one number so that their partner can only see two numbers. Their partner says the missing number. At this stage allow children to use number lines to help them.

Review

You will need the teaching set of Number trios 4. Explain that the game that the children have just played will now be played as a class game. Hold up a card, covering the number that represents the total of the other two. Say the two visible numbers and say: *What is the other number? How did you work that out?* Repeat this for another number, just covering the total number each time to begin with. As the children become more confident, cover a different number in a trio so that children have the total and one number. Now ask:

● *Tell me what you have learned this week.*
● *Tell your partner which number facts you think you can find.*
● *Tell your partner how you work out the answers.*

Groups and shares

Expected prior learning

Children should be able to:

- count in twos and fives from 0 to at least 20 and back again
- count out accurately at least 20 objects.

Topic	Curriculum objectives	Expected outcomes
Multiplication and division	**Lesson 1**	
	To solve one-step problems involving multiplication and division, calculating the answer using concrete objects, pictorial representations and arrays with the support of the teacher.	Use objects to make equal groups.
	Lesson 2	
	To solve one-step problems involving multiplication and division, calculating the answer using concrete objects, pictorial representations and arrays with the support of the teacher.	Use pictures to make equal groups.
	Lesson 3	
	To solve one-step problems involving multiplication and division, calculating the answer using concrete objects, pictorial representations and arrays with the support of the teacher.	Use objects to share into equal groups.
	Lesson 4	
	To solve one-step problems involving multiplication and division, calculating the answer using concrete objects, pictorial representations and arrays with the support of the teacher.	Use pictures to share into equal groups.
	Lesson 5	
	To solve one-step problems involving multiplication and division, calculating the answer using concrete objects, pictorial representations and arrays with the support of the teacher.	Solve simple grouping and sharing problems.

■SCHOLASTIC

Preparation

Lesson 2: copy 'Adding groups', one per child; copy and enlarge 'Adding groups' for less confident learners; prepare two rings and six counters on interactive teaching resource 'Grouping'

Lesson 4: copy 'Sharing (2)', one per child; copy and enlarge 'Sharing (2)' to A3

You will need

Photocopiable sheets
'Adding groups'; 'Sharing (2)'
General resources
Interactive teaching resource 'Grouping'
Equipment
Interlocking cubes; paper plates

Further practice

Photocopiable sheets
'Groups of cubes'; 'Sharing cubes'

Oral and mental starters for week 3

See bank of starters on pages 160 to 161. Oral and mental starters are also on the CD-ROM.

50 Counting in 2s to 50

51 Counting in 5s

48 Everyone count to 100

Overview of progression

Children begin by making several equal groups of cubes. They write repeated addition sentences to show the groupings. They then count pictures of flowers in vases and write the repeated addition sentences for these. They share given numbers of cubes equally onto given numbers of plates. They progress to using pictures to show equal sharing. They write simple sharing sentences such as '6 shared by 2 is 3'. In Lesson 5, they compare equal groupings with equal sharings, such as '2 groups of 3 is 6' and '6 shared by 2 is 3'.

Watch out for

Check that children do make equal groups, and that they share equally. If children are unsure about this, provide further practical experiences of grouping and sharing counters or 1p coins.

Creative context

Encourage the children to think about where they might see examples of grouping or sharing, such as where perhaps sweets are arranged in pairs in a packet, or biscuits arranged in stacks of three, with maybe four stacks in the pack.

Vocabulary

equals, group, how many?, share

Curriculum objectives
• To solve one-step problems involving multiplication, calculating the answer using concrete objects with the support of the teacher.

Success criteria
• I can work out how many there are altogether in equal groups.

You will need
Equipment
Interlocking cubes

Differentiation
Less confident learners
Decide whether to ask the children to make two groups of three, then three groups of two.

More confident learners
Challenge the children to make five groups of six and to write the total.

Lesson 1   Oral and mental starter 50

Main teaching activities

Whole-class work: Explain that in this lesson the children will learn about finding how many there are altogether in equal groups. Ask a child to make four equal groups of two cubes. Invite four children to stand at the front of the class, each holding out one group of two. Ask the children to count in twos with you to find how many there are in total. Say together: *2 add 2 add 2 add 2 makes 8.* Write onto the board 2 + 2 + 2 + 2 = 8. Repeat this for two groups of four, and write 4 + 4 = 8.

Paired work: Ask the children to work in pairs with some cubes. They make two groups of six, three groups of four, four groups of three and six groups of two. Write this onto the board so that they can all see.

Progress check: Ask pairs to demonstrate how they made the groups and counted to find how many. Ask, for example: *How did you count the groups of 2?*

Review
Invite the children to say the totals for the different numbers of groups of particular sizes. Write onto the board: 6 + 6 = and ask for the answer. Repeat this for 4 + 4 + 4; 3 + 3 + 3 + 3 and 2 + 2 + 2 + 2 + 2 + 2. Now suggest that they make 3 groups of 5. Invite three children to each hold five cubes and count in 5s to find the total. Say: *5 + 5 is 10, and 5 more is 15.* Repeat this for five groups of three.

Curriculum objectives
• To solve one-step problems involving multiplication and division, calculating the answer using pictorial representations with the support of the teacher.

Success criteria
• I can work out how many there are altogether in equal groups.

You will need
Photocopiable sheets
'Adding groups'

General resources
Interactive teaching resource 'Grouping'

Differentiation
Less confident learners
Work with more confident partners on the task. Support using the 'Grouping' interactive.

More confident learners
Ask the children to draw seven vases and put into each five flowers. They decide how to find the total.

Lesson 2   Oral and mental starter 50

Main teaching activities

Whole-class work: Reveal the interactive teaching resource 'Grouping' on the CD-ROM (screen 1). Explain that each of the two rings needs three counters. Drag and drop the counters in as the children watch. Ask: *How many counters are there in this ... and that ring? So how many is that altogether?* Write on the board
3 + 3 = 6. Repeat with two groups of four.

Independent work: Provide photocopiable page 'Adding groups' from the CD-ROM. Ask the children to write the addition sentences for the groups and the totals.

Progress check: Ask: questions such as: *How did you find the answer?*

Review
Place the A3 version of 'Adding groups' on the board. Ask the children to take turns to explain how they counted. Encourage, where appropriate, counting up in 2s and 5s, rather than counting in 1s. Use the interactive teaching resource 'Grouping' to check children's understanding of other groups of counters (groups of 2, 3, 4 or 5 if time is available)

Curriculum objectives
● To solve one-step problems involving division, calculating the answer using concrete objects with the support of the teacher.
Success criteria
● I can share into equal groups.

You will need
Equipment
Interlocking cubes; paper plates

Differentiation
Less confident learners
Decide whether to use six cubes to begin with, sharing between two and then three plates.
More confident learners
Challenge the children to share 15 cubes between three plates, then five plates.

Lesson 3 — Oral and mental starter 51

Main teaching activity

Whole-class work: Put out eight cubes and two paper plates, and explain: *Today we are going to share into equal groups. Ask: How many will go on each plate if we share these cubes equally?* Invite a child to share out the cubes. Say: *How many cubes are on each plate? So eight shared between two plates is four.* Write onto the board '8 shared by 2 is 4'.

Paired work: Ask the children to work in pairs with 12 cubes and six plates. Ask them to share the 12 cubes equally between two, three, four and six plates. Write onto the board: two plates; three plates; four plates; six plates, as a reminder. The children write a sharing number sentence each time. For example: 12 shared by 2 is 6.

Progress check: Ask pairs to read out their number sentences. Also invite them to demonstrate how they grouped the cubes. Ask: *How many groups of ... did you make?*

Review

Ask children to say the sharing sentence for two plates, then three and so on. Now put out 16 cubes and four plates. Ask a child to share out the cubes equally. Ask: *How many cubes are on each plate? What is the sharing sentence?* Write onto the board: '16 shared by 4 is 4'.

Curriculum objectives
● To solve one-step problems involving division, calculating the answer using pictorial representations with the support of the teacher.
Success criteria
● I can share pictures into equal groups.

You will need
Photocopiable sheets
'Sharing (2)'
General resources
Interactive teaching resource 'Grouping'
Equipment
Interlocking cubes; paper plates

Differentiation
Less confident learners
Provide cubes and plates for the children to model each sharing sentence.
More confident learners
Challenge the children to share 18 cakes between three plates. They model this by drawing the sharing on the reverse of photocopiable page 'Sharing (2)'.

Lesson 4 — Oral and mental starter 51

Main teaching activities

Whole-class work: Reveal the interactive teaching resource 'Grouping' on the CD-ROM (screen 1) with two rings and six counters. Explain that the children have to share the counters equally between the two rings. Demonstrate moving the counters one at a time: one for this ring; one for that ring; and so on. When each ring has 3 counters say: *six shared between two is three.*

Independent work: Provide photocopiable page 'Sharing (2)' from the CD-ROM. This has pictures of cakes and plates. Children work out the correct number of cakes that must go on each plate so that they are shared equally between them. The children then write the matching sharing sentence. There are also opportunities for children to draw their own pictures to represent sharing.

Progress check: Ask individual children how they have shared out the cakes. Ask them to say their sharing sentence, then ask: *So how many cakes are on each plate?*

Review

Put the A3 version of photocopiable page 'Sharing (2)' onto the board. Ask a child to demonstrate how they shared the cakes by joining each cake to a plate. Discuss whether the sharing is equal and say the sharing sentence together. Repeat this for the other sharings. Invite some of the more confident learners to demonstrate their sharing of 18 cakes between three plates. They can model this for the other children to see with cubes and paper plates. Invite all of the children to say the sharing sentence: *18 shared by three is six.*

Oral and mental starter 48

Curriculum objectives

● To solve one-step problems involving multiplication and division, calculating the answer using concrete objects, pictorial representations and arrays with the support of the teacher.

Success criteria

● I can solve grouping and sharing problems.

You will need

Equipment

Interlocking cubes; individual whiteboards; paper plates

Differentiation

Less confident learners

Decide whether to provide 10 cubes and ask the children to make two groups of five, then five groups of two. They can share between two plates, then five plates.

More confident learners

Ask the children to compare the answers for the two tasks and to look for a pattern.

Lessons 5

Main teaching activities

Whole-class work: Explain that in this lesson children will be grouping and sharing. Put out several cubes and ask a child to make two groups of three. Say: *How many groups of 3 are there? Yes, two. Three add three equals six.* Now put out 2 plates and ask a child to place the 6 cubes, shared equally onto the plates. Say together: *six shared by two is three.*

Paired work: Ask the children to work in pairs, and give each pair 16 cubes. Ask the children to make equal groups with the 16 cubes by making 8 groups of two, four groups of four and two groups of eight. To remind the children, write these onto the board. They write an addition sentence to show how many there are altogether in the equal groups.

Progress check: Invite pairs to show one of their groupings. Ask them to say their addition sentence for this grouping.

Paired work: Provide eight paper plates for each pair. Ask the pairs to share 16 cubes equally between two, four and eight plates and to write a sharing sentence for each one, such as '16 shared between 2 is 8'.

Review

With the children's help, write up the addition sentences to show how many there are altogether in the equal groups. Repeat this for the sharing sentences. Invite the more confident learners to say what patterns they have found. Discuss how, for example, two groups of eight total 16, and 16 shared by two is eight. Encourage the children to look for the links between the other group totals and the sharings. Ask questions such as: *How many do you think two groups of three is? How did you work that out? So what is six shared between two?* Now ask the children to talk to their partner about what they have learned this week.

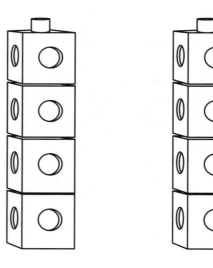

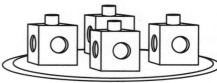

■ SCHOLASTIC

Shape, position and movement

Expected prior learning

Children should be able to:

- name 2D and 3D shapes
- name some of the properties of the shapes.

Topic	Curriculum objectives	Expected outcomes
Geometry: properties of shapes	**Lesson 1**	
	To recognise and name common 2D and 3D shapes, including: • 2D shapes [for example, rectangles (including squares), circles and triangles] • 3D shapes [for example, cuboids (including cubes), pyramids and spheres].	Sort 2D and 3D shapes by their properties.
	Lesson 2	
	To recognise and name common 2D and 3D shapes, including: • 2D shapes [for example, rectangles (including squares), circles and triangles] • 3D shapes [for example, cuboids (including cubes), pyramids and spheres].	Sort 2D and 3D shapes by their properties.
Geometry: position and direction	**Lesson 3**	
	To describe position, direction and movements, including half, quarter and three-quarter turns.	Describe where things are, including quarter, half and whole turns.
	Lesson 4	
	To describe position, direction and movement, including half, quarter and three-quarter turns.	Describe where things are, including quarter, half and whole turns.
	Lesson 5	
	To describe position, direction and movement, including half, quarter and three-quarter turns.	Describe where things are, including half and whole turns.

Preparation

Lesson 1: prepare 'Cubes' and 'Not cubes' labels. Enlarge 'Work mat' to A3, one per child; prepare 'Has 4 sides' and 'Does not have 4 sides' labels.

Lesson 3: this lesson requires large PE apparatus in the hall

Lesson 4: copy 'Town and country jigsaw', one per child; copy and enlarge 'Town and country jigsaw' to A3

You will need

Photocopiable sheets
'Town and country jigsaw'

General resources
'Work mat'

Equipment
2D shape tiles for each group: rectangles, squares, circles and triangles; 3D shapes for each group: cubes, cuboids, pyramids, cylinders and spheres; feely bag with a range of 2D shape tiles in for each group; teaching set of 2D and 3D shapes and a feely bag; access to the hall; hoops, one per child; large PE apparatus; scissors; glue sticks; temporary adhesive

Further practice

● Children work in pairs. They take turns to take a shape, 2D or 3D, from the feely bag and say its name. Their partner says two properties of the shape.
● Provide some jigsaws for the children to complete. Discuss with them how they have to move or turn the pieces to make them fit.
● Provide further experiences of following movement instructions, perhaps in the playground. Use specific vocabulary of turning and moving for the children to follow.

Oral and mental starters for week 4

See bank of starters on pages 160 to 161. Oral and mental starters are also on the CD-ROM.

57 Telling the time

54 Number trios 3

48 Everyone count to 100

Overview of progression

Children begin the week with revising the properties of 2D and 3D shapes. They recognise the shapes by their names and by their properties. They follow instructions for moving and turning themselves, then moving objects into position. They recognise the movements and turns that they make with the object.

Watch out for

Some children may still confuse 2D shapes with 3D shapes, for example calling a cube a square. Reinforce the concepts by asking children to hold the shapes, look at them and feel them. Explain that, for example, a cube has six square faces.

Creative context

During PE lessons, encourage the children to respond to commands using the vocabulary of position and movement.

Vocabulary

above, back, below, beside, between, centre, **circle**, **cone**, corner, **cube**, **cuboid**, curved, **cylinder**, direction, edge, face, far, flat, front, grid, half turn, half way, inside, left, near, next to, on top of, outside, point, position, **pyramid**, **rectangle**, right, side, solid, **sphere**, **square**, straight, **triangle**, underneath, whole turn

Curriculum objectives
- To recognise and name common 2D and 3D shapes.

Success criteria
- I can sort 2D and 3D shapes by their properties.

You will need

General resources
'Work mat'

Equipment
For each group: 2D shape tiles: rectangles, squares, circles and triangles; 3D shapes: cubes, cuboids, pyramids, cylinders and spheres; feely bag; teaching set of 2D and 3D shapes and a feely bag; 'Cubes' and 'Not cubes' labels

Differentiation

Less confident learners
Limit the range to just two types of shape each time.

More confident learners
Ask the children to sort 2D shapes by '3 sides' and 'Not 3 sides', and sort 3D shapes by 'Has 6 faces' and 'Does not have 6 faces'.

Lesson 1
Oral and mental starter 57

Main teaching activities

Whole-class work: Ask the children to shut their eyes and imagine shapes: *Imagine a big square... rectangle... triangle... painted on the floor. How many corners does it have? How many sides?* Then use a feely bag with a shape inside it. Pass it around the group and let the children feel the shape. Ask: *What shape is it? Repeat for other shapes.* Repeat for 3D shapes, for example: *Imagine a big cube... sphere... cylinder. How many corners does it have? How many faces?*

Independent work: Provide general resource 'Work mat' from the CD-ROM, with heading labels 'Cubes' and 'Not cubes'. Ask the children to sort all the shapes on the diagram.

Progress check: Ask the children to say which shapes they have placed in the 'Cubes', then 'Not cubes' regions of the table. Ask: *Why is that a cube? Why is that not a cube?*

Independent work: Ask the children to use the 2D shape tiles and sort for 'Has 4 sides' and 'Does not have 4 sides'. Prepare labels and a 'Work mat' for this task.

Review
Discuss the sortings that the children have made. Now say: Tell me where in the classroom you can see a circle, triangle, square... cube, cuboid...

Curriculum objectives
- To recognise and name common 2D and 3D shapes.

Success criteria
- I can sort 2D and 3D shapes by their properties.

You will need

Equipment
2D shape tiles for each group: rectangles, squares, circles and triangles; 3D shapes for each group: cubes, cuboids, pyramids, cylinders and spheres; feely bag with a range of 2D shape tiles in for each group; teaching set of 2D and 3D shapes and a feely bag

Differentiation

Less confident learners
Ask an adult to work with this group in order to encourage them to use shape vocabulary correctly.

More confident learners
Repeat the activity, this time using 3D shapes.

Lesson 2
Oral and mental starter 57

Main teaching activities

Whole-class work: Explain to the children that in the feely bag you have a 2D shape tile. Invite them to ask you questions to work out what the shape is. They need to ask questions such as: *Does it have four sides?* Explain that they cannot ask whether it is a particular shape until at least one other question has been asked. They repeat this until someone says its correct name. Repeat for another shape.

Group work: Ask the children to work in groups of four. They take turns to feel inside the feely bag and choose a shape tile. They say a property, such as: *It has four sides.* They say other properties until someone says the name.

When everyone has described a shape, ask the children to take turns to hold the feely bag, and to choose a shape. They do not say its name. The other children take turns to ask questions about its properties until someone can say the name.

Progress check: Ask the children to think about the properties they might say. Say, for example:

- *If the shape in the bag is a square, how would you describe it?*

Review
Repeat the whole-class activity, but this time use 3D shapes. Place some 3D shapes in front of the children to help them to think of good questions to ask.

Curriculum objectives
● To describe position, directions and movements.
Success criteria
● I can describe where things are.

You will need
Equipment
Access to the hall; hoops, one per child; large PE apparatus

Differentiation
Less confident learners
Decide whether to limit the children to a smaller range of positions and movements, so that they become familiar with these words. The activity can be repeated at a later date to introduce different vocabulary.

More confident learners
Challenge the children to include words such as 'turn' and 'centre'.

Lesson 3

Main teaching activities

Whole-class work: This could be set as a PE lesson in the hall. Explain that this lesson is about using the vocabulary of position, direction and movement. Ask the children to put out some hoops around the edge of the hall, then run around the hall. When you say *Stop*, they move to stand inside a hoop. Now ask them to hold the hoop above their heads when you say *Stop*. Repeat for other position vocabulary, such as: *stand outside/inside the hoop; four of you stand around it....*

Ask the children to put the hoops away and put out the large apparatus. Now ask them to move in pairs carefully around the hall, finding which pieces of apparatus they can go over or under. Then invite some pairs to demonstrate what they have found out, using the appropriate vocabulary. Repeat for words such as 'top', 'bottom', 'side', 'on', 'in', 'in front of', 'behind'....

Group work: The children work in groups of four to six. Assign each group to a piece of apparatus. Ask them to develop a sequence of movements.

Progress check: After a few minutes, invite each group to show the others their sequence of movements. Say, for example:

- *What movement was that?*
- *Where did she start?*
- *Where did she finish?*

Group work: Ask the groups to move around the apparatus to a different piece and to repeat the activity.

Review

Ask each group in turn to demonstrate its sequence. Ask the other children to describe what they see, using the vocabulary of position, direction and movement. Check that they can use the vocabulary appropriately. When the floor is clear, ask the children to stand up and then to move quietly around the hall. Say:

- *Move forwards.*
- *Stop.*
- *Stretch up as far as you can.*

Then say:

- *Find a partner*
- *One of you lead, the other one is the shadow.*
- *The shadow copies the moves of the other person.*

Now say:

- *Stand on your own.*
- *Move forwards; backwards; sideways; turn left/right...*

As part of a cool-down activity, say:

- *Think of the classroom.*
- *What is in front of the board... beside the board...?*

Curriculum objectives

● To describe position, directions and movements, including turns.

Success criteria

● I can describe where things are.

You will need

Photocopiable sheets

'Town and country jigsaw'

Equipment

Scissors; glue sticks; temporary adhesive

Differentiation

Less confident learners

Let these children see the A3 version of photocopiable page 'Town and country jigsaw' as they work.

More confident learners

Challenge these children to make ten cuts in the pictures and reassemble the pieces.

Lesson 4   Oral and mental starter 48

Main teaching activities

Whole-class work: Show the children the A3 version of photocopiable page 'Town and country jigsaw' from the CD-ROM . Discuss what the children can see, so that the pictures are familiar to them. Ask them to cut up the pictures as indicated on the sheet, then arrange the pieces to make the pictures again.

Independent work: Remove the A3 version of photocopiable page 'Town and country jigsaw', then ask the children to start working. They can glue their reassembled pictures onto paper.

Progress check: Check that the children understand their task. Ask questions such as:

● *What happens if you make that piece turn through half a turn?*
● *Which piece do you think will fit here? Why do you think that?*

Review

Ask the children how they solved the puzzle. Discuss how the pieces needed to be turned, and moved in order to make the puzzle. Cut up the A3 version of photocopiable page 'Town and country jigsaw' and ask some children to help you reassemble the pictures. If a temporary adhesive is used, the pictures can be moved around the board. Ask questions such as:

● *What shape is ___?*
● *How did that help you?*

Curriculum objectives

● To describe position, directions and movements, including turns.

Success criteria

● I can describe where things are.
● I can follow instructions for position, direction and movement.

Differentiation

This can be done in mixed-ability groups, but check that the more confident do not dominate the group and that the less confident take an active part.

Lesson 5   Oral and mental starter 48

Main teaching activities

Whole-class work: Play 'I spy', using position vocabulary and invite the children to find things in the classroom. For example, say: *I spy with my little eye something above the computer... in front of the window... next to the door.* Then play 'Simon says' and include turning on the spot.

Group work: Encourage the children to take turns to be Simon and play 'Simon says'. Check that they include turns. Listen in to the instructions that 'Simon' says to each group.

Progress check: Invite the children to repeat some of the instructions they've given so far. Ask, for example:

● *What other instructions could you say?*

Review

Play both 'I spy' and 'Simon says' again. Observe which children follow the instructions with ease and which need more practice at hearing and understanding the vocabulary of position and movement.

Now ask the children to tell their partner what they have learned this week and which aspects of the work they need to practise further.

Measuring and time

Expected prior learning

Children should be able to:
- recite some of the days of the week
- use non-standard units for measuring length, weight and capacity.

Topic	Curriculum objectives	Expected outcomes
Measurement	**Lesson 1**	
	To recognise and use language relating to dates, including days of the week, weeks, months and years.	Know the days of the week and the months of the year, in chronological order.
	To measure and begin to record the following: lengths and heights; mass/weight; capacity and volume; time (hours, minutes, seconds).	Tell o'clock and half past times.
	Lesson 2	
	To measure and begin to record the following: lengths and heights; mass/weight; capacity and volume; time (hours, minutes, seconds).	Measure time in minutes and hours.
	To compare, describe and solve practical problems for: lengths and heights [for example, long/short, longer/shorter, tall/short, double/half]; mass or weight [for example, heavy/light, heavier than, lighter than]; capacity/volume [full/empty, more than, less than, quarter]; time (quicker, slower, earlier, later).	Use sand timers and stop clocks to measure time passing.
	Lesson 3	
	To measure and begin to record the following: lengths and heights; mass/weight; capacity and volume; time (hours, minutes, seconds).	Begin to use standard units: metres; 100g and kg; 100ml and litre.
	Lesson 4	
	To measure and begin to record the following: lengths and heights; mass/weight; capacity and volume; time (hours, minutes, seconds).	Begin to use standard units: metres; 100g and kg; 100ml and litre.
	Lesson 5	
	To measure and begin to record the following: lengths and heights; mass/weight; capacity and volume; time (hours, minutes, seconds).	Begin to use standard units: metres; 100g and kg; 100ml and litre.

■SCHOLASTIC

Preparation

Lessons 3 to 5: prepare the equipment for the different activities you will be using each lesson; copy 'Measures', one per child

You will need

Photocopiable sheets
'Measures'

General resources
Interactive activities3 'Days of the week' and 'Months of the year'; interactive teaching resource 'Clocks'

Equipment
Blu-Tack®; individual clock faces; 1-minute sand timers, stop clocks; 2D shape tiles; 100g weights, 1kg weights, bucket balances, pan and dial balances that read in 100g; Litre containers marked in 100ml; empty containers marked A, B, C and so on; metre sticks; string; scissors; teaching clock, clock faces, 1-minute sand timers, stop clocks; 2D shape tiles

Further practice

All of these activities in this week's work are practical. Consider using any activity suggestions not used in lessons 3 to 5 for further practice.

Oral and mental starters for week 5

See bank of starters on pages 160 to 161. Oral and mental starters are also on the CD-ROM.

50 Counting in 2s to 50

51 Counting in 5s

54 Number trios 3

53 Add numbers to 5

Overview of progression

Children begin the week by learning the names of the months of the year. They revise telling the time to o'clock and half past times. They estimate short periods of time, such as 1 minute, then find out what can be done in 1 minute, and how long a given task takes. They use sand timers and stop clocks. They then begin to name and use standard units of measure: metre, 100ml, litre, 100g and kilogram. They use these in practical activities where they estimate then measure. They learn that there are ten 100g to balance 1kg, and ten 100ml to fill 1 litre. Great care needs to be taken when using the 1kg weight and it is suggested that this activity is supervised by an adult.

Watch out for

Children may have no sense of the passing of time as yet. Tell them how long an activity has taken, so that they begin to have a 'feel' for the passing of time.

For measures at this stage, they are using standard units as they used non-standard units before. Check that children are as accurate as they can be. For example, they look carefully at the balance to check that it is in balance; they bend down to look at the litre jug to make sure that they have filled it as accurately as they can to the 100ml mark.

Creative context

Encourage the children to discuss the date and month in other subjects. Also discuss the changing seasons, perhaps taking a photograph of a tree in the school grounds each month, or painting it each month to see how it changes over time.

Vocabulary

about, afternoon, balance, clock, day, days of the week, estimate, evening, hands, hour, kilogram, litre, metre, midnight, month, months and seasons of the year, morning, night, time, week, year, 100 grams, 100 millilitres

● To recognise and use language relating to dates, including days of the week and months.
● To measure and begin to record time (hours).

Success criteria
● I can say the names of the days of the week and the months of the year.
● I can read o'clock and half past times.

You will need

General resources
Interactive activities 'Days of the week' and 'Months of the year'; interactive teaching resource 'Clocks'

Equipment
Blu-Tack®; individual clock faces

Differentiation

Less confident learners
Decide whether to work with these children as a group. Encourage them to say the time and to use other time vocabulary.

More confident learners
Challenge the children to include quarter past times.

Lesson 1

Main teaching activities

Whole-class work: As a class, say the names of the days of the week in order. Display the interactive activity 'Months of the year' on the CD-ROM. Prompt individual children to drag and drop the months of the year onto a grid in the correct order. Ask: *How many of you have a birthday in January... February... December?* Count how many and ask: *Which month has most birthdays? Which has least?* Now ask the children to think of something special for each month, such as: *January is winter. In February, we have pancake day. In March, it can be very windy....*

Next, display the interactive activity 'Days of the week' on the CD-ROM. Prompt individual children to drag and drop the days of the week onto a grid in the correct order. Ask: *What day is it tomorrow? Yesterday? What is your favourite day of the week? Why?*

Use the interactive teaching resource 'Clocks' on the CD-ROM and set it to display randomly o'clock and half past times. Ask the children to put up their hands to say the time. Choose, over the session, children from each ability group to say the time. Ask:

● *What time is this? How do you know that?*
● *What does the hour hand show? What does the minute hand show?*

When the children are confident with this, ask some time questions, such as:

● *How long is it between getting up at 7 o'clock and eating lunch at 12 o'clock?*
● *My favourite television programme begins at half past 7 and ends at 9 o'clock. How long does it last?*

For each question, invite a child to explain how he or she worked out the answer. Less confident children may benefit from using individual clock faces to help them with these questions.

Paired work: Ask the children to work in pairs. They take turns to say a time, and their partner sets the clock to show that time. Ask the children to say o'clock and half past times.

Progress check: Ask questions such as:

● *Which clock hand shows the hours?*
● *Which one shows the minutes?*
● *If the hour hand points to 12 and the minute hand points to 12 what time is it?*

Independent work: Ask the children to draw pictures for each month. Discuss with them what they might draw, and provide paper for their pictures. If time is available, give children the interactive activities, 'Days of the week' and 'Months of the year' to complete themselves.

Review

Ask more time questions, such as:

● *At 3 o'clock James goes to his grandpa's house. He comes back home at 6 o'clock. For how long is he out?*
● *Sarah watches her favourite TV programme. The programme starts at 4 o'clock and finishes at half past 4. How long does it last?*
● *Maisie leaves home to go to her grandma's at half past 2. She comes home at 7 o'clock. How long was she away from home?*

For each question, invite the children to explain how they worked out the answer. Now choose twelve children to bring out one of their pictures depicting a month. Ask them to stand in month order. Discuss what has been drawn to depict each month and ask the children to think of other things that could have been drawn.

Make a class month calendar, choosing from all the pictures. Pin this to the wall, with the name of the relevant month under each picture. Discuss which months fall into which seasons.

SCHOLASTIC

Curriculum objectives

● To measure and begin to record time (minutes).
● To compare, describe and solve practical problems for time [quicker, slower, earlier, later].

Success criteria

● I can measure time in minutes and in hours using sand timers and stop clocks.

You will need

Equipment

One-minute sand timers, stop clocks; 2D shape tiles

Differentiation

Less confident learners

The children may need support with recording their results.

More confident learners

Challenge the children to think of things that they could do that they estimate would take 2, 3, 4 or 5 minutes to complete.

Lesson 2

Oral and mental starter 50

Main teaching activities

Whole-class work: Ask the children to shut their eyes, and to keep them shut until they think that a minute has gone. Keep a check of the time, and when a minute has passed, ask everyone to open their eyes and explain that a minute has passed. Now use a one-minute sand timer, and ask the children to watch as the sand goes through the timer. Explain that this has taken just 1 minute. Ask questions such as:

● *Did that feel like a long time or a short time?*
● *What do you think you could do in 1 minute?*

Now show the children the stop clock. Explain that this can be set to find out how long something takes. Show the children how this operates.

Group work: Ask the children to work in groups of four. There are two activities for them to try. Half way through the allotted time ask them to swap timing equipment with another group, and to begin the other activity.

1. Using a sand timer

Provide a 1-minute sand timer. Ask the children to think of things that they can do in 1 minute. For example, they might find out how many times they can write their name. Ask them to think of at least four different things, then try them, setting the sand timer each time. One of the children can be in charge of the sand timer and tell the others when to start and when to stop. They record for example, how many times they can write their name in 1 minute.

2. Using a stop clock

Provide a stop clock. Ask the children to make a repeating pattern of shape tiles. One of the children times them using the stop clock to see how long this takes. They can also try writing their name ten times very neatly and see how long that takes. They write a sentence to record: It took me __ minutes to write my name 10 times.

Progress check: Review each group as they work. At an appropriate time (so as not to interrupt timing) ask them to stop work. Ask questions such as:

● *What have you found out?*
● *Did it feel like 1 minute... 2 minutes...?*

Review

Invite each group to tell the other children what they discovered for one of the two activities, so that both activities are covered. Ask questions such as:

● *Do you think you know how long a minute is?*
● *How would you know?*
● *How long did it take to write your name very neatly? Were you surprised by how long it took?*

Curriculum objectives

● To measure and begin to record the following: lengths and heights; mass/weight; capacity and volume; time (hours, minutes, seconds).

Success criteria

● I can measure using a metre stick.
● I can weigh using 100 grams weight.
● I can find capacity using 100 millilitres measure.

You will need

Photocopiable sheets

'Measures'

Equipment

Metre sticks; string; scissors; 100g weights; 1kg weights; bucket balances; pan; dial balances that read in 100g; litre containers marked in 100ml; empty containers marked A, B, C and so on

Differentiation

Less confident learners

Decide whether to ask an adult to work with this group to encourage the children to talk about their work using the vocabulary of measures.

More confident learners

Activity 8 is a challenge for the children to tackle. Check that they measure accurately, placing each metre stick against the other.

Lessons 3 to 5   Oral and mental starters 54 53

Main teaching activities

Whole-class work: Show the children the metre stick and say: *We have been using different things to measure how long something is, such as straws, cubes, and so on. We can use a metre stick to measure how long something is.* Put the metre stick beside the teacher's table, or a cupboard and ask: *Is the table taller or shorter than the metre stick? How can you tell?* Invite a confident child to stand by the metre stick and ask: Is __ taller or shorter than the metre stick?

Show the children a 100g weight. Say: *We have used sand and cubes to find out how heavy something is. Today we are going to use a weight. This weight weighs 100 grams.* Pass the weight around so the children can feel its weight. Ask: *What do you think weighs about 100 grams?* Then, put the 100g weight into one side of a bucket balance and a book into the other side and ask the children: *Is the book heavier or lighter than 100 grams? How can you tell?*

Show the children the container marked in 100ml. Explain that when this is full to the top mark it holds 1 litre. Show the children the marks up the side of the jug, and explain that each one of these is 100ml, and that ten of those make 1 litre. Pass the jug around the room for the children to examine.

Group work: These activities could be set up as a circus of activities for the children to complete during lessons 3 to 5.

Activity 1 Provide several lengths of string, some shorter than, and some longer than a metre. Ask the children to order the strings by length. Then ask them to use a metre stick to find those that are longer than, and those that are shorter than, 1 metre. They show you their sorting.

Activity 2 Ask children to use the metre stick in the classroom. They find three things longer/taller/wider than 1metre, three things about the same length as 1 metre, and three things shorter than 1 metre. Ask them to record in a chart with three headings: 'Shorter than 1 metre', 'About 1 metre' and 'Longer than 1 metre'.

Activity 3 Ask children to estimate then use the 100g weight and use cupfuls of sand to balance it. They record how many cupfuls they estimated and needed.

Activity 4 The children use a pan and dial balance. They pour in sand, cubes, dried peas in order to find how much they need to weigh out 100g.

Activity 5 Provide a litre jug marked in 100ml. The children estimate, then find by filling and pouring how many egg cups of water measure 100ml.

Activity 6 Provide some containers without scales, but labelled A, B, C and so on. Children fill the litre jug to the 100ml measure mark, then pour into one of the containers. They repeat this to find how many 100ml the container will hold. They record their estimate, and measure on photocopiable page 'Measures'.

Activity 7 Place a 1kg weight into one bucket of the bucket balance. Ask the children to find out how many 100g weights will balance the 1kg weight.

Activity 8 Challenge: provide several metre sticks. Ask the children to devise a way to find how long the classroom is using the metre sticks.

Progress check: Use these questions for any of the activities. Invite the children to explain what they are doing. *What do you need to find out? Have you estimated first? Did you make a good estimate? How do you know that? How close were you able to measure?*

Review

Each lesson review one of the activities in detail. Invite a group to explain what they did, how they made their estimate, and how they checked by measuring. Encourage the other children to ask them questions. If the children are not sure about this, say, for example: *Why did you do it this way? How could you improve what you did? Was it easy to measure this? Why do you think that was?*

Addition and subtraction totals to 10

Expected prior learning

Children should be able to:

- use mental counting on or back methods to find solutions to addition and subtraction sentences.

Topic	Curriculum objectives	Expected outcomes
Addition and subtraction	**Lesson 1**	
	To add and subtract one-digit and two-digit numbers to 20, including zero.	Have rapid recall of addition and subtraction facts to 10.
	Lesson 2	
	To add and subtract one-digit and two-digit numbers to 20, including zero.	Have rapid recall of addition and subtraction facts to 10.
	Lesson 3	
	To add and subtract one-digit and two-digit numbers to 20, including zero.	Have rapid recall of addition and subtraction facts to 10.
	Lesson 4	
	To add and subtract one-digit and two-digit numbers to 20, including zero.	Have rapid recall of addition and subtraction facts to 10.
	Lesson 5	
	To solve one-step problems that involve addition and subtraction, using concrete objects and pictorial representations, and missing number problems.	Use knowledge of addition and subtraction facts to 10 to solve problems.

Preparation

At the start of the week: set up a class newsagent's shop, and label the items for sale using the 1p–20p price labels. Provide a 'till' from the metal or wooden box with some 1p, 2p, 5p, 10p and 20p coins in it.

Lesson 1: prepare price labels 1p–10p, one set per pair; prepare cards price labels 11p–20p for more confident children as appropriate

Lesson 2: copy 'The fairground game'; copy and enlarge 'The fairground game' to A3

Lesson 3: copy 'Subtraction (1)', one per child as appropriate

Lesson 4: prepares sets of 'Number cards 0–20'; one set per pair; copy 'Number line 0–20' for less confident learners as appropriate

Lesson 5: copy 'Number line 0–20' for less confident learners as appropriate

You will need

Photocopiable sheets

'The fairground game'; 'Subtraction (1)'

General resources

'Number cards 0–10'; 'Number line 0–20'

Equipment

A pot of coins (all values from 1p– £2); Price labels 1p–20p; 1–6 dice for each pair; items for a class newsagent's shop, such as newspapers, comics and sweet boxes; metal or wooden box; pad of paper

Further practice

Photocopiable sheets

'Complements of 10'; 'Add and subtract to 10 (2)'

Oral and mental starters for week 6

See bank of starters on pages 84, 85, 160 and 161. Oral and mental starters are also on the CD-ROM.

52 Show me complements of 10

25 Add and subtract to 5

23 Add and subtract to 10

57 Telling the time

Overview of progression

This week children review their learning about addition and subtraction to 10. The aim is to help children to have quick recall of these facts, as they will need these facts to help them to derive 10 + 5, and so on, in Summer 1. This includes using coins in the class shop to purchase items and work out the change from 10p. Lesson 5 gives an opportunity to use facts already known in order to find solutions to a problem.

Watch out for

Some children may still need support with recalling these facts. Encourage them to use mental counting on or back methods.

Creative context

Use stories which include money and shopping. Children can talk about their experiences with family and friends when they go shopping.

Vocabulary

add, altogether, answer, calculate, calculation, compare, difference, equals (=), explain, how many more/less, less, method, minus (−), more, number sentence, order, pattern, plus (+), problem, solution, subtract, sum, total

Curriculum objectives
● To add and subtract one-digit numbers to 10.
Success criteria
● I can find the solutions to all addition and subtraction facts to 10.

You will need
Equipment
A pot of 1p, 2p, 5p and 10p coins per pair; price labels 1p–20p; class 'shop' as described on page 154

Differentiation
Less confident learners
If the children are unsure about equivalent coin values, limit the range of prices to 1p–5p and change from 5p until they understand how to count up in 2p coins as well as 1p coins.

More confident learners
If the children are confident about giving change from 10p, extend the price label range to 12p.

Lesson 1   Oral and mental starter 52

Main teaching activities

Whole-class work: Choose some items from the 'shop' priced between 1p and 10p. Choose a child to be the customer. In role as the shopkeeper, say: *This costs 3p. If the customer gives me 5p to pay for it, how much change will I need to give?* As you count out pennies into the customer's hand, say: *Let's count up together. 3p: 4p, 5p. So I need to give 2p change.* On the board, write 5p – 3p = 2p. *What if the customer gave me a 10p coin: what change would I give then?* As you put the 1p coins into the customer's hand, say: *Count up again. 3p: 4p, 5p, 6p, 7p, 8p, 9p, 10p. So the change is 7p.* On the board, write 10p – 3p = 7p. Children may find it helpful to keep a tally on their fingers as they count up. Repeat for the other items the 'customer' has chosen.

Now say: *Does change always come in pennies? Can we give other coins too?* Demonstrate the change from 5p for a 1p purchase. Ask the children to count up with you in steps of 2p: *1p and 2p is 3p, and 2p more is 5p. So I can use 2p coins to give 4p in change.* Repeat this for other amounts, such as the change from 10p for spending 4p: *4p and 1p is 5p, and 5p more is 10p. The change is 6p: 1p and 5p coins.*

Group and paired work: Ask one group to work in the shop. They take turns to be shopkeeper and customer, choosing items and paying for them using a 10p coin. The shopkeeper counts out the change. Encourage the children to use coins other than 1p to give change.

The other children work in pairs, using a set of price labels 1p–10p and a pot of 1p, 2p, 5p and 10p coins. They take turns to be shopkeeper and customer. The customer chooses a price label and offers the shopkeeper a 10p coin; the shopkeeper counts out the change into the customer's hand. Encourage the children to use coins other than 1p to give change. They can write a subtraction sentence for each transaction.

Decide whether to ask another group to work in the shop so that more children have the opportunity to try this.

Progress check: Invite children to demonstrate how they found the change. Ask questions such as:

● *Who 'knew' the answer?*
● *What addition fact could you use to help you find the answer quickly?*

Review

Invite pairs of children to act as shopkeeper and customer, giving change for prices to 10p. Encourage the other children to suggest alternative ways of giving the change. Ask:

● *Is there another way to give this change?*
● *Which way uses the fewest number of coins?*

Curriculum objectives
● To add and subtract one-digit numbers to 10.
Success criteria
● I can find the solutions to all addition and subtraction facts to 10.

You will need
Photocopiable sheets
'The fairground game'
Equipment
A pot of 1p, 2p, 5p and 10p coins per pair; class 'shop' as described on page 154

Differentiation
Less confident learners
Ask a talk partner to support with the calculations.
More confident learners
Suggest that they use the addition fact so that they can derive the subtraction fact. Ask them to write their own fairground cards.

Lesson 2
Oral and mental starter 25

Main teaching activities

Whole-class work: Repeat the whole-class activity from lesson 1, encouraging the children to count up using larger coins, so that fewer coins are used and use the vocabulary relating to addition and subtraction.

Group and paired work: Ask the children to work in pairs on photocopiable page 'The fairground game' from the CD-ROM.

Decide whether a group should also work in the class shop, as in Lesson 1. Then decide whether the group who is working in the shop should swap with another group so that across the week everyone has a turn in the class shop.

Progress check: Ask questions of everyone such as:
- *How would you work out how much two 5p rides are?*
- *Who does it a different way?*
- *Who 'knows' the answer? Well done!*

Review
Play 'The fairground game' as a class, using the A3 version of the game. Ask questions such as:
- *How did you work out the change?*
- *Which way of giving the change would use the fewest number of coins?*

Curriculum objectives
● To add and subtract one-digit numbers to 10.
Success criteria
● I can find the solutions to all addition and subtraction facts to 10.

You will need
Photocopiable sheets
'Subtraction (1)'
Equipment
Class shop as described on page 154

Differentiation
Less confident learners
Support the children by modelling the two problems on the 'Subtraction (1)' sheet with counters or similar.
More confident learners
Encourage the children to answer the questions quickly and accurately, and to tell their partner how they found the answer.

Lesson 3
Oral and mental starter 23

Main teaching activities

Whole-class work: Explain that today, the children will be revising what they know about subtraction. Ask subtraction questions that use a range of vocabulary, such as: *What is 9 subtract 4? How many more is 8 than 2? How many fewer is 3 than 6? What is the difference between 6 and 9?*

Check that the children remember the strategy of counting on. So for 9 – 4, they could count: *4: 5, 6, 7, 8, 9. That is 5 more. So 9 – 4 is 5.* Emphasise how to record their work.

Independent work: Provide copies of photocopiable page 'Subtraction (1)' from the CD-ROM. The children work individually to answer the questions. Decide whether a group should work in the shop, as lesson 1.

Progress check: Target the children who you think have rapid recall of these number facts. Ask them questions such as: *How did you work that out? Did you 'know' any answers? Well done!* Check that they are using known facts to derive those that they do not know yet.

Review
Review some of the examples from the photocopiable page. Ask individual children to explain how they worked out their answer, and which strategy they used. Ask questions such as:
- *What is 9 subtract 2? How did you work that out?*
- *Do some of you remember the answers to these? Well done.*

Invite the children to discuss with a partner what they know about using addition and subtraction. Ask those children who you are targeting for assessment to give feedback about their discussion.

Curriculum objectives
● To add and subtract one-digit numbers to 10.

Success criteria
● I can find the solutions to all addition and subtraction facts to 10.

You will need

General resources
'Number cards 0–20'; 'Number line 0–20'

Equipment
Class 'shop' as described on page 154

Differentiation

Less confident learners
Provide number lines. Encourage them to use recall, or count on or back mentally before using the number lines.

More confident learners
Challenge the children to try to recall the facts rather than resorting to using mental counting on or back methods.

Lesson 4   Oral and mental starter 57

Main teaching activities

Whole-class work: Say a number and ask the children to use that number to make an addition that totals 10. If you say 4, the children should say 6 + 4 = 10 or 4 + 6 = 10. Write the children's number sentences on the board. Ask: *How did you find the answer?*

Now say: *If I say 4, tell me the subtraction sentence from 10.* The children should say 10 − 4 = 6 or 10 − 6 = 4.

Repeat for other numbers from 1 to 10. This time ask the children to say two addition and two subtraction sentences.

Paired work: Provide each pair with a set of 0–10 number cards. They take turns to turn over one of the cards, then both write down two addition and two subtraction sentences with that number and 10. They compare their number sentences, and use counting on or back to check their solutions.

Decide whether a group should work in the class shop as in lesson 1.

Progress check: Ask:
● *What do I add to 7 to make a total of 10?*
● *What other addition and subtraction sentences can you make with these three numbers?*

Review

Explain that you will ask the children to hold up fingers to show the answers to questions when you say *Show me.* Say, for example:
● *What is 5 + 5?*
● *What do I add to 8 to make 10?*
● *What is the difference between 7 and 10?*
● *What is the total of 4 and 6?*
● *How many more is 10 than 1?*
● *How many fewer is 3 than 10?*

Curriculum objectives
● To solve simple one-step problems that involve addition and subtraction.

Success criteria
● I can use addition and subtraction to solve word problems.

You will need

General resources
'Number line 0–20'

Differentiation

Less confident learners
Decide whether the children need number lines to support them.

More confident learners
Challenge the children to include the number 5, and to see what number greater than 10 they can make with 1, 2, 3, 4 and 5.

Lesson 5   Oral and mental starter 57

Main teaching activities

Whole-class work: Explain that in this lesson you will set the children a problem to solve. Write onto the board: 4 + 1 + 2. Ask: *How would you find the solution?* Children may suggest that 4 + 1 is 5, and 5 + 2 is 7. Write up correct solutions.

Now set the problem. Say to the children: *Paul took four number cards. The cards were 1, 2, 3, and 4. Your task today is to try to make all the numbers from 5 to 10, using just these numbers and addition.* Ask the children to discuss in pairs how they could go about this task. Invite them to explain to others how they think they could do the task. Give the children plenty of time to carry out the task.

Progress check: Ask pairs to explain how they are finding solutions. Ask: *Which numbers can you make using just two of the numbers 1, 2, 3 and 4? So what do you do to find the other numbers?*

Review

Say: *Now you may use the number 5 as well.* Ask for suggestions of how to make 5 (1 + 4 or 2 + 3), 6 (2 + 4 or 1 + 5), 7 (2 + 5 or 3 + 4), 8 (1 + 2 + 5 or 1 + 3 + 4), 9 (4 + 5 or 2 + 3 + 4) and 10 (4 + 5 + 1 or 2 + 3 + 5). Ask:
● *What decisions did you make?*
● *What patterns did you discover?*
● *How did you record your work?*

Invite children to say how they used the number facts that they know in order to work out new ones.

Curriculum objectives
● To solve one-step problems that involve addition and subtraction.

You will need
1. Check
Oral and mental starter

54 Number trios 4

'Number line 0–20'

2. Assess
'Missing number problems';
'Number line 0–20'

3. Further practice
Oral and mental starters

52 Show me complements of 10

53 Add numbers to 5

Photocopiable sheets
'Dice roll add'; 'Adding'

Curriculum objectives
● To solve one-step problems involving multiplication and division.

You will need
1. Check
Oral and mental starter

50 Counting in 2s to 50

'Number line 0–20'

2. Assess
12 interlocking cubes for each child; 4 paper plates for each child

3. Further practice
Oral and mental starters

50 Counting in 2s to 50

51 Counting in 5s

Photocopiable sheets
'Groups of cubes'; 'Sharing cubes'

Addition and subtraction: missing number problems

Most children should be able to use strategies to find the solutions to problems.

Some children will not have made such progress and will require additional practice of using mental counting on or back strategies, or using a number line.

1. Check
54 Number trios 4

Observe how children respond to the number trio questions. Note which children lack confidence and provide number lines to help them to find the solutions. Invite more confident children to explain how they calculated to find the solutions.

● *How did you find the answer?*
● *Who used a different method?*
● *Who 'knew' the answer? Well done!*

2. Assess
Observe how children tackle photocopiable page 'Missing number problems' on page 162. Note those who are less confident and offer number lines to help them. For those who are more confident ask them to explain their strategies, such as counting on mentally, using known facts and adding on or subtracting. Record the outcomes.

3. Further practice
The suggested oral and mental starters give further practice in recall of number bonds to 10 and beyond 10. Use the photocopiables suggested on pages 165 and 166 to provide further experience in finding solutions where the answers are greater than 10.

Groups and sharing

Most children should be able to find out how many there are altogether in several equal groups and use sharing equally to find solutions.

Some children will not have made such progress and will require further support with equal groups and sharing in twos.

1. Check
50 Counting in 2s to 50

Observe which children count confidently and which are unsure. For the less confident children provide number lines to help them to count forward and back in twos. Challenge the more confident to continue the count in twos to 100 and back again.

● *When counting forwards in twos what number comes after 18…?*
● *When counting back in twos what number comes before 14…?*

2. Assess
Ask the children to make six equal groups of two cubes and say how many cubes they have altogether. They record this as 'six groups of two is 12'. Now ask them to use the same cubes to show how to share them out equally into two sets. They record this as '12 shared by two is six'. They repeat this for 4 groups of 3 and sharing 12 into four sets. Observe who responds confidently and who needs further practice. Record the outcomes.

3. Further practice
Use the suggested oral and mental starters to provide further practice in counting in twos and fives. The photocopiables provide further practice in equal groups and sharing.

Curriculum objectives

● To measure and begin to record the following: lengths and heights; mass/weight; capacity and volume; time (hours, minutes, seconds).

You will need

1. Check

Oral and mental starter

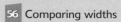 Comparing more than two lengths

2. Assess

Metre sticks; 'Metre measure recording sheet'

3. Further practice

Oral and mental starter

56 Comparing widths

Photocopiable sheets

'Butterfly wings'

Comparing and ordering lengths

Most children should be able to identify three things that are longer or shorter.

Some children will not have made such progress and will require further experience of making comparisons of length.

1. Check

55 Comparing more than two lengths

Observe how the children holding the strips of paper put these together to make a direct comparison. The less confident may need further practice in making direct comparisons. Challenge the more able to order more than three strips.

● *Which is longest... shortest?*
● *How did you work that out?*

2. Assess

Provide metre sticks. Children find things in the classroom wider and narrower than a metre stick, and about a metre, and record their results on photocopiable sheet 'Metre measure recording sheet' from page 163. Observe how the children make their estimates. Less confident children may need further support. Challenge the more confident children to find as many things as they can in the classroom that are about 1 metre wide. Record the outcomes.

3. Further practice

Use the suggested oral and mental starters to provide further practice of comparing three or more widths. Completing the suggested photocopiable sheet 'Butterfly wings' on page 164 will give further practice of making comparisons, this time with four items. You may wish to limit the less confident children to comparing two, then three, then four butterflies.

Curriculum objectives

● To describe position, direction and movement including half, quarter and three-quarter turns.

You will need

1. Check

Oral and mental starter

58 58 Simon says

2. Assess

Individual whiteboards

3. Further practice

Oral and mental starters

58 Simon says

59 I spy

Follow instructions for whole, half and quarter turns

Most children should be able to follow the instructions for turning themselves through whole, half and quarter turns.

Some children will not have made such progress and will require more practice in understanding and following the instructions.

1. Check

 Simon says

Encourage all the children to follow the instructions. Observe which children are less confident and include some simpler instructions for them. Make the instructions more complex for the more confident children, such as 'a quarter turn, then a step forward'.

● *What instructions did I just give you?*
● *What instruction do you need to move you back to where you were before?*

2. Assess

In groups of four, children take turns to play 'Simon says'. Decide whether an adult should work with the less confident group to give help with the vocabulary. Challenge the more confident children to make their instructions more complex, including two things to do each time. Check that they use appropriate vocabulary and that the others follow the instructions carefully. Record the outcomes.

3. Further practice

Use both oral and mental starters to give the children practice in recognising the vocabulary of position, direction and motion and following the instructions.

Oral and mental starters

Number and place value

48 Everyone count to 100

Ask the children to count with you, from 0 to 100 and back again. Keep the pace sharp. Repeat this, this time, counting around the class. Ask questions such as:

- *If Tom says 25, what will Sara say?*
- *What number comes between 36 and 38?*

49 Count the cubes

Ask the children to count out 10 cubes. Remind them to touch, say the number, and move the cube in a coordinated way. Now say: *Count out 12 cubes. Check the number by touching, counting and moving the cubes. Count out 15... 20... cubes. Count them in a different order. How many are there now?*

Repeat this for other quantities.

50 Counting in 2s to 50

Ask the children to count with you in twos from zero to 20 and back again. Extend the counting range to 30, then to 40, then 50. Keep the pace sharp.

51 Counting in 5s

Ask the children to count with you in fives from zero to 20 and back again. Extend the counting range to 30, 40, 50 and keep the pace sharp.

Addition and subtraction

52 Show me complements of 10

Provide individual whiteboards and pens. Ask the children to write the number that goes with the number you will say to make a total of 10. For example, if you say 6, they write 4. When you say *Show me*, they hold up their whiteboards for you to check. Say, for example: *How much do I add to 3 to total 10? What do I add to 8 to make 10? 4 and what makes 10?*

53 Add numbers to 5

Ask the children to add larger numbers to 5. Say, for example: *What is 6 add 5? How did you work it out? What is 8 add 5? What is 5 add 9? Tell me two numbers that will total 12.*

Keep the totals to up to 15, at this stage.

54 Number trios 4

Use the teaching set of cards from 'Number trios 3' from the CD-ROM. Hold up a card, covering the total and ask the children to find the missing number. Ask *How did you work that out?* Now cover a different number on the same card and ask for the missing number, again asking for how the answer was found. Repeat for the third number. Repeat this for the other cards.

Measurement

55 Comparing more than two lengths

Ask three children to choose some strips of paper or ribbons and to hold them out so that the other children can see how long these are. Say: *Which do you think is the longest... shortest?* Now ask the three children to hold the strips out by one end, so that their hands match the ends up. Ask: *Did you make a good estimate? Which one is the longest... shortest?* Invite the children to order the strips starting with the shortest, then the middle one then the longest one. Repeat this with another three children and three different strips. Extend to four strips.

56 Comparing widths

Show the children three sheets of paper, each with a different width. Ask: Which do you estimate is the widest... narrowest? *How did you make that estimate? How should we compare these to find whether we made good estimates?* If children are unsure, they can place one sheet of paper on another to compare the widths, and repeat this so that all three sheets have been compared. Repeat with another three things, such as books of varying widths.

57 Telling the time

Use the interactive teaching resource 'Clocks' on the CD-ROM and the random time feature. Set to whole and half hours only. Explain that you will show the children a time on the clock, and you would like them to read it aloud when you say *Go*

Extension

Ask questions such as: *What time does the clock show? What time will it be in half an hour... one hour... two hours? The clock shows 2 o'clock. If I turn the hands to half past 4, how much later would that be?*

Invite the children to suggest a time that another child can set on the teaching clock. Ask: *Where will the hour hand go? And the minute hand?*

Geometry

58 Simon says

Ask the children to follow the directions you give. Remind them that if you do not say 'Simon says', and they follow the directions, they must sit down. Begin by saying: *Simon says stand up. Simon says put your hands on your head. Simon says turn half the way around. Sit down.* Continue like this, including turns, movement and change of position.

59 I spy

Explain that the children will be playing a version of 'I spy'. Say, for example: I spy something with hands that turn (clock). I spy something with a knob that turns (door). I spy something that has two finger spaces that will turn (scissors). Now ask the children to think of anything else that will turn that is in the classroom.

Name: _____   Date: _____

Missing number problems

- Tom spilled some paint onto his work.
- Write the missing number in the box.
- Do this for each number sentence.

1. $6 + ⬛ = 11$ ☐

2. $12 - ⬛ = 4$ ☐

3. $5 + 7 = ⬛$ ☐

4. $⬛ - 6 = 6$ ☐

5. $16 - 9 = ⬛$ ☐

6. $13 - ⬛ = 4$ ☐

7. $⬛ + 4 = 11$ ☐

8. $14 - ⬛ = 6$ ☐

9. $7 + ⬛ = 13$ ☐

10. $15 - ⬛ = 8$ ☐

I can solve one-step addition and subtraction problems.

How did you do?

Name: _____   Date: _____

Metre measure recording sheet

- ■ Work with a partner.
- ■ You will need a metre stick.
- ■ Find things that you estimate are wider than a metre.
- ■ Find things you estimate are narrower than a metre.
- ■ Find things you estimate are about a metre.
- ■ Write them into the sheet.
- ■ Check by comparing with the metre stick.

If you made a good estimate put a tick in the box.

Wider than a metre	Narrower than a metre	About a metre in width	I made a good estimate

I can measure and compare length.

How did you do?

Butterfly wings

- You will need scissors, paper and a glue stick.

- Cut out the butterfly wings.
- Compare the width of the butterfly wings.
- Put them in order from narrowest to widest.
- Glue them in order onto some paper.

Name: _____ Date: _____

Dice roll add

- Work with a partner.
- You will need two 1–9 dice.
- Take turns to roll both dice.
- Add the scores.
- Write an addition sentence.
- There is space to write jottings if this helps you.
- Do this another 9 times.

1.	□ + □ = □
2.	□ + □ = □
3.	□ + □ = □
4.	□ + □ = □
5.	□ + □ = □
6.	□ + □ = □
7.	□ + □ = □
8.	□ + □ = □
9.	□ + □ = □
10.	□ + □ = □

I can recall number bonds to 10.

How did you do?

Adding

■ Join the number sentence to its answer.

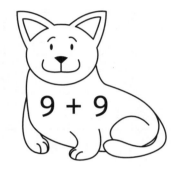

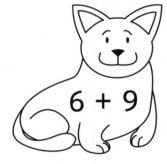

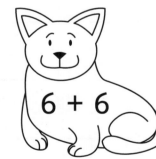

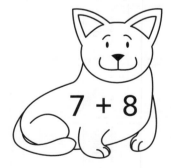

I can add two numbers to make a total of more than 10.

How did you do?

Groups of cubes

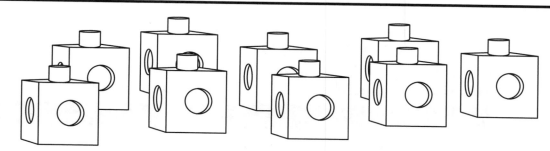

- Work with a partner.
- You will need some interlocking cubes.
- Follow the instructions.
- Write the number sentences.

1. Make 2 sets of 3.   3 + 3 = ☐

2. Make 2 sets of 4.   4 + 4 = ☐

3. Make 2 sets of 5.   5 + 5 = ☐

4. Make 3 sets of 3.   3 + 3 + 3 = ☐

5. Make 3 sets of 4.   4 + 4 + 4 = ☐

6. Make 3 sets of 5.   5 + 5 + 5 = ☐

7. Make 2 sets of 10.   ☐ + ☐ = ☐

8. Make 3 sets of 6.   ☐ + ☐ + ☐ = ☐

9. Make 4 sets of 5.   ☐ + ☐ + ☐ + ☐ = ☐

I can share into equal groups.

How did you do?

Addition to totals to 10

Expected prior learning

Children should be able to:

- count in ones to at least 50
- count in 2s, 5s and 10s to at least 20.

Topic	Curriculum objectives	Expected outcomes
Number and place value	**Lesson 1**	
	To count to and across 100, forwards and backwards, beginning with 0 or 1, or from any given number.	Count to and from 100 from any starting number.
	To count, read and write numbers to 100 in numerals, count in multiples of twos, fives and tens.	Read and write numbers to 100.
	Lesson 2	
	To count, read and write numbers to 100 in numerals, count in multiples of twos, fives and tens.	Count in twos, fives and tens. Read and write numbers to 100.
	Lesson 3	
	To read and write numbers from 1 to 20 in numerals and words.	Read and write numbers from 1 to 20 in words.
	Lesson 4	
	To identify and represent numbers using objects and pictorial representations including the number line, and use the language of: equal to, more than, less than (fewer), most, least.	Recognise place value, knowing which is the tens and which is the units digit, and their worth.
	Lesson 5	
	To identify and represent numbers using objects and pictorial representations including the number line, and use the language of: equal to, more than, less than (fewer), most, least.	Recognise place value, knowing which is the tens and which is the units digit and their worth.

Preparation

Lesson 1: prepare number cards 0–9 two sets per pair; copy 'Hundred square', one per pair; copy and enlarge 'Hundred square' to A3

Lesson 2: copy 'Hundred square', one per pair; copy and enlarge 'Hundred square' to A3

Lesson 3: prepare a teaching set of number word cards zero to twenty. Copy 'Number words', one per child

Lesson 4: prepare number cards 0–9 two sets per pair

Lesson 5: copy 'Tens and units on the abacus', one per child; copy and enlarge 'Hundred square' to A3

You will need

Photocopiable sheets
'Tens and units on the abacus'; 'Number words'

General resources
'Hundred square'; 'Two-spike abacus'; 'Number cards 0–20'; interactive teaching resource 'Number square'

Equipment
Two different-coloured pencils per pair; individual whiteboards and pens; straws and elastic bands; Blu-Tack®

Further practice

Children should practise counting in 2s, 5s and 10s, to 100 and back to 0, regularly, in order to encourage fluency in their counting skills. This should be practised orally at this stage.

Oral and mental starters for week 1

See bank of starters on pages 160 and 204. Oral and mental starters are also on the CD-ROM.

48 Everyone count to 100

60 Counting in 2s to 100

61 Counting in 5s to 100

62 Counting in 10s

Overview of progression

This week children learn about counting patterns to 100, reading and writing number words, and place value. They begin with counting in 2s, 5s and 10s to 100, recognising the number patterns that these counts make, using a hundred square to help them. They investigate which numbers appear in the counts of two, five and ten (decade numbers). They then learn to read and write number words to 20. In lessons 4 and 5, they use numeral cards, straws and elastic bands and two-spike abaci to represent tens and units digits. They recognise how many tens and how many units each number has, and which digit each is.

Watch out for

Some children may confuse tens and units, and not be clear about which unit is which. Provide two sets of 1–9 number cards and ask the children to put out cards to represent the numbers that you say. Check that the children understand the order in which the cards must be placed.

Creative context

Ask the children to look at the house numbers in the street where they live. Ask them to find out if odd numbers are on one side of the street, and even numbers on the other side, or whether the house numbers count on in 1s. The results of this could be shown pictorially, with odds one side of the street and even other side, for some children, and consecutive numbers for other children.

Vocabulary

digit, exchange, first, hundred, one, two, three..., ones, 'teens' numbers, **tens, units**

Curriculum objectives

● To count to 100, forwards and backwards, beginning with 0 or 1, or from any given number.
● To count, read and write numbers to 100 in numerals.

Success criteria

● I can count to 100 starting from any number.
● I can read and write any number up to 100.

You will need

General resources

'Number cards 0–20'; interactive teaching resource 'Number square'; 'Hundred square'

Equipment

Two different-coloured pencils per pair; individual whiteboards and pens

Differentiation

Less confident learners

Decide whether to limit the game to the numbers up to 40 or 50. The children can fold their copy of photocopiable page 'Hundred square' so that the other numbers are hidden.

More confident learners

Encourage the children to circle both numbers that they could make from each pair of cards.

Lesson I 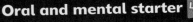 Oral and mental starter 48

Main teaching activities

Whole-class work: Count to and from 100, including starting from any number.

Write the numbers 16, 21, 39 and 45 on the board. Reveal interactive teaching resource 'Number square' on the CD-ROM and say: *Where is 16?* Invite a child to highlight the number. Now ask: *Where is 21...39... 45...?* and ask other children to select these numbers. Repeat this for another set of numbers such as 87, 92, 56, 73....

Now ask the children to look for some number patterns on interactive teaching resource 'Number square'. Say: *What number comes below 1... 11...? And what comes below 2... 12...?* Repeat this for all the columns of numbers, and check that the children recognise how the units digit is always the same, and that it is the tens digit that changes.

Paired work: Provide each pair with two sets of shuffled number cards from 0–9. Each pair also needs photocopiable page 'Hundred square' from the CD-ROM and two different-coloured pencils. They take turns to take the top two cards, and make a two-digit number with them. For example, for 2 and 5, they can make 25 or 52. They circle the number that they make with their coloured pencil on the 'Hundred square'. If a number has already been circled, they think about how they could make a different number. For example, if they have a 3 and a 7 they can make 37 or 73. They continue until the cards are used, then shuffle the cards and continue the game.

Progress check: Ask children to read the numbers that they have circled, and to say which two cards they used. Ask, for example: *What number is this? Which cards did you use to make that number?*

Review

Reveal interactive teaching resource 'Number square' again. Explain that you will select a number on the square. Ask the children to read it together. Keep the pace of this sharp. Ask, for example:

● *What number patterns can you see on the number square?*
● *What number comes just after 70?*
● *What number comes just before 31?*

Hide individual numbers on the Number square and ask children to write down the missing numbers on their individual whiteboards.

Leave interactive teaching resource 'Number square' visible. Provide individual whiteboards and pens and explain that you will say a number. Ask the children to write that number, and when you say *Show me*, they turn their boards so that you can read their number. Check that they write the numbers correctly, and note any child who needs help with this.

Curriculum objectives

● To count, read and write numbers to 100 in numerals, count in multiples of twos, fives and tens.

Success criteria

● I can count in 2s, 5s and 10s.
● I can read and write numbers to 100.

You will need

General resources

Interactive teaching resource 'Number square'; 'Hundred square'

Differentiation

Less confident learner

Check that the children can read the numbers, so that they recognise each number.

More confident learners

Challenge the children to count in threes from 0 and to find all the numbers 'visited' on photocopiable page 'Hundred square' by all the counts of 2, 3, 5 and 10. (30, 60 and 90).

Lesson 2

Oral and mental starter 60

Main teaching activities

Whole-class work: Ask the children to count with you from 0 to 100 and back again. Keep the pace of this sharp. Now count together in 2s, from 0 to at least 50 and back again. Repeat this, counting to 100 and back again. If children falter, say the numbers loudly so that they hear the pattern. Now count forwards and back from 0 to 100 in fives. Check that the children recognise the pattern of saying either 5 or 0 for the units digit. Repeat this count several times. Now count in 10s from zero to 100 and back again. Again, repeat this several times.

Reveal interactive teaching resource 'Number square' on the CD-ROM. Ask a child to select the numbers said in the counting in 2s from 0 pattern. Ask: *What sort of numbers are these?* Agree that these are all even numbers. Repeat this for the count in 5s, and agree that all of these have either a 5 or a 0 as their units digit. Repeat this for the count in 10s, and agree that all of the numbers said have a 0 as their units digit.

Paired work: Provide each child with photocopiable page 'Hundred square' from the CD-ROM. Ask them to circle all of the numbers in the count of 2s; tick the numbers in the count of 5s; and cross the numbers in the count of 10s. Ask them to write at the top of photocopiable page 'Hundred square' the numbers which appear in all the counts of 2s, 5s and 10s (decade numbers).

Progress check: Ask pairs to explain which numbers they know will be in the count of 2s and how they know that. Repeat this for the count of fives, then of tens.

Review

Review the activity that the children did on photocopiable page 'Hundred square'. Reveal interactive teaching resource 'Number square'. Ask a child to use the annotation tool to circle all the numbers in the count of 2, as the other children say the count slowly. Repeat this for the count of 5 – this time ask a child to put a tick in the square of each number said. Then repeat this with another child who puts a cross in the square of each number in the count of tens. Ask, for example:

● *How do you know which numbers come in the count of 2s... 5s... 10s?*
● *Which numbers come in all of these counts?*
● *What is special about these numbers?* (They are all decade numbers, or in the count of 10.)

Curriculum objectives
● To read and write numbers from 1 to 20 in words.

Success criteria
● I can read and write numbers from 1 to 20 in words.

You will need
Photocopiable sheets
'Number words'

General resources
Number word cards zero to twenty

Equipment
Washing line and pegs; individual whiteboards and pens

Differentiation
Less confident learners
Work with the children on the link between the words and the numerals using word and numeral cards.

More confident learners
Challenge the children to read and write number words to thirty.

Lesson 3
Oral and mental starter 61

Main teaching activities

Whole-class work: Use the teaching set of number cards. Explain that you will hold up each number word card, but that these will not be in number order. Ask the children to put up their hands to read aloud the number word. Choose a child to read the number word, and if correct, ask the child to come to the front of the class and peg the number word onto the washing line where the child thinks it should go. Continue until the number words are all on the washing line, and in order. Read the words together from 'zero' to 'twenty'. Now say, for example: *Who will take the number four... fifteen... twenty... from the washing line?* Continue, until all the number words have been removed.

Independent work: Provide each child with photocopiable page 'Number words'. Ask them to join the number word to its numeral. Then ask them to write the answers to the questions on the sheet.

Progress check: Ask individuals to read some of the number words that they have joined correctly to the numeral. Say, for example: *Point to the number word which is next after twelve....*

Review
Explain that you will write a number, in numerals, on the board and that the children should write its number word on their individual whiteboards. Give the children time to write the word before saying *Show me*. Now repeat the activity this time saying, for example:
● *Write the word that is after 7....*
● *Write the word that is before 11....*
● *Write the word that is between ... and .....*

Curriculum objectives
● To identify and represent numbers using objects.

Success criteria
● I can use straws to show tens and units.
● I can say the tens digit in a number.
● I can say the units digit in a number.

You will need
General resources
'Number cards 0–20'

Equipment
Straws and elastic bands

Differentiation
Less confident learners
Use a set of 1–4 cards to represent the tens and the 1–9 cards the units.

More confident learners
Ask the children to write each two-digit number that they make.

Lesson 4
Oral and mental starter 62

Main teaching activities

Whole-class work: Provide each pair with elastic bands and straws. Explain that you will say a number and write it as a number on the board. Ask the children in pairs to make the number, using straws: bundles of ten for the tens unit, and loose straws for the units. Say: *Make fifteen.* Check that the children have made one bundle of ten, and have five loose straws. Repeat for other numbers to 20. Now say: *Make the number twenty-one. How many tens are there and how many units?* Repeat this for other two-digit numbers to 99.

Paired work: Provide each pair with two sets of number cards from 0–9, straws and elastic bands. One child turns over two number cards from the shuffled stack, and makes a two-digit number with these cards. Then they both make the number using the straws. They check each other's work. If they disagree, ask them to count the straws they took to check that they have the number that they wanted.

Progress check: Invite a pair to show their last number to the class. Ask questions such as: *What number did you just make with the cards? So how many tens is that? How many units?*

Review
Hold up three bundles of ten and two more straws and ask: *What is this number? How many tens are there? How many units?* Repeat this for other numbers up to 99. Now write '54' onto the board and ask: *What is this number? How many tens does it have? How many units does it have? How do you know that?* Repeat this for other two-digit numbers to 99.

Lesson 5

Curriculum objectives
● To identify and represent numbers using objects and pictorial representations.

Success criteria
● I can say the tens digit in a number.
● I can say the units digit in a number.

You will need

Photocopiable sheets
'Tens and units on the abacus'

General resources
'Hundred square'; 'Two-spike abacus'

Equipment
Blu-Tack®

Differentiation

Less confident learners
Children may find photocopiable page 'Hundred square' a help when working out which two-digit numbers to write in the second activity on photocopiable page 'Tens and units on the abacus'.

More confident learners
Challenge the children to draw their own abacus numbers on the back of the photocopiable sheet. They challenge their partner to say how many tens, how many units, and what the number is.

Main teaching activities

Whole-class work: Show the children the two-spike abacus and explain that it can be used to show tens and units digits. Show 14 on the abacus, and ask: *What number does this show? So how many tens are there? How do you know that? How many units are there? How do you know that?* Repeat this for other TU numbers, up to about 50. Each time check that the children recognise which is the tens spike and which is the units.

Independent work: Provide photocopiable page 'Tens and units on the abacus' from the CD-ROM. Ask the children to complete the photocopiable page, as a check of their knowledge and understanding about place value.

Progress check: Ask:
- *How do you know how many tens there are in 15?*
- *How do you know how many units there are in 15?*
- *How many beads will you put on each spike for 15?*
- *In the second activity, what number does the first abacus show?*
- *How do you know?*

Review

Stick up the A3 version of photocopiable page 'Hundred square'. Ask a child to point to a two-digit number. Invite another child to use the two-spike abacus to show that number. Invite the other children to say the number together and to say how many tens and how many units it has. Ask another pair of children to repeat the choosing and making of a two-digit number and repeat the questions. Do this several times. Now ask:

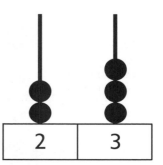

- *How do I know how many tens a number has?*
- *How do I know how many units a number has?*

Ask the children to talk with their partner for a brief moment about what they have learned this week, what they feel confident about, and what they still need to learn.

Addition and subtraction to 20

Expected prior learning

Children should be able to:

- recall addition facts to 10
- derive subtraction facts to 10.

Topic	Curriculum objectives	Expected outcomes
Addition and subtraction	**Lesson 1**	
	To represent and use number bonds and related subtraction facts within 20. To add and subtract one-digit and two-digit numbers to 20, including zero.	Begin to know number bonds from 10 + 0 to 10 + 10. Add and subtract one-digit numbers, including zero.
	Lesson 2	
	To represent and use number bonds and related subtraction facts within 20. To add and subtract one-digit and two-digit numbers to 20, including zero.	Begin to know addition and subtraction facts to a total of 20, using patterns such as 4 + 5 = 9 and 14 + 5 = 19. Add and subtract a one-digit number and a two-digit number.
	Lesson 3	
	To represent and use number bonds and related subtraction facts within 20. To add and subtract one-digit and two-digit numbers to 20, including zero.	Begin to know addition and subtraction facts to a total of 20, using patterns such as 4 + 5 = 9 and 14 + 5 = 19. Add and subtract a one-digit number and a two-digit number.
	Lesson 4	
	To represent and use number bonds and related subtraction facts within 20. To add and subtract one-digit and two-digit numbers to 20, including zero.	Begin to know addition and subtraction facts to a total of 20, using patterns such as 4 + 5 = 9 and 14 + 5 = 19. Add and subtract a one-digit number and a two-digit number.
	Lesson 5	
	To solve one-step problems that involve addition and subtraction, using concrete objects and pictorial representations, and missing number problems such as 7 = ☐ – 9.	Solve addition and subtraction problems, including missing number problems.

Preparation

Lesson 1: copy 'Adding and subtracting to 20 (1)', one per child'; copy and enlarge 'Adding and subtracting to 20 (1)' to A3

Lesson 2: copy 'Add and subtract (2)', one per child; prepare a teaching set of cards from 'Addition to 10 trio cards'

Lesson 3: copy 'Subtraction (2)', one per child

Lesson 4: prepare 'Number cards 0–9', one set per pair

Lesson 5: copy 'Add and subtract: missing numbers', one per child; copy and enlarge 'Add and subtract: missing numbers' to A3

You will need

Photocopiable sheets
'Adding and subtracting to 20 (1)'; 'Add and subtract (2)'; 'Subtraction (2)'; 'Add and subtract: missing numbers'; 'Addition to 10 trio cards'

General resources
'Number cards 0–20'

Equipment
Blu-Tack®

Further practice

Photocopiable sheets
'Adding and subtracting to 20'; 'Adding to 20'; 'Subtracting to 20'

Oral and mental starters for week 2

See bank of starters on pages 160 to 204. Oral and mental starters are also on the CD-ROM.

48 Everyone count to 100

60 Counting in 2s to 100

61 Counting in 5s to 100

62 Counting in 10s

Overview of progression

This week, children use addition and subtraction facts that they already know in order to derive others. For example, $2 + 5 = 7$ helps with $12 + 5 = 17$. In lesson 1, they add a one-digit number to 10, and derive three other facts, another addition and two subtractions, from the first fact. In subsequent lessons, they use the addition of two one-digit numbers with a total less than 10 to derive addition and subtraction facts involving a teen number. In lesson 5, children solve problems involving missing numbers, for example $14 + \square = 17$ by writing a number sentence to help them: $4 + 3 = 7$.

Watch out for

Check that children can find one-digit addition and subtraction number trios quickly as these are needed for this week's work. If children are unsure, provide further practice with number trios with totals to 10.

Creative context

Children may enjoy writing their own addition and subtraction stories that involve teen numbers. For example: *I have 13 toy cars. My brother has 4 toy cars. So we have 17 toy cars altogether.*

Vocabulary

add, altogether, answer, compare, count, difference, explain, how many?, how many fewer is ＿＿ than ＿＿?, how many more is ＿＿ than ＿＿?, how many more to make ＿＿?, how much less is ＿＿?, how much more is ＿＿, leaves, makes, minus (−), number sentence, operation, order, **pattern**, plus (+), read, record, show me, sign, subtract, sum, take away, total, what is the difference between ＿＿?, write

Curriculum objectives
● To represent and use number bonds and related subtraction facts within 20.
● To add and subtract one-digit and two-digit numbers to 20, including zero.
Success criteria
● I can add a one-digit number to 10.
● I can work out the subtraction number sentence from 10 + 0 to 10 + 10.

You will need
Photocopiable sheets
'Adding and subtracting to 20 (1)'
Equipment
Blu-Tack®

Differentiation
Less confident learners
Ask more confident talk partners to explain the method and work with the children on the number sentences.
More confident learners
Ask the children to write other number trios to 20 in the same format as the sheet.

Lesson 1   Oral and mental starter 48

Main teaching activities

Whole-class work: Explain that in this lesson, the children will begin to learn some addition sentences. Write on the board 10 + 0 and ask: *What is the total? How do you know that?* Repeat this for 10 + 1, 10 + 2, 10 + 3... up to 10 + 10. Ask the children to look carefully at what has been written on the board and to find any patterns. Discuss how adding a one-digit number to 10 just changes the units digit.

$$10 + 0 = 10$$
$$10 + 1 = 11$$
$$10 + 2 = 12$$
$$10 + 3 = 13$$
$$10 + 4 = 14$$
$$10 + 5 = 15$$
$$10 + 6 = 16$$
$$10 + 7 = 17$$
$$10 + 8 = 18$$
$$10 + 9 = 19$$
$$10 + 10 = 20$$

Now say: *10 + 5 is 15. What is 15 take away 5? How did you work that out?* Discuss how, if children know the addition sentence, then they can find another addition sentence and two subtraction sentences using these three numbers.

Independent work: Provide photocopiable page 'Adding and subtracting to 20 (1)' from the CD-ROM. Children first complete an addition fact and then use it to derive another addition and the two subtraction facts.

Progress check: Ask children to explain how they worked out their answers. Encourage them to look carefully at the first addition sentence. Ask: *What happens to the units digit in the answer? How can you use this to help you to work out the other answers?*

Review

Stick the A3 version of photocopiable page 'Adding and subtracting to 20 (1)' onto the board. Invite children to give answers, first to the addition sentence to be completed then to derive the other answers. Ask questions such as:

● *How did you work that out?*
● *What happens when we add a one digit number to 10?*
● *How can you use that to help you to find the other addition sentence?*
● *How does that help you to find the two subtraction sentences?*

■SCHOLASTIC

Lesson 2 — Oral and mental starter 60

Main teaching activities

Whole-class work: Write the numbers 4, 5 and 9 on the board. Ask the children to suggest two addition sentences and two subtraction sentences that use these three numbers. They should suggest: 4 + 5 = 9; 5 + 4 = 9; 9 − 4 = 5; 9 − 5 = 4. Now repeat this with the numbers 19, 14 and 5: 14 + 5 = 19; 5 + 14 = 19; 19 − 5 = 14; 19 − 14 = 5. Explain that the children can use what they already know about addition to 10 to find new facts. Discuss how, if they know one fact of the three, they can work out the others.

Independent work: Provide each child with a copy of photocopiable page 'Add and subtract (2)' from the CD-ROM.

Progress check: Say: *Explain how you used the questions in the first activity to help answer the questions in the second activity. How did 6 + 3 = 9 help you to answer 19 − 3?*

Review

Show a card from photocopiable page 'Addition to 10 trio cards' from the CD-ROM. Ask the children to provide four different number facts for a trio of numbers such as: 16, 12 and 4. Ask:

● *What are the addition facts?*
● *What are the subtraction facts?*
● *How can you work out a subtraction fact from an addition fact?*

Ask the children to use known facts to help them with these problems:

● *There are 14 chicks in the henhouse. Three chicks escape. How many chicks are left? How did you work that out?*
● *There are 16 cows in the field. The farmer takes four cows away. How many cows are left in the field?*

Invite the children to give examples of methods they can use to add and to subtract.

Lesson 3 — Oral and mental starter 60

Main teaching activities

Whole-class work: Explain that today the children will be subtracting from 'teens' numbers. Ask them to work out, for example, 7 − 5, by counting up from 5 to 7, and then 17 − 5. Ask them to explain their answers and to discuss the pattern that they see. Repeat this for other pairs of subtraction sentences, including 10 − ☐ and 20 − ☐.

Independent work: Provide each child with a copy of photocopiable page 'Subtraction (2)' from the CD-ROM to complete individually.

Progress check: Ask individual children to explain how they use the subtraction facts to 10 to find other facts. For example, ask: *If 9 − 2 is 7, what is 19 − 2? And what is 19 − 7? How did you work that out?*

Review

Review some of the examples from photocopiable page 'Subtraction (2)'. Ask questions such as: *What is 9 − 4? What is 19 − 4? How do you know this?*

Curriculum objectives
- To represent and use number bonds and related subtraction facts within 20.
- To add and subtract one-digit and two-digit numbers to 20, including zero.

Success criteria
- I can use addition facts to 10 to work out new facts.

You will need
General resources
'Number cards 0–20'

Differentiation
Less confident learners

Provide a number line as an aid if children need further support.

More confident learner

Decide whether to extend this to calculations beyond 20, such as 4 + 3 = 7 and 24 + 3 = 27.

Curriculum objectives
- To solve one-step missing number problems that involve addition and subtraction.

Success criteria
- I can find the answers to missing number problems.

You will need
Photocopiable sheets
'Add and subtract: missing numbers'

Equipment
Blu-Tack®

Differentiation
Less confident learners

Decide whether to work as a group to find the solutions to photocopiable page 'Add and subtract: missing numbers'.

More confident learners

Encourage the children to work quickly and accurately to find the solutions. They can discuss with their partner which number sentences helped them to find the solutions.

Lesson 4
Oral and mental starter 60

Main teaching activities

Whole-class work: Write on the board 3 + 4 and ask: *What is 3 add 4?* Write up the answer. Now ask: *What other facts can you find?* Write up 4 + 3 = 7, 7 − 4 = 3 and 7 − 3 = 4. Ask the children to say other facts they can find, using teens numbers. They should say 14 + 3 = 17, 3 + 14 = 17, 17 − 14 = 3 and 17 − 3 = 14. Repeat this for another addition, such as 3 + 6.

Paired work: Ask the children to work in pairs. They will need a set of 1–9 number cards. They shuffle the cards, then take turns to take the top two cards. They make two addition and two subtraction sentences from the two numbers, and write these down. Then they change the first number into a teens number. So, for '6 and 2', they make '16 and 2' and write the two addition and subtraction sentences for these numbers.

Progress check: Ask pairs to explain how they use what they know to find other answers. For example, say *What is 5 + 3? So how can you use this to find 15 + 3?*

Review

Explain that you will write on the board two numbers. The children then suggest two addition sentences and two subtraction sentences. So, for 5 and 9, they say 5 + 4 = 9, 4 + 5 = 9, 9 − 5 = 4, 9 − 4 = 5. Now say: *What is 15 + 4?* Ask the children to find both addition and subtraction sentences for these numbers. Ask, for example:
- *How did you work that out?*
- *Did anyone use a different way?*
- *What other facts can we find?*

Lesson 5
Oral and mental starter 62

Main teaching activities

Whole-class work: Write on the board 19 − ☐ = 14. Ask: *What facts can we use to find the missing number?* Discuss how 4 + 5 = 9 can be used to solve this.

Independent work: Provide photocopiable page 'Add and subtract: missing numbers' from the CD-ROM. Ask the children to use what they know to find the solutions. There is room for the children to write the fact that they know to help them.

Progress check: Check that children understand that an addition or subtraction sentence for one-digit numbers will help them to find the solution. For question 1, for example, ask: *What number sentence will help you?* Agree that 2 + 3 = 5 will help them to find the missing number.

Review

Stick the A3 version of 'Add and subtract: missing numbers' onto the board. Ask children to explain how they solved each problem. Ask questions such as:
- *Which number sentence helped you?*
- *How did it help you?*

Now ask the children to discuss, in pairs, what they have learned this week, and what they feel confident with.

Fractions

Expected prior learning

Children should be able to:

- find and name half of a small quantity, shape or measure.

Topic	Curriculum objectives	Expected outcomes
Fractions	**Lesson 1**	
	To recognise, find and name a half as one of two equal parts of an object, shape or quantity.	Find halves of shapes, measures and quantities.
	Lesson 2	
	To recognise, find and name a quarter as one of four equal parts of an object, shape or quantity.	Find a quarter of shapes.
	Lesson 3	
	To recognise, find and name a half as one of two equal parts of an object, shape or quantity.	Find halves of shapes, measures and quantities.
	To recognise, find and name a quarter as one of four equal parts of an object, shape or quantity.	Find a quarter of shapes.
	Lesson 4	
	To recognise, find and name a half as one of two equal parts of an object, shape or quantity.	Find halves of shapes, measures and quantities.
	To recognise, find and name a quarter as one of four equal parts of an object, shape or quantity.	Find a quarter of shapes.
	Lesson 5	
	To recognise, find and name a half as one of two equal parts of an object, shape or quantity.	Find halves of measures.
	To recognise, find and name a quarter as one of four equal parts of an object, shape or quantity.	Find a quarter of measures.

Preparation

Lesson 1: cut out some large paper shapes, such as squares, equilateral triangles, circles and rectangles

Lesson 2: cut out some large paper shapes, such as squares, circles and rectangles

Lesson 3: prepare large paper rectangles; prepare sufficient paper squares so that each child can have three

You will need

General resources

Interactive activity 'Halves and quarters'

Equipment

Large paper shapes, such as squares, equilateral triangles, circles and rectangles; shape tiles; scissors; large paper rectangles; paper squares, three per child; four hoops; tube of interlocking cubes; four paper plates per pair; string; strips of paper

Further practice

Photocopiable sheets

'Finding halves';
'Finding quarters'

Oral and mental starters for week 3

See bank of starters on pages 160 and 205. Oral and mental starters are also on the CD-ROM.

48 Everyone count to 100

65 Make my total to 10

67 Addition and subtraction to 20

66 Add and subtract beyond 10

Overview of progression

This week, children explore quarters of shapes, quantities and lengths, as well as halves. Lesson 1 gives children the opportunity to re-visit finding halves of shapes and quantities. In lesson 2, quarters are introduced through shapes. In subsequent lessons, children find halves and quarters of quantities and use sharing methods to find quarters of lengths through cutting string and paper. They also revise that two halves make a whole and begin to understand that four equal quarters make a whole.

Watch out for

Check that children are accurate in folding paper to find quarters, and similarly they are accurate when folding string or strips of paper to find halves and quarters of lengths.

Creative context

Children can make paint blot pictures, fold them in half, then open them to see if the pattern is the same both sides. They will need a safety mirror to check this.

Vocabulary

equal, **fraction**, half, halves, quarter, share, whole

Curriculum objectives
● To recognise, find and name a half as one of two equal parts of a shape or quantity.

Success criteria
● I can find half of a shape and a quantity.

You will need

Equipment
Large paper shapes, such as squares, equilateral triangles, circles and rectangles; shape tiles; scissors; interlocking cubes

Differentiation

Less confident learners
Decide whether to limit the number of cubes used for finding half to up to 10.

More confident learners
Challenge the children to find half of larger numbers of cubes, such as 24.

Lesson 1

Oral and mental starter 65

Main teaching activities

Whole-class work: Explain to the children that in this lesson they will be finding half of shapes and of objects. Hold up the large paper square and ask: *How can I find half of this square?* Agree that it can be folded to make two identical parts. Do this to show the children. Open it up again, point to one part and ask: *What is this?* Agree it is half of the square. Repeat this for the other part. Now ask: *What do two halves make?* Agree that it makes a whole. Repeat this for another shape. Write the words 'half' and 'whole' onto the board so that the children can see and read these.

Paired work: Provide some shape tiles, scissors, paper and ask the children to draw around a shape, cut it out, then fold it in two. They write 'half' on each of the two halves. They repeat this for another shape.

Progress check: After about 10 minutes of work, ask the children to pause. Invite a child to show everyone a shape they have cut out and to name each half and the whole. Repeat this with another child and another shape. Ask: *How many halves do we need to make a whole one?*

Whole-class work: Ask the children to quickly put away the scissors and shape tiles. Ask them to work in pairs and count out eight cubes. Ask them to discuss with their partner how to find half of the cubes. Now ask for suggestions for finding half. If the children are unsure, suggest that they could share them out: *one to me and one to you, one to me...*, or they could make a tower and break the tower into two equal pieces. Ask the children to choose their favourite method and to find half of the eight cubes. Invite a pair to bring out their halved group of eight cubes for everyone to see. Say together: *four is half of eight.*

Paired work: Ask the children to find half of 12 cubes, then to find half of 14 cubes. They write a sentence such as 'Half of 12 is 6', and so on.

Progress check: Invite a pair to demonstrate how they found half of the quantity. Ask questions such as:

- *If you make a tower and break it equally in two, how many is that each?*
- *So what is half of ...?*
- *If you shared the cubes out, one for you and one for me, and so on, would you get the same answer?*

Review

Invite four children to come to the front of the class. Put them into pairs. Ask the first pair to count out and make a tower of 16 cubes. Ask them to count the cubes aloud to show everyone that there are 16. Now ask them to break the tower into two equal parts and to count each part. Ask: *What is half of 16?* Now ask the second pair to count out 16 cubes, then share them into two piles: *one for this pile, and one for that pile, one for this pile....* When they have done this, ask them to count the cubes in one pile and to say how many there are. Ask them to check the second pile and to say the total. Ask: *What is 16 shared by 2? Yes, 8. So sharing by 2 and finding half gives the same answer.* Repeat this with another two children and 18 cubes.

Curriculum objectives

● To recognise, find and name a quarter as one of four equal parts of a shape.

Success criteria

● I can find a quarter of a shape.

You will need

Equipment

Large paper shapes, such as squares, equilateral triangles, circles and rectangles; shape tiles; scissors

Differentiation

Less confident learners

Encourage the children to use the correct vocabulary of halves, quarters and wholes.

More confident learners

Children fold and cut octagon to make two halves, then to make four quarters.

Lesson 2

Main teaching activities

Whole-class work: Hold up the large paper square and explain that it can be folded in half and in half again. Demonstrate this then open it out again and show the folds. Ask: *How many pieces can you see? What do you notice about them?* Elicit from the children that there are four pieces and they all look the same. Explain that the square has been folded into four equal parts and that these are called quarters. Point to each quarter, and count them together. Say to the children: *Four quarters make a whole one.* Repeat this for another shape, such as the circle. Write 'quarter' onto the board so that the children can see this.

Paired work: Provide a square, circle and rectangle shape tile for each pair, paper and scissors. Ask the children to draw round the square, cut it out, then fold it to make quarters. They write 'quarter' onto each piece. They repeat this for the other shapes.

Progress check: Ask pairs to show one of their shapes and ask them: *How many quarters are there? So how many quarters make a whole one?*

Review

Invite children to show their shapes. Ask:

● *How many quarters make a whole one in this shape?*

Repeat this for another large paper shape.

Curriculum objectives

● To recognise, find and name a half as one of two equal parts of a shape.
● To recognise, find and name a quarter as one of four equal parts of a shape.

Success criteria

● I can find a half of a shape.
● I can find a quarter of a shape.
● I can show that four quarters make a whole shape.

You will need

Equipment

Large paper rectangles; paper squares, three per child; scissors

Differentiation

Less confident learners

Check that the children do not cut the central folds that hold the shape together.

More confident learners

Challenge the children to cut out circles and repeat the activity, folding into quarters, and cutting out through all layers.

Lesson 3

Main teaching activities

Whole-class work: Hold up a paper square and ask: *How shall we fold this to make halves? What do we have to do first?* Invite suggestions, and encourage the children to use 'half'. Demonstrate folding the square into half. Write 'half' on each part. Now fold another paper square into quarters. Ask: *What do we call each part? How many quarters make one whole?*

Hold up a rectangle, fold it into quarters, then use a pair of scissors to cut a shape around the edge, making sure that the central part of the rectangle is not cut into. Open out the paper and discuss what shapes the children can see. Fold it into quarters again, show the shape, then unfold it slowly to show the whole shape. Now ask: *How many equal pieces make a whole?*

Independent work: Provide each child with two or three paper squares, and scissors. Ask the children to fold their paper in half, then into quarters. They need to identify the centre of the paper, which has the folds that must not be cut. Ask the children to draw a shape freehand, then cut through all four layers to see what they have made. They write 'quarter' onto each of the quarters of the shape. They repeat this making a different quartered pattern.

Progress check: Ask questions such as: *How many quarters make a whole? How many halves make a whole one?*

Review

Invite children to bring one of their shapes to the front and open it out to show what they have made. Ask questions such as:

● *How many quarters are there in this whole shape?*
● *How many halves are there in this whole shape?*

Curriculum objectives
● To recognise, find and name a half as one of two equal parts of a quantity.
● To recognise, find and name a quarter as one of four equal parts of a quantity.

Success criteria
● I can find a half of a quantity.
● I can find a quarter of a quantity.
● I can show that four quarters make a whole quantity.

You will need
General resources
Interactive activity 'Halves and quarters'
Equipment
Four hoops; tube of interlocking cubes; four paper plates per pair

Differentiation
Less confident learners
Decide whether to begin with 4 cubes, then 8, then 16.
More confident learners
Challenge children to repeat the activity this time with 24 cubes.

Lesson 4 — Oral and mental starter 66

Main teaching activities

Whole-class work: Explain to the children that in this lesson they will be finding a half and a quarter of quantities such as cubes and counters. Put out two hoops so that the children can see them. Now take 12 cubes and ask a child to count them. Ask the child to share the cubes equally between the two hoops. Ask: *How many cubes are there in each hoop? So what is half of 12? Yes, half of 12 is 6.* Collect the cubes up again, and put out another two hoops. Explain that this time you would like a child to share the cubes between four hoops in order to find a quarter of 12. When this is completed ask: *How many cubes are in each ring? So what is a quarter of 12? Yes, a quarter of 12 is 3.* Repeat this for eight cubes. This time write onto the board: Half of eight is four. A quarter of eight is two

Paired work: Provide each pair with four paper plates, a tub of interlocking cubes and some paper. Ask the children to count out 16 cubes, share these out between two plates to find half, and write a sentence which begins 'Half of 16 is...'. They repeat this by sharing the cubes between four plates and writing 'A quarter of 16 is...'. When they have completed this, suggest that they repeat the activity, this time using 20 cubes.

Progress check: Observe how the children share out their cubes. Then ask questions such as:
● *How did you find half of the cubes?*
● *How did you find a quarter of the cubes?*

Independent work: Ask children to complete the interactive activity 'Halves and quarters' on the CD-ROM. This might also be used as a half-term assessment activity.

Review

Review the work with the children. Ask questions such as:
● *How many is half of 16?*
● *How many is a quarter of 16?*
Repeat this for 20 cubes. Then extend to 24 cubes, and model the sharing to find half then a quarter as before.

Curriculum objectives
- To recognise, find and name a half as one of two equal parts of an object.
- To recognise, find and name a quarter as one of four equal parts of an object.

Success criteria
- I can find a half of a length.
- I can find a quarter of a length.
- I can show that four quarters make a whole length.

You will need

Equipment

String; scissors; strips of paper

Differentiation

This activity can be carried out in mixed ability pairs. Check that all the children are actively involved.

Lessons 5

Main teaching activities

Whole-class work: Explain that in this lesson children will find halves and quarters of a length. Ask two children to take some string and match it to the length of a book. Cut the string off for them then hold up the string to show the class. Ask: *How do we find half the length of the book?* Agree that the string can be folded in half, then cut. Now ask: *How can we find a quarter of the length of the book?* Agree that a halved piece of string can be halved again. One piece of the string is one quarter.

Paired work: Provide some strips of paper for each pair. Ask the children to use a strip to find the length of, for example, a shoe, pencil, ruler, and so on. They then fold it and cut it to find half. They repeat this with one half to find a quarter. They mount their pieces of paper onto paper and write 'quarter' and 'half' as appropriate. They repeat this for other objects.

Progress check: Ask a pair:
- *How did you find the length of the pencil?*
- *So how did you find half?*
- *How did you find a quarter?*

Review

Ask two children to use the string to find how wide a table is in the classroom. They cut off the string and show the others what they have. Now ask: *How shall we find half the length of the table?* Agree that the string should be folded in two then cut. *How shall we find a quarter of the length of the table?* Agree that one half can be folded again and cut. Now ask the two children to hold out the half length of string, and other children to join them to hold out the two quarters, so that these join together again to show the length of the table. Ask one of the children holding one quarter to step forward. Ask: *How long is this piece of string?* Agree it is a quarter of the length of the table.

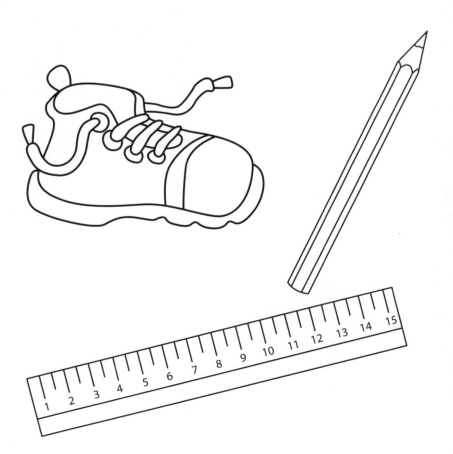

■SCHOLASTIC

Multiplication and division

Expected prior learning

Children should be able to:

- use cubes to find multiples
- count in 2s, 5s and 10s to 20 and beyond.

Topic	Curriculum objectives	Expected outcomes
Multiplication and division	**Lesson 1**	
	To solve one-step problems involving multiplication and division, by calculating the answer using concrete objects, pictorial representations and arrays with the support of the teacher.	Use doubling and halving facts to understand multiplication.
	Lesson 2	
	To solve one-step problems involving multiplication and division, by calculating the answer using concrete objects, pictorial representations and arrays with the support of the teacher.	Use doubling and halving facts to understand division.
	Lesson 3	
	To solve one-step problems involving multiplication and division, by calculating the answer using concrete objects, pictorial representations and arrays with the support of the teacher.	Use arrays to understand multiplication.
	Lesson 4	
	To solve one-step problems involving multiplication and division, by calculating the answer using concrete objects, pictorial representations and arrays with the support of the teacher.	Use arrays to understand multiplication.
	Lesson 5	
	To solve one-step problems involving multiplication and division, by calculating the answer using concrete objects, pictorial representations and arrays with the support of the teacher.	Use arrays to understand multiplication.

Preparation

Lesson 1: copy 'Doubling problems', one per child; copy and enlarge 'Doubling problems'

Lesson 2: copy 'Halves (2)', one per child

Lesson 3: prepare five towers of two interlocking cubes

Lesson 4: prepare 'Number cards 1–10', one set per pair; prepare two towers of five interlocking cubes

Lesson 5: prepare 'Number cards 1–10', one set per group; prepare 10 towers of 10 interlocking cubes

You will need

Photocopiable sheets

'Doubling problems'; 'Halves (2)'

General resources

'Number cards 1–10'

Equipment

Blu-Tack®; interlocking cubes; two different colours of 20 counters per pair

Further practice

Photocopiable sheets

'Counting in 2s (2)'; 'Doubling and halving';

Oral and mental starters for week 4

See bank of starters on page 205. Oral and mental starters are also on the CD-ROM.

66 Add and subtract beyond 10

67 Addition and subtraction to 20

68 Halving and doubling

71 Telling the time

Overview of progression

This week, children begin with doubling and halving, with numbers to 20. They make simple vertical arrays with towers of two cubes and count how many in total, counting in twos. They repeat this for arrays of towers of five cubes, then ten cubes. They answer 'division' questions in the Review section of lessons 3 to 5, such as: *I have 12 cubes. How many towers of 2 can I make?* They solve these problems by counting up in 2s, 5s or 10s, until they reach the required number. They use their fingers to help them to keep a record of how many 2s, 5s or 10s they have counted.

> ## Watch out for
>
> Check that children can count reliably in 2s, 5s and 10s. If they falter, provide further experience of counting aloud in 2s, 5s and 10s until they are confident.

Creative context

Take opportunities during the school day to count children in 2s, 5s or 10s, for example, when children line up to leave the classroom.

Vocabulary

counting numbers, double, half, halves, twice

Lesson 1 — Oral and mental starter 67

Curriculum objectives
● To solve one-step problems involving multiplication.

Success criteria
● I can use doubling to solve problems.

You will need

Photocopiable sheets
'Doubling problems'

Equipment
Blu-Tack®

Differentiation

Less confident learners
Decide whether to work as a group to solve the problems on photocopiable page 'Doubling problems'.

More confident learners
Challenge the children to write their own problem and swap this with their partner.

Main teaching activities

Whole-class work: Ask the children to find doubles of numbers to 10. Say, for example: *What is double 2? ... double 6? ... double 9? How did you work that out? Who 'knew' the answer? Well done!* Now explain that in this lesson the children will be using doubling facts in order to solve word problems. Say: *I have eight grapes. My sister has double that number of grapes. How many grapes does my sister have? How did you work that out?* Introduce the vocabulary of 'twice' and explain that 'twice' can be used to mean double. Say, for example: *Jon has four books. Peter has twice as many books as Jon. How many books does Peter have?* Discuss with the children how they found the answer.

Independent work: Provide photocopiable page 'Doubling problems' from the CD-ROM. Read through the problems together as a class before the children begin work.

Progress check: Ask individual children: *How did you work that out? So double ... is?* Check that children can read the questions, and provide support if needed.

Review

Put up the A3 enlargement of photocopiable page 'Doubling problems' onto the board. Read the first question together then ask for the answer. Discuss how the children worked this out. Some of them by now should have rapid recall of the doubling facts. Repeat this for the second and subsequent questions. Repeat the whole-class activity, and keep the pace sharp as you ask double questions.

Lesson 2 — Oral and mental starter 66

Curriculum objectives
● To solve one-step problems involving division.

Success criteria
● I can use halving to solve problems.

You will need

Photocopiable sheets
'Halves (2)'

Equipment
Two different colours of 20 counters per pair

Differentiation

Less confident learners
If needed, provide interlocking cubes to help children to find half of a number.

More confident learners
Challenge the children to find doubles of numbers from 11 to 15.

Main teaching activities

Whole-class work: Explain that in this lesson, children will be finding halves. Say: *Use the double facts you know to find halves. What is half of 10? Half of 16...? How did you work that out?*

Paired work: Ask the children to work in pairs. They will need two colours of counters and photocopiable page 'Halves (2)' from the CD-ROM.

Progress check: Ask pairs to explain how they found the half fact for the double that had just been chosen. If children find this difficult, remind them to use the double fact so that they can work back to the half.

Review

Ask the children to put some counters in front of them. For every half fact that you say, that they find correctly, they take one of the counters. Say, for example:
● *What is half of 8?*
● *What is half of 10?*
● *What is half of 16?*
● *If double 2 is 4, what is the half fact for 4?*
● *What is half of 20...14... 18...?*

● To solve one-step problems involving multiplication, by calculating the answer using concrete objects and arrays with the support of the teacher.

Success criteria
● I can count in 2s to find how many there are in an array with rows of 2.

You will need
Equipment
Interlocking cubes

Differentiation
Less confident learners
Ask an adult to encourage the children to count in 2s aloud for each vertical array of towers of 2.

More confident learners
Challenge the children to try 11, 12,...15 rows of 2 and to count in 2s to find how many cubes there are.

Curriculum objectives
● To solve one-step problems involving multiplication, by calculating the answer using concrete objects and arrays with the support of the teacher.

Success criteria
● I can count in 5s to find how many there are in an array with towers of 5.

You will need
General resources
'Number cards 0–20'
Equipment
Interlocking cubes

Differentiation
Less confident learners
Encourage children to count aloud in fives. If they are unsure, say the count for them, then repeat, so they become confident in counting in fives.

More confident learners
Challenge the children to predict what 11 and then 12 towers of five will be.

Lesson 3
Oral and mental starter 68

Main teaching activities

Whole-class work: Ask a child to make three towers of two cubes. Put these out, so that they are side to side and ask: *How many towers of two are there? So how many cubes are there altogether?* Count together in twos: *two, four, six. There are six cubes.* Now ask a child to make five towers of two. Again place these, side by side so that there is a vertical array (five columns, two rows). Say: *How many towers of two are there? So how many cubes are there? Let's count in twos: two, four, six, eight, ten. So there are ten cubes.*

Paired work: Ask the children to work in pairs with 20 interlocking cubes. They make towers of two and then count in twos to find how many cubes there are in one tower, two towers, three towers, and so on up to ten towers. Ask them to record their work like this: one tower of two has two cubes. two towers of two has four cubes...

Progress check: Ask the children to demonstrate how they counted in twos. Say, for example: *So you counted in twos. How many cubes are there in ... towers of two?*

Review

Put out one tower of two and say: How many cubes are there? So one tower of two has two cubes. Put out two towers of two and say: How many cubes are there? Let's count in twos: two, four. So two towers of two have four cubes. Repeat this for three, four....ten towers, counting in twos each time.

Lesson 4
Oral and mental starter 68

Main teaching activities

Whole-class work: Begin by counting in fives from 0 to 100 and back again. Repeat this several times so that the children feel confident with this. Now put out two towers of five cubes. Place these side by side to make a vertical array. Ask: *How many towers are there? How many cubes in each tower? Let's count the cubes, counting in fives: five, ten. So two towers of five has ten cubes.*

Paired work: Ask the children to work in pairs. They begin by making ten towers of five cubes. They will need a set of shuffled 1–10 number cards. Ask them to take turns to turn over a card. They take that number of towers of 5, place them side by side to make a vertical array. They count how many cubes there are by touching each tower and counting in fives. They write a sentence: ☐ towers of five cubes has ☐ cubes altogether.

Progress check: Invite a pair to demonstrate counting the cubes in the towers. Check that they count in fives. Ask the children to say the number sentence: ☐ towers of five cubes has ☐ cubes altogether.

Review

With the children, review their work. Put out one tower of five and say together: *one tower of five has five cubes.* Repeat with two towers, counting in fives to find the total and say together: *two towers of five has ten cubes.* Continue with three, four... ten towers.

Curriculum objectives
● To solve one-step problems involving multiplication, by calculating the answer using concrete objects and arrays with the support of the teacher.

Success criteria
● I can count in 10s to find how many there are in an array with towers of 10.

You will need

General resources
'Number cards 0–20'

Equipment
Interlocking cubes (100)

Differentiation

Less confident learners
Ask an adult to work with this group. Encourage the children to count aloud in 10s.

More confident learners
Ask the children to continue with 11 and 12 towers of 10 and work out how many cubes that would be.

Lesson 5
Oral and mental starter 71

Main teaching activities

Whole-class work: Explain that in this lesson children will be counting in tens. Begin by counting in tens from 0 to 100 and back again. Repeat the count several times. Now put out one tower of ten cubes. Ask: *How many cubes is that? So one tower of ten has ten cubes.* Put out another tower of ten, and ask: *How many cubes is that? So, 10, 20. Two towers of ten have 20 cubes.* Repeat this up to ten towers.

Group work: Ask the children to work in groups of four to six. They will need 100 interlocking cubes and a set of shuffled 1–10 number cards. Ask them to begin by making towers of ten. They take turns to turn over a card, then they take turns to take the required number of towers of ten. Together they count in tens to find the total number of cubes. They write a number sentence each time: ☐ towers of ten have ☐ cubes.

Progress check: Ask a group to count together in tens to demonstrate finding how many cubes there are in the towers that they have put out. Ask: *So how many cubes are there in total? How do you know that?*

Review

Put out five towers of ten and say:

- *Tom has five packs of sweets. Each pack has ten sweets in it. How many sweets is that in total?*

Use the towers of cubes to help the children with their count. Now say:

- *Sally has six notebooks. Each notebook has ten pages. How many pages are there altogether?*

Encourage the children to count aloud to find the solution. They can use their fingers to help them to keep check of their count. Say, for example:

- *There are four boxes of eggs. Each box has ten eggs. How many eggs is that in total?*
- *There are seven bundles of straws. Each bundle has ten straws in it. How many straws are there in total?*

Remind the children of what they have learned this week: doubling and halving; counting in twos, fives and tens to solve problems.

Measuring

Expected prior learning

Children should be able to:

● use uniform non-standard units of measure.

Topic	Curriculum objectives	Expected outcomes
Measurement	**Lesson 1**	
	To measure and begin to record the following: ● lengths and heights ● mass/weight ● capacity and volume ● time (hours, minutes, seconds).	Use a simple ruler to measure a short line.
	Lesson 2	
	To measure and begin to record the following: ● lengths and heights ● mass/weight ● capacity and volume ● time (hours, minutes, seconds).	Begin to use standard units: 100ml and litre.
	Lesson 3	
	To measure and begin to record the following: ● lengths and heights ● mass/weight ● capacity and volume ● time (hours, minutes, seconds).	Begin to use standard units: 100g and kg.
	Lesson 4	
	To measure and begin to record the following: ● lengths and heights ● mass/weight ● capacity and volume ● time (hours, minutes, seconds).	Use a stop watch to measure a short amount of time in seconds.
	Lesson 5	
	To measure and begin to record the following: ● lengths and heights ● mass/weight ● capacity and volume ● time (hours, minutes, seconds).	Begin to use standard units: metres; 100g and kg; 100ml and litre.

Preparation

Lesson 1: prepare trays of items for children to measure, some longer than 10cm, some shorter than 10cm, and some about 10cm in length

Lesson 3: copy 'Measures chart (1)', one per child

Lesson 5: copy 'Match the units', one per child; copy and enlarge 'Match the units'

You will need

Photocopiable sheets

'Measures chart (1)'; 'Match the units'

Equipment

Metre stick marked in decimetre; rulers or 10cm lengths of paper; trays of items for children to measure, some longer than 10cm, some shorter than 10cm, and some about 10cm in length; litre container and 100ml container; 20ml and 10 ml scoops; straight-sided unmarked containers with an elastic band around each one; containers of sand; Plastic bags and ties; 100g weights; bucket balances, scale balance; simple stop clocks or stop watches that mark seconds

Further practice

All of these activities in this week's work are practical. Consider using any activity suggestions not used in lessons 3 to 5 for further practice.

Oral and mental starters for week 5

See bank of starters on pages 204 to 205. Oral and mental starters are also on the CD-ROM.

61 Counting in 5s to 100

63 Writing numerals

64 Writing number words

68 Halving and doubling

71 Telling the time

Overview of progression

This week, children use some metric units for estimating and measuring. They begin by estimating longer than 10cm, shorter than 10cm or about the same length as 10cm. They learn that there are ten 10cm lengths in a metre. Then they use 20ml scoops to estimate and measure capacity. For weight, they make their own 100g weight by balancing 100g of sand and use this to estimate and compare the weight of items in the classroom. They estimate 10 seconds of time, and find out what things they can do in 10 seconds. In lesson 5, they make decisions about which units from a choice of metric and uniform non-standard units they would choose for measuring given items.

Watch out for

Check that children work accurately. For measuring length, some may need to be reminded to match the 10cm strip to the beginning of the length of the item being compared.

Creative context

When cooking at school, ask the children to read how much packets of flour, sugar, and so on weigh. They find the weight on the packet. Repeat this with liquid containers, such as milk.

Vocabulary

balance, capacity, centimetre, **clock**, compare, container, day, estimate, hour, length, measure, measuring jug, metre, metre stick, minute, scales, second, week, weight

Curriculum objectives
● To measure and begin to record lengths.
Success criteria
● I can use a simple ruler for measuring lengths.

You will need
Equipment
Metre stick marked in decimetres; rulers or prepared 10cm pieces of paper; trays of items for children to measure, some longer than 10cm, some shorter than 10cm, and some about 10cm in length

Differentiation
This is an activity in which all the children can be actively involved. The group work can be in mixed groups, or by confidence.

Lesson I
Oral and mental starter 61

Main teaching activities

Whole-class work: Show the children a metre stick marked in decimetres. Explain that each of the sections measures 10cm. Count together in tens from 0 to 100, along the metre stick. Say: *Each count represents another 10cm*. Ask two children to hold the metre stick horizontally. Now hold a book along the metre stick. Ask: *About how long is the book?* Explain the measurement is about ... centimetres long.

Group work: Children can work in groups of four to six, with a tray of items to measure. Provide each child with rulers, metre sticks or prepare some pieces of paper which are exactly 10cm in length for this task. Ask the children to find things that they think are longer than 10cm, shorter than 10cm and about 10cm. They write these into the chart, then check with the cut-off 10cm measurer. Explain that the crocodile shows where to start measuring at its tail, and the end of the 10cm is the end of the crocodile's mouth.

Progress check: Ask each group to show something they found that was longer than 10cm, shorter than 10cm or about the same length as 10cm, and to demonstrate how they measured. Check that they matched the 10cm measure to the end of the item. Ask: *Did you make a good estimate? How do you know?*

Review

Invite individual children to show an item that they estimated was less than 10cm. Ask the child to demonstrate how they measured. Repeat this for items estimated as longer than 10cm and those about the same as 10cm. Ask:

- *Did you make a good estimate?*
- *Was the ... a bit longer or shorter than 10cm?*
- *How many 10cm are there in a metre?*

Curriculum objectives
● To measure and begin to record capacity and volume.
Success criteria
● I can measure how much something holds.

You will need
Equipment
Litre container and 100ml container; 20ml and 10ml scoops; straight-sided unmarked containers with an elastic band around each one; containers of sand

Differentiation
Less confident learners
Children may need help in counting how many scoopfuls of sand they use.
More confident learners
Ask the children to repeat the activity using a 10ml scoop. Explain that they will need to be as accurate as they can as 10ml of sand is a very small amount each time.

Lesson 2
Oral and mental starter 68

Main teaching activities

Whole-class work: Explain that in this lesson children will measure how much something holds. Show the children the litre container and explain that this holds 1 litre. Pass the container around the class so that all the children can see the mark for 1 litre. Explain that the litre is split into smaller units called millilitres. Write litre and millilitre onto the board. Show the children the 20ml scoop that they will be using in this lesson. Pass the scoop around so that the children can see its size and capacity. Explain that 50 scoopfuls will fill the litre container.

Group work: Give each group a clear container with an elastic band around it. Ask the children to estimate how many 20ml scoops of sand are needed to reach the band. The children estimate, then check. They can record this on paper. Ask them to move the band to a different position and repeat. This activity should help the children to improve in estimating capacity.

Progress check: Invite the groups to show their estimates and measures. Ask: *Did you find it easier to make a good estimate when you moved the elastic band for your second go? Why do you think that was?*

Review

Invite a group to say whether their estimates improved as they repeated the activity. Ask: *Why do you think that is?* Now show the children the litre and 100ml containers. Ask: *How many 100ml do you think will fit in the litre container?* Ask the children to count each time sand is poured into the litre container, using the 100ml container. Explain that ten 100ml will fill 1 litre.

Curriculum objectives
● To measure and begin to record mass/weight.
Success criteria
● I can make a 100g weight.

You will need
Photocopiable sheets
'Measures chart (1)'
Equipment
Containers of sand; plastic bags and ties; 100g weights; bucket balances, scale balance

Differentiation
Less confident learners
Check that the children make reasonably accurate sand weights. Discuss with them that these weigh 100 grams.
More confident learners
Challenge the children to make other sand weights, such as 50g, 30g, 200g. They should then find items in the classroom that they estimate weigh about the same as each of these.

Lesson 3   Oral and mental starter 71

Main teaching activities

Whole-class work: Pass round some 100g weights. Ask the children to take turns to feel the weight of this, then pass it to the next child. Explain that ten of these will weigh a kilogram. Demonstrate this with ten 100g weights, and a scale balance. Ask the children to watch as the weights are added, and to count as each weight is added to the pan.

Group work: Provide each group with a 100g weight, some sand, plastic bags and ties, and a bucket balance. Ask the children to estimate how much sand they need to balance the 100g weight. Then they measure it accurately. They put the measured sand into a bag and tie the top firmly. Now they try to find items in the classroom that they estimate weigh about 100g. Then check by balancing with the bag of sand, recording on photocopiable page 'Measures chart (1)' from the CD-ROM.

Progress check: Ask a group to demonstrate their weighing. Check that they place the sand weight in the centre of the bucket, and add the item to be balanced to the centre of the second bucket. Ask:

- *How much does your bag of sand weigh?*
- *How many of these bags weigh the same as a kilogram?*

Review

Invite a group to show the items that weighed about 100g. Now ask, for example:

- *How many 100g will balance 1 kilogram?*
- *How do you know?*

Using the scale balance, ask the children to suggest things in the classroom that would balance 200g. Point to the 200g mark on the scale. When there is a reasonably accurate balance of 200g, ask:

- *How many 100g weights would we need to make 200g?*
- *How do you know? How can you check?*

Suggest to the children that they look at packets of food, at home, to find their weight in grams.

Curriculum objectives
● To measure and begin to record time (minutes, seconds).

Success criteria
● I can use a stop watch to measure seconds passing.

You will need

Equipment
Simple stop clocks or stop watches that mark seconds; teaching clock

Differentiation
This activity can be completed in mixed ability groups. All the children should take a full part in the activities.

Main teaching activities

Whole-class work: Ask the children how we measure the passing of time. Give answers such as days, weeks, hours, minutes if the children do not suggest these. Ask: *How many days are there in one week?* If children do not know this, say the names of the days of the week in order, and ask the children to keep a count with their fingers. Now ask: *How many minutes are there in 1 hour?* If the children are unsure, use the teaching clock and count round the clock face in fives, from the 12 and back to the 12. Explain that each minute can be divided into seconds and that there are 60 seconds in one minute. Ask the children to shut their eyes when you say *Shut*. Tell them you will say *Open* when 60 seconds have passed. The time may seem quite a long expanse to the children.

Explain that you would like the children to try out some activities and see how many they can do in 10 seconds each time.

Activity 1 Ask them to see how if they can write their name neatly in 10 seconds. They wait for you to say *Start* then *Stop*. Show them the stop clock face at the start and finish of the 10 seconds.

Activity 2 Ask the children to see how many cubes they can pick up one at a time and put into a margarine tub in 10 seconds.

Activity 3 Ask the children to put their hands on their heads, then fold their arms, and to count how many times they can repeat these movements in 10 seconds.

Activity 4 Ask the children to squat down, then stand up, taking 10 seconds to stretch as far as they can.

Group work: Ask the children to work in groups of four. They firstly suggest things that they might do that they think will take 10 seconds. They write down their suggestions, then take turns to time the 10 seconds using a stop clock while the others try out the ideas. They write if they made a good estimate.

Progress check: Ask questions such as: *How well did you estimate the time? Do you think you recognise 10 seconds now?* Ask the children to shut their eyes, when you say *Shut,* then open them again when they think 10 seconds has passed. Ask: *Did you make a good estimate?*

Review

Ask the children to say, in their groups, things that they tried that took about 10 seconds. Choose a couple of the suggestions that can be done easily by everyone, and time the children as they try these out. Ask questions such as:

- *How many days are there in a week?*
- *How many minutes are there in 1 hour?*
- *How many seconds are there in 1 minute?*

Curriculum objectives
- To measure and begin to record the following: lengths and heights; mass/weight; capacity and volume.

Success criteria
- I can say which units to use.

You will need
Photocopiable sheets
'Match the units'

Equipment
Various measuring equipment for measuring length, mass and capacity

Differentiation
Less confident learners
Ask an adult to work with these children, encouraging them to explain their decisions.

More confident learners
Encourage the children to suggest something at home that could be measured using each of the units on the sheet.

Lesson 5   Oral and mental starter 64

Main teaching activities

Whole-class work: Ask the children to suggest things in the classroom that could be measured for length (or width, or height) using rulers, garden canes, matchsticks, metre sticks. Now repeat this for weighing (or balancing) with cubes, marbles, cups of sand, 100g weights. Repeat this for finding capacity with egg cups, scoops, litre jugs of water.

Independent work: Ask the children to complete photocopiable page 'Match the units' from the CD-ROM, which asks them to choose the most appropriate units to measure the length, weight and capacity of various objects.

Match the units

■ Which units would you use to measure these things? Draw a line to match each thing to the right unit.

Length

Weight

Capacity

I can say which units to use.

Progress check: Ask questions such as:
- *Why did you choose that unit?*
- *Which unit would you choose to measure a ...?*

Review
Review the work on the A3 copy of photocopiable page 'Match the units'. Ask questions such as:
- *Why did you choose that unit?*
- *Who chose something else?*
- *Which unit would be better for measuring that? Why?*

Moving and turning

Expected prior learning

Children should be able to:

- follow simple instructions for moving.

Topic	Curriculum objectives	Expected outcomes
Geometry: position and direction	**Lesson 1**	
	To describe position, direction and movement, including whole, half, quarter and three-quarter turns.	Follow instructions to move, change direction and turn.
	Lesson 2	
	To describe position, direction and movement, including whole, half, quarter and three-quarter turns.	Follow instructions to move, change direction and turn.
	Lesson 3	
	To describe position, direction and movement, including whole, half, quarter and three-quarter turns.	Follow instructions to move, change direction and turn.
	Lesson 4	
	To describe position, direction and movement, including whole, half, quarter and three-quarter turns.	Follow instructions to move, change direction and turn. Begin to recognise and use the clockwise direction to turn in.
	Lesson 5	
	To describe position, direction and movement, including whole, half, quarter and three-quarter turns.	Follow instructions to move, change direction and turn. Begin to recognise and use the clockwise direction to turn in.

■SCHOLASTIC

Preparation

Lesson 1: arrange access to the hall or playground

Lessons 2 to 4: copy 'Home to the shops', one per child in the group who will do the corresponding activity

You will need

Photocopiable sheets

'Home to the shops'

Equipment

Access to the hall or playground; roamer; models (a doll's house with furniture, a garage with cars, a farm with animals); large sheets of sugar paper; interlocking cubes; scissors

Further practice

These activities are essentially practical. Provide further opportunities for children to follow instructions, both in PE and dance, but also during class lesson time. For example, turning the page of a book, observing which way the clock hands move, and replicating that movement with their hands, opening a door and observing how that turns.

Oral and mental starters for week 6

See bank of starters on page 205. Oral and mental starters are also on the CD-ROM.

65 Make my total to 10

67 Addition and subtraction to 20

66 Add and subtract beyond 10

68 Halving and doubling

Overview of progression

This week children build on their knowledge and respond to instructions for moving. The vocabulary of turning is introduced. They use the vocabulary in practical situations, giving instructions to each other, and saying what they are doing so that others can follow their movements. They are introduced to the idea of inanimate objects 'turning' such as the page of a book, a door handle, and so on.

Watch out for

Some children may be unsure of 'left' and 'right' and 'clockwise'. For 'left' and 'right' ask the children to hold something, such as a cube, in their right hand as a reminder of which is which, then ask them to follow instructions for moving and turning.

Creative context

Children can follow more instructions in PE and dance lessons. Include the vocabulary used in these lessons for them to follow instructions, then give instructions to a partner to follow.

Vocabulary

above, back, below, beside, between, centre, clockwise, direction, far, front, grid, half turn, half way, inside, left, near, next to, on top of, outside, position, quarter turn, right, three-quarter turn, underneath, whole turn

Curriculum objectives
- To describe position, direction and movement.

Success criteria
- I can follow instructions to move.
- I can give instructions for someone else to move.

You will need

Equipment

Access to the hall or playground

Differentiation

Less confident learners

Check that the children understand left and right. If children are unsure about which is their right or left, provide all the children in the class with a beanbag or quoit to hold in their right hand, as a reminder.

More confident learners

Challenge the children to make more complex moves, for example quarter, half and three-quarter turns.

Lesson I

Main teaching activities

Whole-class work: This activity should be taught in the hall or playground. Explain to the children that they will learn more about moving. Ask them to follow your instructions. Say: *Face me. Step forward; step back; step to the right; step to the left; now two steps forward; turn in a circle and face me again.* Repeat instructions like these. You may wish to move in the children's direction (your right is their left) in order to help everyone to move correctly.

Paired work: Ask the children to make a sequence of moves that they can describe, and practise them.

Then ask each pair to join another. Ask the children to take turns to say their moves for the other pair to follow.

Progress check: Ask pairs to show their moves and to describe each move as they make it. Ask questions such as: *Which is your right... left side?*

Whole-class work: Invite groups to demonstrate their moves with their backs to the other children as their start position. Ask the other children to say what they see and to join in with the moves.

Group work: Ask the children to invent another set of moves, including up, down.

Review

Ask each group in turn to show their new moves, starting with their backs to the children. Ask the other children to say the moves as they see them. When everyone has demonstrated their moves, say, for example:

- *Hold up your right hand.*
- *Now hold up your left hand.*
- *Move your right hand up, down, out to your left side, out to your right side....*

Check that children know which is their right and which is their left side.

Curriculum objectives
● To describe position, direction and movement, including whole, half, quarter and three-quarter turns.

Success criteria
● I can turn in a circle.
● I can move a quarter, half, three-quarters and all the way round in a circle.

You will need
Photocopiable sheets
'Home to the shops'
Equipment
Roamer; models (a doll's house with furniture, a garage with cars, a farm with animals); large sheets of sugar paper

Differentiation
Less confident learners
Activity 1 can be simplified by including just one left or right turn.
More confident learners
Activity 1 can be made more challenging by asking the children to program a route that involves a number of turns.

Lesson 2

Oral and mental starter 68

Main teaching activities

Whole-class work: Play 'I spy' with the whole class. Explain that you will say where something is, and the children should raise a hand to tell you what it is. Use the language of position and direction. For example: *I spy something on top of the cupboard, near to the window. I spy something blue in the left-hand room of the doll's house...* When the children have played this game four or five times, ask them to stand up and follow your directions in a game of 'Simon says'. Decide whether to make this a forfeit game for those who respond to instructions without being told 'Simon says'. For example: *Simon says put your hands on your head. Simon says turn to your left. Simon says turn all the way round. Turn to the right! Make a quarter turn, make a half turn, turn three-quarters of the way round.* Demonstrate these turns, in the clockwise direction, if necessary. Check that the children can follow your directions to identify the objects.

Invite a child to give instructions for 'Simon says'.

Group work: Set up a circus of activities for lessons 2, 3 and 4.

Activity 1: Ask the children to work in a group of three or four. They program a Roamer to move from one place in the classroom to another, making left and/or right turns on the way. They will find it helpful to record the Roamer's moves.

Activity 2: Ask the children to work in groups of three or four to arrange the furniture in a doll's house according to agreed placements. This activity works best if an adult gives position, direction and movement instructions to the children as they work. Other groups can work on the same activity, using a model garage and cars, or a model farm and animals.

Activity 3: Provide a large sheet of sugar paper and a toy car for each group of three or four. Ask the children to draw their own roadway on the paper. Ask them to put in turns to the left and right, and a roundabout. They should also include somewhere marked 'Home' and somewhere marked 'Shops'. They then try out the roadway, moving the car from 'Home' to the 'Shops' and back again. Ask them to write down their instructions for carrying out the journey on photocopiable page 'Home to the shops' from the CD-ROM.

Progress check: Ask the children to say the moves that they are making. Now give some direction such as: *Turn it to the right... left. Turn it quarter, half, three-quarters of the way round.* Check that the children are confident with this vocabulary.

Review

Invite some children who have tried the Roamer activity to demonstrate what they have done. Invite the other children to describe the movements that they see. Encourage them to use words such as left, right and turn as they make their descriptions. Ask questions such as:
● *Which way did the Roamer turn?*
● *How can you make the Roamer turn left/right?*
● *How can you make the Roamer turn all the way round?*

Curriculum objectives

- To describe position, direction and movement, including whole, half, quarter and three-quarter turns.

Success criteria

- I can turn in a circle.
- I can move a quarter, half, three-quarters and all the way round in a circle.

You will need

Equipment

Roamer; models (a doll's house with furniture, a garage with cars, a farm with animals); large sheets of sugar paper

Differentiation

Less confident learners

Ask an adult to work with them to say the vocabulary in sentences, then ask the children to do the same.

More confident learners

Challenge the children to combine two moves in one set of instructions. Such as *Move the ... on top of the ... and turn it a quarter.*

Lesson 3   Oral and mental starter 67

Main teaching activities

Whole-class work: Place an object in front of the children, such as a toy car. Ask them to describe where it is. Now ask them to shut their eyes. Move the object to another location, but still where the children will be able to see it. Ask them to open their eyes and to look for the object. Ask questions such as *Where is it now? What is it near? Is it on or under the...?*

Group work: Choose from the circus of activities for lesson 2 for each group. Ask each group to work at a different activity from the previous lesson.

Progress check: Invite children to demonstrate what they are doing and to describe the movements made. Ask questions such as: *Where is the ...? Tell me how to move it to ....*

Review

Review the 'Home to the shops' activity. Invite the children who carried out this activity to explain what they did as they show the roadway they drew. Ask questions as you point to the roadway, such as: *Which way does the car need to go? Where is the right... left turn? Which way around the roundabout will the car need to go?*

Curriculum objectives

- To describe position, direction and movement, including whole, half, quarter and three-quarter turns.

Success criteria

- I can move in a clockwise direction.
- I can turn in a circle.
- I can move a quarter, half, three-quarters and all the way round in a circle.

You will need

Equipment

As lesson 3; interlocking cubes; scissors

Differentiation

Less confident learners

Provide experience of opening and closing scissors and turning pages of books for the children to try themselves, and to observe how the objects are turning.

More confident learners

Encourage the children to suggest other objects that can be turned in some way.

Lesson 4   Oral and mental starter 66

Main teaching activities

Whole-class work: Play 'Simon Says' again (without the forfeits). Encourage the children to respond rapidly to directions and turns, and check that they know their left from their right. If they find this activity difficult, suggest that they keep a cube in their right hand.

Show the children a pair of scissors. Open and close the scissors and explain that the scissors turn about a point. Point to the rivet join in the centre of the scissors. Ask for a suggestion of something else in the classroom that turns about a point, such as the clock hands. Explain that the hands turn in a clockwise direction. Ask the children to stand up and move an arm in a clockwise direction. Demonstrate this by turning round and moving your arm for the children to follow. Now open and close the classroom door and explain that the door turns about a line, and point to the hinged area of the door, from top to bottom. Ask for a suggestion of something else that turns about a line, such as a book when the pages are turned.

Group work: Choose from the circus of activities for lesson 2 for each group. Ask each group to work at a different activity from the previous lesson.

Progress check: Invite children in each group to explain to the rest of the class what they are doing. Encourage them to speak in sentences, and to use the vocabulary of position, direction and motion.

Review

Review the doll's house activity from lesson 2. Invite children from different groups to place the furniture, following your instructions: Put the bed in the room upstairs, on the left, and next to the window.... Ask questions such as: *Where is the ...? What is next to the ...? What is on the left/right of the ...?*

Lesson 5 — Oral and mental starter

Curriculum objectives
● To describe position, direction and movement, including whole, half, quarter and three-quarter turns.
Success criteria
● I can follow instructions to place, move and turn objects.

You will need
Equipment
Interlocking cubes

Differentiation
Less confident learners
Check that the children give instructions carefully using the new vocabulary.
More confident learners
Challenge the children to move the cubes, including building up with them.

Main teaching activities

Whole-class work: Explain to the children that in this lesson they will be working with a partner, and taking turns to give instructions for placing cubes on the table. Place a cube where the children can see it. Now ask a child to place another cube next to the first on the right. Repeat this, with different instructions, including left, right, behind, in front of, turn and so on.

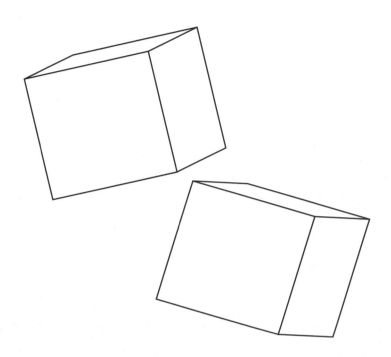

Paired work: Provide each pair with several cubes. Ask them to take turns to give instructions for placing the cubes.

Progress check: Listen to the instructions that a pair give each other. Ask questions such as: *Which side of the cube is the left side? Turn this cube halfway round.*

Review

Play 'Simon says' again, but without the forfeits. Say, for example: *Simon says stand up. Simon says turn halfway round. Simon says turn three-quarters of the way round. Sit down.* Include the vocabulary of turning. Now ask the children to sit down, facing you and say:

- *Show me your right hand.*
- *Now show me your left hand.*
- *Stand up. Turn three-quarters of the way round.*
- *Now turn another quarter and sit down.*
- *Tell me what you have learned this week.*

Curriculum objectives
● To count, read and write numbers to 100 in numerals, count in different multiples including twos, fives and tens.

You will need
I. Check
Oral and mental starter

61 Counting in 5s to 100

2. Assess
'Hundred square'; two sets of cards from 'Number cards 0–20' per group

3. Further practice
Oral and mental starters

60 Counting in 2s to 100

61 Counting in 5s to 100

62 Counting in 10s

Photocopiable sheets
'Count in twos'; 'Count in fives'; 'Count in tens'

Curriculum objectives
● To represent and use number bonds and related subtraction facts within 20.
● To add and subtract one-digit and two-digit numbers to 20, including zero.

You will need
I. Check
Oral and mental starter

67 Addition and subtraction to 20

2. Assess
'Number line 0–20'

3. Further practice
Oral and mental starters

66 Add and subtract beyond 10

Photocopiables sheets
'Adding to 20'; 'Subtracting to 20'; 'Adding and subtracting to 20'

Counting in twos, fives and tens

Most children should be able to count in 2s, 5s and 10s to 100 and back again.

Some children will not have made such progress and will require more practice, counting in 2s, then moving on to 5s and 10s.

I. Check

61 Counting in 5s to 100

Observe which children join in the counting in a confident manner, and which children are less confident. Extend the more confident children, asking them to say a number which comes in the count of 2s as well as 5s.

- *What do you say after 20 in the count of 5s?*
- *What number comes before 35 in the count of 5s?*

2. Assess

Ask the children to take turns to turn over two number cards and make a 2-digit number. They decide whether the number that is made is in the count of 2s, 5s or 10s. They mark a number on photocopiable sheet 'Hundred square' on page 206 by putting a cross through it. Decide whether to fold photocopiable page 'Hundred square' so it just shows numbers to 30 for the less confident. Challenge the more confident children to explain how they know that the number is in the count of 2s, 5s or 10s. Record the outcomes.

3. Further practice

Use the oral and mental starters suggested to reinforce the counting patterns. The photocopiable sheets on pages 207 to 209 give further experience of identifying which numbers come in the count of 2s, 5s or 10s.

Addition and subtraction facts to 20

Most children should be able to use mental strategies to find solutions.

Some children will not have made such progress and will require consolidation practice of addition and subtraction to 10 before moving on.

I. Check

67 Addition and subtraction to 20

Encourage the children to use mental strategies to find answers. Keep the pace of this sharp. Note who is confident and who needs further practice. Extend to subtraction questions such as $17 - 7$, $16 - 10$ and so on to extend the more confident children.

- *How did you work that out?*
- *What number fact did you use to help you?*
- *Who used a different way?*

2. Assess

Ask the children to find all the addition facts that they know or can derive with an answer of 15. Then ask them to write a corresponding subtraction fact for each answer. Provide the less confident children with photocopiable page 'Number line 0–20' from the CD-ROM to support them. Challenge the more confident children to provide another addition and two subtraction sentences using the number trios they have from their original addition sentences. Record the outcomes.

3. Further practice

Use the oral and mental starters to provide further practice of recalling these facts. The photocopiable sheets on pages 210 to 212 will give children further opportunities to derive and recall these facts.

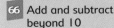

Curriculum objectives
● To recognise, find and name a half as one of two equal parts of an object, shape or quantity.

You will need
1. Check
Oral and mental starter
68 Halving and doubling

2. Assess
Cubes

3. Further practice
Oral and mental starter
69 Finding half

Photocopiable sheets
'Finding halves'

Finding half of quantities

Most children should be able to find half of a quantity.

Some children will not have made such progress and will require further support and practice of finding halves of quantities.

1. Check

68 Halving and doubling

Observe which children answer confidently and which will need further practice. Extend the more able by saying an even number such as 8, and asking for the double, then for the half of the original number.

- *How did you work that out?*
- *Who used a different way?*
- *Who 'knew' the answer?*

2. Assess

Provide each child with 20 cubes. Ask them to find half of 20, and write 'Half of 20 is …'. Then repeat this by removing two cubes each time, until they have none left. Observe how the children find the answers. Challenge the more confident children to try to recall the answers. Support the less confident children by limiting the number of cubes to ten, to begin with. Record the outcomes.

3. Further practice

Use the suggested oral and mental starters to practise finding half of an even quantity, gradually moving to recall of the facts to 20. The photocopiable sheet provides links between halving and sharing and gives children further practice in finding half.

Curriculum objectives
● To recognise, find and name a quarter as one of four equal parts of an object, shape or quantity.

You will need
1. Check
Oral and mental starter
70 Finding half and half again

2. Assess
20 interlocking cubes per child; four paper plates per child

3. Further practice
Oral and mental starters
70 Finding half and half again (extension)

Photocopiable sheets
'Finding quarters'

Finding a quarter of quantities

Most children should be able to find a quarter of a quantity of cubes by sharing.

Some children will not have made such progress and will require further practice in sharing out quantities to find a quarter.

1. Check

70 Finding half and half again

Encourage children to count to see how much half is, then find half again. Observe which children are confident with this, and which need further practice. Extend to larger quantities, divisible by four, for the more confident children.

- *What is half of 12? So what is half of 6? How much is a quarter of 12?*
- *How did you work that out?*

2. Assess

Ask the children to share out the 20 cubes between the four plates to find a quarter. Ask them to write the sentence 'A quarter of 20 is …'. They repeat this for 12, then 16 cubes. Decide whether to provide eight cubes for the less confident children to share out. Observe how children share. Check that they make equal shares. Record the outcomes.

3. Further practice

Use the oral and mental starters suggested, with the extension, in order to practise finding a quarter of quantities. The photocopiable sheet suggested provides further practical experience of finding a quarter of quantities.

Oral and mental starters

Number and place value

60 Counting in 2s to 100

Ask the children to start with you, from 0, to 30, counting in 2s and back to 0. Repeat this, extending the counting to 40, 50, and so on, up to 100. Repeat this starting from 1, for odd numbers. Now start from any number, odd or even, and count in twos forwards then back again. Ask questions such as:

- *What is the next number after 28...?*
- *If I count back in twos from 40, what number do I say after 30...?*
- *Start on 26... Count on in twos three... times. What number do you say?*
- *Start at 43... Count back in twos four... times. What number do you say?*

61 Counting in 5s to 100

Ask the children to count with you in 5s from 0, to 30, 40, 50... up to 100, and back again. Keep a good pace for this. Now repeat this starting from any number in the 'counting in fives' pattern. Children may find it helpful to quietly slap their knees as they count in order to keep the rhythm of the count. Ask questions such as:

- *What is the next number after 40...55...70...?*
- *Count back. What number do we say after 85...70...55...?*
- *Now let's count in 5s, starting from 1. Say 1, then 2, 3, 4, 5 in your heads, and 6 out loud and so on.*

62 Counting in 10s

Count from 0 to 100 in tens and back again. Repeat the count starting from any 'decade' number such as 10, 20, 30 .... Count up to 100, back to zero and on to the start number. Say, for example:

- *If I start at 20..., what will my next number be? And my next?*
- *Count back three tens from 70... What number do you say?*
- *Now let's count in tens starting on 1. What is the next number? And the next? How do you know that?*

63 Writing numerals

Explain that you will say a number. Ask the children to write the numerals onto their individual whiteboards and when you say *Show me*, they hold up their boards for you to see. Say, for example: *Write 5, 8, 10, 12, 15, 20, 18... Write the number that is one more than 13; one less than 16... Write 30, 40, 100...*. Ask questions such as:

- *Write 15. Which is the tens digit? Which is the units digit?*
- *Write 20. How many tens are there? How many units?*
- *Write 35. How many tens are there? How many units?*

64 Writing number words

Explain that you will say a number. Ask the children to write the number word onto their individual whiteboards. When you say *Show me*, they hold up their boards for you to see. Say, for example: *Write 3, 6, 9, 11, 17.... Write the number that is one less than 14. Write the number that is one more than 19.* Ask questions such as:

- *Which are the teens numbers?*
- *So is thirteen a teen number?*
- *Is twenty a teen number? How do you know that?*

Addition and subtraction

65 Make my total to 10

Explain that you will say a total. Ask the children to write on their individual whiteboards and pens an addition to give this total. For example, if you say 8 the children might write 1 + 7, 2 + 6.... Invite children with different responses to come to the front of the class and hold their boards so that everyone can see the responses. Now ask, for example: *What other additions with a total of 8 are there?*

Now ask the children to write a subtraction sentence that begins '8 take away ...'. Again, invite children with different responses to come to the front for everyone to see. Ask: *Do we have all the possible answers? How do you know this?* The children can be put in an order at the front of the class, for example: 8 − 0 = 8, 8 − 1 = 7, and so on. Repeat this for other totals and subtractions up to 10.

66 Add and subtract beyond 10

Explain that you will begin with addition questions such as: 12 + 6, 16 + 3, 13 + 7.... Ask the children to use addition facts to 10 to find the answers. They put up their hands to answer. Ask each time:

- *What fact did you use to help you?*
- *How did you use that fact?*

Over time repeat this for subtraction such as: 18 − 4, 19 − 6, 15 − 2.... Ask similar questions in order to remind the children that they can use subtraction to 10 facts to help them find these solutions.

67 Addition and subtraction to 20

Ask the children to write answers to additions such as: 10 + 5, 10 + 7, 10 + 6.... Repeat this, asking subtraction questions such as: 16 − 10, 17 − 7, 20 − 10.... Ask, for example:

- *How did you work that out?*
- *Who tried a different way?*
- *Who 'knew' the answer? Well done!*

68 Halving and doubling

Ask the children to find doubles of numbers to 10. Say, for example: *What is double 2? ... double 6? ... double 9....? How did you work that out? Who 'knew' the answer? Well done!*

Now ask halving questions, such as: *Use the double facts that you know to answer these. What is half of 10? What is half of 14...? How did you work that out?*

Fractions

69 Finding half

Show the children ten cubes and ask: *How can we find out how much half is?* When the cubes have been halved say together: *Half of 10 is 5.* Repeat this for other even quantities to 10, then extend to 20. Ask, for example: *Who worked out the answer in their head? How did you do that? Well done!*

70 Finding half and half again

Put out 12 cubes and ask: *How much is half of these 12 cubes? How much is half of that?* Put the cubes back together and say: *How can we find a quarter?* Children may suggest sharing the cubes into four groups. Ask: *So what is a quarter of 12?* Explain that it is possible to find a quarter by finding half, then half again. Repeat this for 8, 16 and 20 cubes.

Extension

Extend the number range to up to 32.

Hundred square

1	2	3	4	5	6	7	8	9	10
11	12	13	14	15	16	17	18	19	20
21	22	23	24	25	26	27	28	29	30
31	32	33	34	35	36	37	38	39	40
41	42	43	44	45	46	47	48	49	50
51	52	53	54	55	56	57	58	59	60
61	62	63	64	65	66	67	68	69	70
71	72	73	74	75	76	77	78	79	80
81	82	83	84	85	86	87	88	89	90
91	92	93	94	95	96	97	98	99	100

Name: _____   Date: _____

Count in twos

- Some of the numbers in these counting patterns are missing.
- Write in the missing numbers.

1.

| 0 | 2 | 4 | 6 | | | | |

2.

| 6 | 8 | 10 | 12 | | | |

3.

| 10 | | 14 | | 18 | | 22 |

4.
| 14 | | 18 | 20 | | 26 | |

5.
| | | | 18 | 20 | 22 | |

6.
| 20 | 18 | 16 | | | | 8 |

7.
| 24 | | 20 | | 16 | | 12 | |

8.
| 28 | 26 | | 22 | | |

9.
| | | 16 | | 12 | 10 | |

I can count in twos.

How did you do?

Count in fives

- Here are the numbers from 0 to 30.
- Circle the numbers that you say when you count in fives.

0   1   2

30

29

28

3

4

27

5

26

6

25

7

24

23

8

22

9

21

10

20

11

19

12

18

13   14   15   16   17

I can count in fives.

How did you do?

SCHOLASTIC
www.scholastic.co.uk

Count in tens

■ Write the missing numbers.

1.

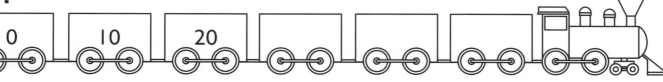

0 | 10 | 20

2.

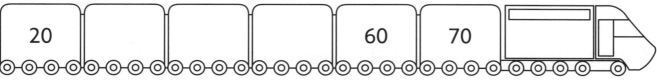

10 | | 30 | | 50

3.

20 | | | | 60 | 70

4.

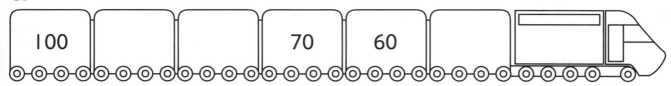

40 | 50 | 60

5.

50 | | | 80 | 90

6.

100 | | | 70 | 60

7.

| | | 60 | 50 | 40

I can count in tens.

How did you do?

Adding to 20

- Play this game with a partner.
- You will need a set of 1–9 number cards.

- Shuffle the cards.
- Take turns to turn over a card.
- Add the card number to 10.
- The first player to say the answer wins a point.
- Write the name of the winner.
- Write the addition sentence and the answer.

Name	Addition sentence	Answer

I can add to 20.

How did you do?

PHOTOCOPIABLE

SCHOLASTIC
www.scholastic.co.uk

Subtracting to 20

- Play this game with a partner.
- You will need a pack of 1–9 number cards.

- Shuffle the cards.
- Take turns to turn over a card.
- Subtract the card number from 19.
- The first player to say the answer wins a point.
- Write the name of the winner.
- Write the subtraction sentence and the answer.

Name	Subtraction sentence	Answer

I can subtract to 20.

How did you do?

Adding and subtracting to 20 (2)

■ Join the answers to the add or subtract sentence.

12 + 7

14 + 2

13

18

19 – 9

10

18

19

12 + 5

12

13 – 2

15 + 3

17

17

16 – 4

19 – 3

14 + 3

16

15 – 3

11

10 + 8

16

12

18 – 5

I can add and subtract.

How did you do?

Number and place value

Expected prior learning

Children should be able to:

- read, write and say numbers in order to at least 50
- recognise place value in numbers to 30.

Topic	Curriculum objectives	Expected outcomes
Number and place value	**Lesson 1** To identify and represent numbers using objects and pictorial representations including the number line, and use the language of: equal to, more than, less than (fewer), most, least.	Recognise place value, knowing which is the tens and which is the units digit, and their worth.
	Lesson 2 To identify and represent numbers using objects and pictorial representations including the number line, and use the language of: equal to, more than, less than (fewer), most, least.	Recognise place value, knowing which is the tens and which is the units digit, and their worth.
	Lesson 3 To identify and represent numbers using objects and pictorial representations including the number line, and use the language of: equal to, more than, less than (fewer), most, least. When given a number, to identify one more and one less.	Recognise place value, knowing which is the tens and which is the units digit, and their worth. Recognise the number that is one more or one less than any number up to 100.
	Lesson 4 To identify and represent numbers using objects and pictorial representations including the number line, and use the language of: equal to, more than, less than (fewer), most, least. When given a number, to identify one more and one less.	Recognise place value, knowing which is the tens and which is the units digit, and their worth. Recognise the number that is one more or one less than any number up to 100.
	Lesson 5 To identify and represent numbers using objects and pictorial representations including the number line, and use the language of: equal to, more than, less than (fewer), most, least. When given a number, to identify one more and one less.	Recognise place value, knowing which is the tens and which is the units digit, and their worth. Recognise the number that is one more or one less than any number up to 100.

SUMMER 2

WEEK 1

Preparation

Lesson 1: prepare 'Number cards 0–20', one set per group

Lesson 2: copy 'Abacus recording sheet', one per child; copy 'Two-spike abacus', one per pair

Lesson 3: copy 'Hundred square', one per pair

Lesson 4: prepare interactive teaching resource 'Number square' with many of the numbers hidden

Lesson 5: prepare 'Number cards 0–9', two sets per pair; copy 'Write one more and one less', one per child

You will need

Photocopiable sheets

'Write one more and one less'

General resources

'Hundred square'; 'Number cards 0–20'; 'Two-spike abacus'; 'Abacus recording sheet'; interactive teaching resource 'Number square'

Equipment

Straws and elastic bands; abacus; 18 counters per pair; individual whiteboards

Further practice

Photocopiable sheets

'Abacus numbers'; 'Tens and units (3)'; 'Find one more and one less'

Oral and mental starters for week 1

See bank of starters on page 246. Oral and mental starters are also on the CD-ROM.

72 Count in 1s

73 Count in 2s

74 Count in 5s

75 Count in 10s

77 Ordinal numbers

Overview of progression

This week brings together children's knowledge of numbers to 100. They begin by bundling straws to make TU numbers. Then they represent TU numbers by completing pictures of abacuses. They use a hundred square to find the number that is one more or one less than a given number, then use this knowledge to complete a hundred square with missing numbers. In lesson 5, they use numeral cards to make TU numbers, then write the numbers that are one more and one less than the card number.

Watch out for

Some children may still reverse the digits, so that, for example 45 is shown as 54. Reinforce how the position of the digits gives their value. Children can write down the numbers on photocopiable page 'Abacus recording sheet' from the CD-ROM to help them to practise reading and writing numbers correctly.

Creative context

Encourage children to look for larger numbers in books that they use in any subject. It might be a book about animals, the planets or a story book. They say the page number for numbers to 100.

Vocabulary

counting numbers 0 to 100, one less than, one more than, ones, **tens**, **units**

Curriculum objectives
● To identify and represent numbers using objects, and use the language of: more than, less than (fewer), most, least.

Success criteria
● I can say which is the tens and which is the units digit.
● I can say tens and units numbers.

You will need
General resources
'Number cards 0–20'
Equipment
Straws and elastic bands

Differentiation
Less confident learners
Decide whether to limit the number cards to 0–12 and extend the range when children are confident.
More confident learners
Ask the children to use two sets of 0–20 cards, and to keep a record of their TU number after each turn. The first child to 100 (or beyond) wins the game.

Lesson 1

Oral and mental starter 72

Main teaching activities

Whole-class work: Provide the children with straws and elastic bands. Explain that in this lesson children will make tens and units numbers by bundling straws. Ask them to make the number 12, making the ten by bundling ten straws and fixing with an elastic band, then have the units separately. Ask: *How many tens are there in 12? How many units?* Invite a child to write 12 onto the board. Repeat this for another number, such as 18, then extend to numbers 30 and beyond, such as 25, 38, 49, 56, 64, 77, 83, 91.... Ask questions each time, such as:

- *How many tens are there in ...?*
- *How many units are there in ...?*
- *Who will write this number onto the board for us?*

Group work: Ask the children to work in groups of four. They will need straws, elastic bands and a set of number cards . They shuffle the cards all together. Ask them to take turns to take the top card. They count out the number of straws to match the card, and if it is ten or more, show it by a bundle of ten and some loose straws. For their next turn, they include the loose straws with new straws, to make another bundle of ten, and so on. When all the straws have been used, the children count their bundles of ten and loose straws, and the winner is the child with the highest score. They can record their final scores on paper. They shuffle the cards and play the game again.

Progress check: Ask questions such as:

- *Tell me what the card number is. How many tens... units is that?*
- *Show me the tens digit.*
- *Show me the units digit.*

Children continue to play the game, writing their final scores.

Review

Ask: *Who won the game?* Invite those children to stand at the front and say their winning scores. Ask the other children to decide who had the greatest score of all. Now write 57 onto the board and ask:

- *What is this number?*
- *How many tens does it have?*
- *How many units?*
- *Which is the tens digit?*
- *Which is the units digit?*

Repeat this for other numbers, such as 64, 78, 81, 95....

Curriculum objectives
● To identify and represent numbers using objects and pictorial representations.

Success criteria
● I can read and write tens and units numbers.
● I can say the tens digit and the units digit.

You will need

Photocopiable sheets

'Abacus recording sheet'

General resources

'Two-spike abacus'

Equipment

Abacus; 18 counters per pair

Differentiation

Less confident learners

Decide whether to work as a group and to limit the numbers to 20, then extend beyond 20 as the children's confidence grows.

More confident learners

Challenge the children to make 20 different numbers.

Lesson 2
Oral and mental starter 73

Main teaching activities

Whole-class work: Show the children the abacus and remind them that they can use it to make numbers from 0 to 99. Show 32 and ask: *How many tens is that? How many units? What is the number?* Repeat this for other two-digit numbers such as 42, 68, 91....

Paired work: Provide each pair with photocopiable page 'Two-spike abacus' from the CD-ROM and each child with photocopiable page 'Abacus recording sheet' from the CD-ROM and 18 counters. Ask the children to take turns to use counters to make a two-digit number. They say the number, and record the tens and units in digits on photocopiable page 'Abacus recording sheet'.

Progress check: Ask a pair to show a two-digit number that they made on the abacus. Ask: *How many tens are there? How many units? How do you know that? So what is this number?* Check that the children understand which is the tens and which is the units digit of the number.

Review

Invite a child to come to the front with their copy of photocopiable page 'Abacus recording sheet', and another child to come to the front too. Explain that the first child will say one of their numbers. The other child will make that number on the abacus. (The child using the abacus might need some help.) Each time ask: *How many tens are there? How many units are there? What is this number?* Repeat this with different children making the abacus numbers.

Curriculum objectives
● To identify and represent numbers using pictorial representations, and use the language of: more than, less than.
● When given a number, to identify one more and one less.

Success criteria
● I can say the tens and units numbers.
● I can say which is the tens digit and which the units digit.
● I can say the number that is one more or one less than a given number.

You will need

General resources

'Hundred square'; interactive teaching resource 'Number square'

Differentiation

Less confident learners

Fold 'Hundred square' down to 40, and children to work with these numbers to begin with.

More confident learners

Invite the children to find 20 sets of three numbers.

Lesson 3
Oral and mental starter 74

Main teaching activities

Whole-class work: Reveal interactive teaching resource 'Number square' on the CD-ROM. Ask the children to say the numbers that you select. Select, for example, 8, 13, 17, 25, 36, 48, 57, 66, 72, 84, 99, 50. Each time ask: *How many tens are there? How many units?* Now point to 45 and say: *Which number is one more than this? Which number is one less than this? How do you know?* Repeat this for other numbers, including decade numbers such as 20, 6, 90.

Paired work: Provide each pair with photocopiable page 'Hundred square' from the CD-ROM. They take turns to say a number, and their partner finds it on the hundred square. They write down the number, and the numbers that are one more and one less, for example: 46, 47, 48. They mark these numbers on the hundred square by putting a ring around all three of them. They repeat this, finding ten sets of three numbers in total.

Progress check: Ask questions such as: *Which number is one more than 79...? One less than 90...?* Each time ask: *How many tens are there? How many units?*

Review

Reveal interactive teaching resource 'Number square'. Explain that you will say a number. Ask a child to select the number, then select the numbers that are one more and one less. For a starting number of 53, invite everyone to say the number sentence: *one less than 53 is 52 and one more than 53 is 54.* Repeat this for different children selecting the starting number of their choice.

■SCHOLASTIC

Oral and mental starter 75

Lesson 4

Main teaching activities

Whole-class work: Repeat the whole-class activity from lesson 3, choosing different numbers.

Paired work: Display the interactive teaching resource, 'Number square' on the CD-ROM with many of the numbers hidden. Ask the children to discuss which numbers are missing and to write the numbers that are 1 more and 1 less than the numbers that are shown on the Number square. The children then use these to find other numbers until they have completed the square.

Progress check: Point to individual numbers and ask: *What number would be next to it? Why? How could you work it out?*

Review

Review the paired activity. Point to an empty space just before a printed number, and ask:

- *What number goes here?*
- *How can you work this out?*

Clear the screen then hide other numbers. Ask the children: *What is this hidden number? How do you know? Which were the easiest numbers to work out? Which numbers did you find most difficult?*

Curriculum objectives
- To identify and represent numbers using pictorial representations.
- When given a number, to identify one more and one less.

Success criteria
- I can say which is the tens digit and which is the units digit.
- I can say the number that is one more or one less than a given number.

You will need

General resources

Interactive teaching resource 'Number square'

Differentiation

Less confident learners

Work with more confident talk partners to explain the positioning of different numbers on the screen.

More confident learners

Challenge the children to explain the position using patterns of numbers, such as the column patterns: all the 1 units are under each other (1, 11, 21), and so on.

Oral and mental starter 77

Lesson 5

Main teaching activities

Whole-class work: Explain to the children that in this lesson they will be making TU numbers, then finding the numbers that are one more and one less. Write on the board 51 and ask: *What number is this? What number is one more than this? What number is one less than this?* Repeat this for other numbers such as 32, 84, 90....

Paired work: Provide each pair with two sets of number cards. Each child will also need paper or individual whiteboards. Ask the children to shuffle the cards. They take turns to turn over two cards. They make a TU number and write this down, as well as the numbers that are one more and one less.

Progress check: Invite a pair of children to show two cards they have turned over. Ask: *What number can you make? What other number can you make with these two cards?*

Review

Invite pairs to say one of their numbers. Write the number onto the board. Ask: *What number is 1 less?* Write this onto the board before the starting number. *What number is 1 more?* Write this after the starting number. Repeat this for other numbers. Now ask:

- *What number comes one before 90... 80...?*
- *What number comes one after 59... 69...?*
- *How do we write the number 100?*

Invite the children to discuss with their partner what they have learned about numbers to 100, what they feel confident with, and what they still need to learn.

Curriculum objectives
- To identify and represent numbers using objects, and use the language of: more than, less than.
- When given a number, to identify one more and one less.

Success criteria
- I can say and write the numbers that are one more and one less than a given number.

You will need

General resources

'Number cards 0–9'

Differentiation

Less confident learners

Children use one pile of 0–9 cards for the units, and a set of 1–5 cards for the tens.

More confident learners

Children challenge them to write another TU number and write the numbers that are 2 more and 2 less. They repeat this for four more TU numbers.

Addition and subtraction to 20

Expected prior learning

Children should be able to:

- recall rapidly addition facts to 10
- derive rapidly subtraction facts to 10 from known addition facts.

Topic	Curriculum objectives	Expected outcomes
Addition and subtraction	**Lesson 1** To add and subtract one-digit and two-digit numbers to 20, including zero. To solve one-step problems that involve addition and subtraction, using objects and pictorial representations, and missing number problems such as $7 = \square - 9$.	Begin to know addition and subtraction facts to a total of 20, using patterns such as $4 + 5 = 9$ and $14 + 5 = 19$. Solve addition and subtraction problems using recall, counting on or back, or recognising addition and subtraction patterns.
	Lesson 2 To add and subtract one-digit and two-digit numbers to 20, including zero.	Begin to know addition and subtraction facts to a total of 20, using patterns such as $4 + 5 = 9$ and $14 + 5 = 19$.
	Lesson 3 To add and subtract one-digit and two-digit numbers to 20, including zero.	Begin to know addition and subtraction facts to a total of 20, using patterns such as $4 + 5 = 9$ and $14 + 5 = 19$.
	Lesson 4 To add and subtract one-digit and two-digit numbers to 20, including zero. To solve one-step problems that involve addition and subtraction, using objects and pictorial representations, and missing number problems such as $7 = \square - 9$.	Begin to know addition and subtraction facts to a total of 20, using patterns such as $4 + 5 = 9$ and $14 + 5 = 19$. Solve addition and subtraction problems using recall, counting on or back, or recognising addition and subtraction patterns.
	Lesson 5 To add and subtract one-digit and two-digit numbers to 20, including zero. To solve one-step problems that involve addition and subtraction, using objects and pictorial representations, and missing number problems such as $7 = \square - 9$.	Begin to know addition and subtraction facts to a total of 20, using patterns such as $4 + 5 = 9$ and $14 + 5 = 19$. Solve addition and subtraction problems using recall, counting on or back, or recognising addition and subtraction patterns.

Preparation

Lesson 1: copy 'Make a ten and add some more', one per child; copy 'Number line 0–20' for less confident learners as appropriate

Lesson 3: prepare number cards 1–9, one set per pair

Lesson 4: copy 'Addition and subtraction (1)', one per child; copy 'Number line 0–20' for less confident learners as appropriate

Lesson 5: prepare price labels, one set per pair

You will need

Photocopiable sheets

'Make a ten and add some more'; 'Addition and subtraction (1)'

General resources

'Number line 0–20'; 'Number cards 0–20'

Equipment

Price labels 1p–20p; interlocking cubes; dice (numbered 2, 2, 3, 3, 4, 4) per group; dice (numbered 1, 2, 3, 4, 5, 5) per group; dice (numbered 1, 1, 2, 2, 3, 3) for less confident learners as appropriate

Further practice

Photocopiable sheets

'Addition'; 'Addition and subtraction (2)'; 'Addition and subtraction grids'; 'Addition and subtraction word problems'

Oral and mental starters for week 2

See bank of starters on pages 246 to 247. Oral and mental starters are also on the CD-ROM.

78 Arrow cards tens and units

76 1 more and 1 less to 100

79 Make 10 and add

Overview of progression

This week children begin by learning a new strategy for adding. For $8 + 5$ they make a ten and add the rest: $8 + 5 = 8 + 2 + 5 − 2 = 10 + 3 = 13$. They use the number trio 8, 5 and 13 to derive another addition and two subtraction sentences. They use the addition facts to 10 to derive new facts, such as $4 + 3 = 7$ and $14 + 3 = 17$. They use this knowledge to find new subtraction facts, such as $8 − 5 = 3$ so $18 − 5 = 13$. In the final lesson they use price labels to make totals to up to 20p, using the strategies that they have practised during these lessons. Then they find the change from 20p.

Watch out for

Check that children are confident with addition facts to 10, as these are needed for deriving facts with totals of more than 10. For those who are unsure, provide further experience of addition to 10, using cubes to make totals, counting on from the larger number, number lines, and mental counting on.

Creative context

Stories about shopping can involve addition and subtraction to find totals. Children can write stories which set problems for others to solve such as *'I bought some toffees for 8p and a chocolate bar for 7p.'*

Vocabulary

add, after, altogether, before, difference, double, equal to, equals (=), half, half way, halve, how many?, how many fewer is ___ than ___?, how many more is ___ than ___?, how many more to make ___?, how much less is ___?, how much more is ___?, leaves, less, makes, minus (−), more, nearly, plus (+), roughly, sign, subtract, sum, take away, total, what is the difference between ___?

Curriculum objectives
● To add and subtract one-digit and two-digit numbers to 20, including zero.
● To solve one-step problems that involve addition and subtraction, using objects.

Success criteria
● I can add by making ten and adding what is left.

You will need
Photocopiable sheets
'Make a ten and add some more'

General resources
'Number line 0–20'

Equipment
Interlocking cubes

Differentiation
Less confident learners
Decide whether to provide photocopiable page 'Number line 0–20'.

More confident learners
Challenge the children to write another addition and two subtraction sentences that use the number trio for each question on photocopiable page 'Make a ten and add some more'.

Lesson 1
Oral and mental starter 78

Main teaching activities

Whole-class work: Explain to the children that in this week they will practise skills for adding and subtracting to 20. Say: *In this lesson we shall be learning another way to add two one-digit numbers, when the total is more than ten.*

Show a tower of eight cubes and a tower of five cubes. Write onto the board 8 + 5 and say:

- *Eight is the larger number so let's start with that.*
- *How much do we need to add to eight to make ten?*
- *Yes two, so let's take two from the five.*

Break two cubes off the five-tower and add them to the eight-tower. Write onto the board 8 + 2 = 10. Say:

- *We've got three left. 10 + 3 = 13*
- *What is 10 + 3? Yes 13. So 8 + 5 = 13.*

Write another addition sentence onto the board such as 9 + 5 and repeat the process making 10: 9 + 1 = 10, 10 + 4 = 14.

Independent work:
Provide photocopiable page 'Make a ten and add some more' from the CD-ROM and ask the children to use the new method to calculate the answers.

Progress check: Ask the children, independently, to show how they are calculating the answers. Ask questions such as:

- *What do I need to add to 7 to make a ten?*
- *So what do I have to subtract from the 6?*

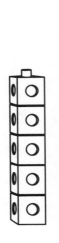

Review

Write onto the board 8 + 6. Ask: *How do we work out the answer?* Encourage the children to say the next step and write up 8 + 2 + 6 − 2 = 10 + 4 = 14. Now ask: *What other subtraction sentence can we make with 8, 6 and 14?* Write up 6 + 8 = 14. Now ask: *What subtraction sentences can we make with these three numbers?* Write up 14 − 8 = 6 and 14 − 6 = 8. Repeat this for another addition such as 9 + 7.

■ SCHOLASTIC

Curriculum objectives
● To add and subtract one-digit and two-digit numbers to 20.

Success criteria
● I can use addition facts I know to find new facts.
● I can use subtraction facts I know to find new facts.

You will need

Equipment
2, 2, 3, 3, 4, 4 dice per group; 1, 2, 3, 4, 5, 5 dice per group; 1, 1, 2, 2, 3, 3 dice for less confident learners as appropriate

Differentiation

Less confident learners
Decide whether to use a 1, 1, 2, 2, 3, 3 dice and a 1, 2, 3, 4, 5, 5 dice.

More confident learners
Challenge the children to write two different 'teens' addition sentences based on the same two dice throws. For example, they could use 4 and 5 to make 14 + 5 = 19 or 15 + 4 = 19.

Lesson 2
Oral and mental starter 76

Main teaching activities

Whole-class work: Remind the children that they know the addition and subtraction facts to 5 + 5. Write 4 + 3 on the board and ask: *What is 4 add 3?* Write the answer. Now write 14 + 3 and ask:

● *What is 14 add 3?*
● *How did you work that out?*
● *What do you notice about 4 + 3 and 14 + 3?*

Discuss how the units are the same in both calculations, because 14 + 3 is the same as 10 + 4 + 3. Discuss how rapid recall of addition facts like this can be used to work out facts that we do not know. Repeat this with, for example, 8 − 5 and 18 − 5.

Now write 5 + 3 and ask:

● *What is 5 add 3?*
● *So what is 15 add 3?*
● *What would 13 + 5 be?*
● *What do you notice?*

Discuss again how rapid recall of a fact can help us to work out facts that we do not know.

Paired work: Ask the children to work in pairs with a dice labelled 2, 2, 3, 3, 4, 4 and a dice labelled 1, 2, 3, 4, 5, 5. They take turns to roll both dice, add the two scores and write an addition sentence (such as 4 + 5 = 9). Then they add 10 to one of their dice scores and write a new addition sentence (such as 14 + 5 = 19). They repeat this until they have rolled the two dice ten times.

Progress check: Ask a group to talk about what they've done so far:

● *How did you find the answer to that addition sentence?*
● *Did anyone work it out a different way?*
● *Tell me another addition sentence that uses those numbers.*
● *Tell me two subtraction sentences that use those numbers.*

Review

Ask children from each group to give examples of number sentences. Invite them to write their number sentences on the board for the other children to solve. Ask questions such as:

● *How did you work that out?*
● *Who used a different way of working?*
● *How does knowing some addition facts help you to add 'teens' numbers?*

Finish by asking some oral questions, such as: 15 + 3, 17 + 2, 13 + 6.

Curriculum objectives
● To add and subtract one-digit and two-digit numbers to 20.

Success criteria
● I can use number trios to find addition and subtraction sentences up to 20.

You will need
General resources
'Number cards 0–20'

Differentiation
Less confident learners
Decide whether to limit the children to number cards 0–9.

More confident learners
Challenge the children to write 15 pairs of subtraction sentences.

Lesson 3 — Oral and mental starter 79

Main teaching activities

Whole-class work: Explain that today, the children will be using subtraction facts that they already know to help them to find other facts that they do not know. Write 8 − 5 on the board and ask: *What is eight subtract five? So what is 18 subtract 5? How did you work that out?* Discuss how these two subtractions involve the same change in the units and no change in the tens. Repeat this for further examples such as 9 − 3 and 8 − 4.

Group work: Ask the children to work in pairs. They shuffle a set of 0-20 number cards. They take turns to take the top two cards (for example, 4 and 9). They arrange the numbers to make a subtraction sentence: 9 − 4 = ? They write this down, then write a 'teens' sentence: 19 − 4 = ? Finally, they write the answers to both sentences. Ask the children to write ten pairs of subtraction sentences in this way.

Progress check: Ask the children to look at one pair of subtraction sentences such as 6 − 2 = 4 and 16 − 4 = 2. Say: *Tell me another pair of subtraction sentences that use these numbers.* Discuss how they worked out the answers.

Review

Review the children's work by asking children from each group to write a set of subtraction sentences on the board for the others to solve. Discuss how rapid recall of subtraction facts can be used to find other facts that are not known. Ask: *How did you work that out? Who did this a different way? How would you work out 19 − 8?*

Curriculum objectives
● To add and subtract one-digit and two-digit numbers to 20, including zero.
● To solve one-step problems involving addition and subtraction, using objects and pictorial representations, and missing number problems.

Success criteria
● I can add and subtract up to a total of 20.

You will need
Photocopiable sheets
'Addition and subtraction (1)'

General resources
'Number line 0–20'; 'Number cards 0–20'

Equipment
Price labels 1p–20p; 2, 2, 3, 3, 4, 4 dice; 1, 2, 3, 4, 5, 5 dice; 1p, 2p, 5p, 10p, 20p coins

Differentiation
Less confident learners
Provide a 'Number line 0–20' for support.

More confident learners
Write more problems, but using different numbers, for another child to solve.

Lesson 4 — Oral and mental starter 79

Main teaching activities

Whole-class work: Review the main teaching activities from lessons 2 and 3 by writing questions on the board (see below). Ask the children to explain how they worked out each answer. Check that they are confident with the strategy of using known number facts and place value to work out unknown facts using Number cards to generate number sentences. If necessary, write and discuss further examples.

Independent work: Provide photocopiable page 'Addition and subtraction 1' from the CD-ROM. This photocopiable page contains a mixture of addition and subtraction sentences for the children to complete. Encourage them to work quickly and efficiently, using number facts they know to work out unknown facts.

Progress check: Invite the children to stop work after a few minutes. Review the first example from the photocopiable sheet together. Ask questions such as: *How did you work out the answer? Who did this a different way?*

$$5 + 2 =$$
$$15 + 2 =$$
$$12 + 5 =$$

$$5 - 2 =$$
$$15 - 2 =$$

Review

Choose examples from the photocopiable sheet. Write the number sentences on the board. Encourage the children to answer swiftly and to explain how they worked out their answers. Ask questions such as: *How did you work that out? Who used a different way? What is 7 + 2? So what is 17 + 2? So what is 12 + 7? What is 7 − 2? So what is 17 − 2?*

SCHOLASTIC

Lesson 5

Curriculum objectives
● To add and subtract one-
digit and two-digit numbers
to 20.
● To solve one-step problems
that involve addition and
subtraction.
Success criteria
● I can add and subtract up
to a total of 20.

You will need
General resources
'Number line 0–20'
Equipment
Price labels 1p–20p; pots
of 1p, 2p, 5p, 10p and 20p
coins

Differentiation
Less confident learners
Decide whether to provide
coins so that the children can
model the addition sentences
with the coins.
More confident learners
Challenge the children to
calculate totals beyond 20p,
such as 11p + 15p.

Main teaching activities

Whole-class work: Explain to the children that in this lesson they will be
adding and subtracting up to 20. They will be using pairs of price labels to
make totals and then finding the change from 20p. Write onto the board
7p + 9p and ask: *How shall we work out this total?* Children may suggest
making it 9p + 7p, then making a 10 and adding what is left. Write the total
onto the board and ask: *How much change will I have from 20p? How will you
work that out?* Discuss methods chosen, such as knowing that 16 + 4 is 20
(from 6 + 4 = 10).

Paired work: Provide each pair with a set of price labels 1p–20p. They spread
the labels out, face up, then take turns to choose two labels whose total they
think is 20p or less. They total to check, then work out the change from 20p.
They record their addition sentence, and a subtraction sentence from 20p
on paper.

Progress check: Ask questions such as:
● *Which labels do you think will total to 20p or less?*
● *How did you make that decision?*
● *How did you total ... and ...?*
● *How did you work out the change form 20p?*

Review

Invite the children to give examples of their addition sentences and ask the
other children to suggest ways of totalling. Write some examples onto the
board. Then ask:
● *How could we find the change from 20p for ...?*
Discuss what the children have learned this week. Encourage them to say what
they feel confident in and in which areas they think they need further practice.

Fractions

Expected prior learning

Children should be able to:

- find half of a quantity, length or shape
- find a quarter of a quantity, length or shape.

Topic	Curriculum objectives	Expected outcomes
Fractions	**Lesson 1**	
	To recognise, find and name a half as one of two equal parts of an object, shape or quantity. To recognise, find and name a quarter as one of four equal parts of an object, shape or quantity.	Find halves and quarters of shapes.
	Lesson 2	
	To recognise, find and name a half as one of two equal parts of an object, shape or quantity. To recognise, find and name a quarter as one of four equal parts of an object, shape or quantity.	Find halves and quarters of lengths.
	Lesson 3	
	To recognise, find and name a half as one of two equal parts of an object, shape or quantity. To recognise, find and name a quarter as one of four equal parts of an object, shape or quantity.	Find halves and quarters of quantities.
	Lesson 4	
	To recognise, find and name a half as one of two equal parts of an object, shape or quantity. To recognise, find and name a quarter as one of four equal parts of an object, shape or quantity.	Identify shapes that have been halved or quartered.
	Lesson 5	
	To recognise, find and name a half as one of two equal parts of an object, shape or quantity. To recognise, find and name a quarter as one of four equal parts of an object, shape or quantity.	Find halves and quarters of shapes and quantities.

Preparation

Lesson 1: prepare paper squares, rectangles and circles, one of each per child (with some spares)

Lesson 2: prepare strips of paper long enough to be folded into quarters; cut a metre long strip of paper

Lesson 4: copy 'Fractions of shapes', one per child; copy and enlarge 'Fractions of shapes' to A3; prepare paper squares, rectangles and circles for less confident learners as appropriate

Lesson 5: copy 'Shade the fraction', one per child; prepare the large paper circle

You will need

Photocopiable sheets

'Fractions of shapes'; 'Shade the fraction'

Equipment

Interlocking cubes; paper squares, rectangles, circles; scissors; large paper circle; black marker; coloured crayons; metre length strip of paper; strips of paper long enough for the children to fold into quarters; Blu-Tack®; squared paper

Further practice

Photocopiable sheets

'Shape fractions'; 'Colour fractions'

Oral and mental starters for week 3

See bank of starters on page 247. Oral and mental starters are also on the CD-ROM.

79 Make 10 and add

80 Add to make 20

81 Subtract from 20

Overview of progression

Children find halves and quarters of shapes. They repeat this for lengths, folding lengths of paper. They then work with quantities, finding halves and quarters, and extend this to three-quarters. They begin to know that two quarters is equivalent to a half, that three-quarters is three quarters, or a half and a quarter. They return to working with shapes for the final two lessons, and work with shapes that have or have not lines to make halves and quarters. By the end of these five lessons children should understand that two halves of a shape, length or quantity are equal, and similarly for quarters, that each quarter is the same size.

Watch out for

Children may not appreciate that, for example, the two halves of a shape, length or quantity must be equal. Provide opportunities to make direct comparisons, by, for example, placing the two halves one on top of the other to see these are equal. The same issue may arise with quarters, and can be resolved in the same way.

Creative context

Encourage the children to use the vocabulary of fractions in other contexts. For example, half an hour; when sharing an orange, are the two halves equal; when cutting a pie into quarters, are all the pieces the same size?

Vocabulary

fraction, half, quarter, whole

Curriculum objectives
● To recognise, find and name a half as one of two equal parts of a shape.
● To recognise, find and name a quarter as one of four equal parts of a shape.

Success criteria
● I can find halves and quarters of shapes.

You will need
Equipment
Paper squares, rectangles, and circles; scissors

Differentiation
Less confident learners
Observe the children working. They will need to fold and cut neatly.

More confident learners
Challenge the children to find a different way to fold the rectangle to make four identical pieces, each of which is a quarter of the rectangle.

Lesson I

Oral and mental starter 79

Main teaching activities

Whole-class work: Explain to the children that in this lesson they will be finding halves and quarters of shapes. Provide every child with a paper square and scissors. Ask the children to follow you as you fold a paper square in half to make a rectangle shape. Hold this up and ask: *What shape have I made? Copy my shape. Hold up your shape now.* Check that the children have folded to make a rectangle. Now show them how to fold this in half again to make a square shape again. Ask the children to hold up the shape they have made for you to check. Now demonstrate how to open out the whole square and cut along the fold lines, first of all to make two halves. Ask the children to cut to make two halves and when you say *Show me*, they hold up their halves, one in each hand. Now ask them to fold each half in half to make the small square and to cut along the fold line. The children should now have four small squares. Ask the children to place their four small squares back into a large square shape for you to observe. Say:

- *Hold up a small square. How much is that? Is it half of the square? Is it a quarter of the square?*
- *How many pieces do you need to make half of the square? Hold them up to show me.*
- *How many pieces do you need to make a whole square? How much is each of those pieces worth?*

Independent work: Provide each child with a paper circle. Ask them to fold it in half, then half again, and to cut along the lines to make four quarters.

Progress check: After a few minutes of cutting, ask the children to hold up a quarter of their circle when you say *Show me.* Repeat this for two quarters, and say: *How much is two quarters of a circle?* Now ask the children to hold up three-quarters of their circle. Ask: *How many pieces is that? How many pieces are left on the table? So how many quarters will make a whole circle?*

Independent work: Repeat the activity this time with a paper rectangle, folding and cutting to make quarters.

Review

Invite children to hold up half of their paper rectangle and ask: *How many pieces are you holding up? So two pieces make a half. How much is one piece?* Ask the children to put the four pieces, one on top of each other. Now ask: *Are the pieces the same shape? Are they the same size?* Agree that all four pieces are the same shape and size. Ask: *How many pieces are there in the whole rectangle?*

Curriculum objectives
● To recognise, find and name a half as one of two equal parts of an object.
● To recognise, find and name a quarter as one of four equal parts of an object.

Success criteria
● I can find halves and quarters of lengths.

You will need
Equipment
Scissors; black marker; metre length strip of paper; strips of paper long enough for the children to fold into quarters

Differentiation
Less confident learners
Observe the children as they fold to ensure that the folds are reasonably accurate.

More confident learners
Ask the children in a group to compare their half-strips by length and then their quarter-strips. What do they notice?

Lesson 2
Oral and mental starter 80

Main teaching activities

Whole-class work: Explain that in this lesson children will find quarters, halves, and whole lengths. Show the metre long strip of paper and ask: *How can I find half of this length of paper?* Fold it in half, name the two pieces as half each, then fold again to show quarters. Unfold it, mark each fold with a black marker so that it is clear, and ask questions such as: *How many halves make a whole length? How many quarters make a half?*

Now invite a child to fold a shorter strip of paper into half, and another child to fold a much longer strip of paper into quarters. Say, for example: *Which is longer? Half of the shorter strip or a quarter of the longer strip?* Discuss how a quarter of a longer strip can be longer than half of a shorter strip.

Independent work: Provide each child with a strip of paper. Ask the children to take one strip, fold it in half, then in quarters.

Progress check: After a few minutes for folding, ask the children to hold up their strip of paper folded in half. Repeat this to show one quarter. Finally ask the children to hold up the paper to show the whole strip.

Group work: Ask the children to work in groups of four. They take turns to say: *Show me half. Show me a quarter. Show me the whole strip.*

Review

Have available various lengths of paper strips. Invite two children to come to the front and each choose a different length strip. Say: *Which do you think will be longer? A quarter of this strip or half of this strip?* Invite the children at the front to fold then make the comparison. Then ask: *Did you make a good estimate?* Repeat this for another pair of strips and two more children.

Curriculum objectives
● To recognise, find and name a half as one of two equal parts of an object, shape or quantity.
● To recognise, find and name a quarter as one of four equal parts of an object, shape or quantity.

Success criteria
● I can find halves and quarters of quantities.

You will need
Equipment
Interlocking cubes

Differentiation
Less confident learners
Work as a group to find quarter, half and three-quarters.

More confident learners
Repeat the activity for 24 cubes.

Lesson 3
Oral and mental starter 79

Main teaching activities

Whole-class work: Invite a child to count out eight interlocking cubes in front of the class. Ask the child to make a tower of eight, then break the tower into two equal pieces. Ask: *How many cubes are in each piece? So four is half of eight.* Now ask the child to break the two four towers into halves again, and ask: *How many are in each of these small towers? So how many towers of 2 do we have? Each tower is a quarter of 8. How many is a quarter of 8? Half of 8?*

Paired work: Ask the children to work in pairs to make a tower of 12. They find half and a quarter of the tower. Ask them to record this as: Half of 12 is ☐. Quarter of 12 is ☐. Write these sentences onto the board for all to see. They can repeat this for 16 cubes, then 20 cubes.

Progress check: Ask pairs to explain how they find half and a quarter of 12. *How much would two halves be? What do we call this?*

Review

Ask the children questions about 16 cubes. For example: *How many is half of 16? How many is a quarter of 16? How many is two quarters of 16? What do we call two quarters? How many is two halves of 16? What do we call two halves?* Repeat this for 20 cubes.

Curriculum objectives
- To recognise, find and name a half as one of two equal parts of a shape.
- To recognise, find and name a quarter as one of four equal parts of a shape.

Success criteria
- I can find shapes that have been cut into halves or quarters.

You will need
Photocopiable sheets
'Fractions of shapes'

Equipment
Paper squares, rectangles, circles; Blu-Tack®

Differentiation
Less confident learners

Children may find it helpful to make quartered shapes by folding paper shapes.

More confident learners

Encourage the children to discuss why a shape is or is not halved or quartered.

Curriculum objectives
- To recognise, find and name a half as one of two equal parts of shapes and quantities.
- To recognise, find and name a quarter as one of four equal parts of shapes and quantities.

Success criteria
- I can find halves and quarters of shapes and quantities.

You will need
Photocopiable sheets
'Shade the fraction'

Equipment
Large paper circle; black marker; coloured crayons; squared paper

Differentiation
Less confident learners

Work as a group. Encourage children to use the vocabulary of fractions.

More confident learners

Provide squared paper and ask children to make their own 12-square rectangle, different from the one on the photocopiable page. Then ask them to shade each quarter a different colour.

Lesson 4   Oral and mental starter 80

Main teaching activities

Whole-class work: Remind the children of the work that they have done so far this week. Ask questions such as: *How many quarters make a whole one? How many halves make a whole one?* Discuss how the two halves, or the quarters, must be equal in size and shape.

Independent work: Ask the children to complete photocopiable page 'Fractions of shapes' from the CD-ROM.

Progress check: Ask questions such as:
- *How do you know that that shape has been cut in half?*
- *How do you know that that shape has been cut into quarters?*
- *How many halves make a whole?*
- *What about this shape? How do you know that it has not been cut in half?*
- *How do you know that that shape has not been cut into quarters?*

Review

Stick the A3 version of photocopiable page 'Fractions of shapes' onto the board. Ask the children to tell you the answer for each of the shapes. Discuss, for example, the square that is not cut into halves. Ask: *How do you know?* Repeat this for other shapes that are not cut into halves or quarters.

Lesson 5   Oral and mental starter 81

Main teaching activities

Whole-class work: Show the large paper circle and ask a child to fold it into two halves. Open out the circle, and draw a line with a black marker along the fold line. Now ask a child to refold the circle along the half line, and then fold again to make quarters. Open out the circle, and mark the quarters fold line with a black marker. Now ask questions such as: *How many halves does the circle have? How many quarters are there in the whole circle? How many quarters are there in half the circle*

Independent work: Provide photocopiable page 'Shade the fraction' from the CD-ROM and a coloured crayon for each child. Read through the instructions for the first part of photocopiable page 'Shade the fraction', and ask the children to follow the instructions to colour in the shapes.

Progress check: Ask about one of the shapes on the photocopiable sheet:
- *Which part of the shape have you shaded?*
- *What fraction have you shaded?*

Independent work: Ask the children to read the rest of the instructions with you and then they can continue with their work.

Review

Draw a circle on the board, and draw a line through the circle, but one which clearly does not cut it into two halves. Ask: *Have I made two halves? Why do you think that?* Explain that a line through a shape will not always make two halves. Repeat this, drawing first a square, then a rectangle, and finally an isosceles triangle. Ask: *What have you learned this week?* Invite the children to talk to their partner about what they have learned, where they feel confident, and where they need further help.

Multiplication and division

Expected prior learning

Children should be able to:

- count in 2s, 5s and 10s.

Topic	Curriculum objectives	Expected outcomes
Multiplication and division	**Lesson 1**	
	To solve one-step problems involving multiplication and division, calculating the answer using objects, pictorial representations and arrays with the support of the teacher.	Use counting in twos to find multiplication and division facts.
	Lesson 2	
	To solve one-step problems involving multiplication and division, calculating the answer using objects, pictorial representations and arrays with the support of the teacher.	Use counting in twos to find multiplication and division facts.
	Lesson 3	
	To solve one-step problems involving multiplication and division, calculating the answer using objects, pictorial representations and arrays with the support of the teacher.	Use counting in twos, fives and tens to find multiplication and division facts.
	Lesson 4	
	To solve one-step problems involving multiplication and division, calculating the answer using objects, pictorial representations and arrays with the support of the teacher.	Use counting in twos, fives and tens to find multiplication and division facts.
	Lesson 5	
	To solve one-step problems involving multiplication and division, calculating the answer using objects, pictorial representations and arrays with the support of the teacher.	Use counting in twos, fives and tens to find multiplication and division facts.

Preparation

Lesson 1: copy 'Ladybird doubles', one per pair

Lesson 2: use 'Ladybird doubles' from lesson 1, or copy 'Ladybird doubles', one per pair

Lesson 3: copy 'Equal groups', one per child

Lesson 4: copy 'Sharing equally', one per child

Lesson 5: copy 'Arrays', one per child; copy and enlarge on to squared paper and 'Arrays' to A3

You will need

Photocopiable sheets

'Ladybird doubles'; 'Equal groups'; 'Sharing equally'; 'Arrays'

General resources

Squared paper

Equipment

Scissors; interlocking cubes; paper plates; Blu-Tack®

Further practice

Photocopiable sheets

'Groups'; 'Fair shares'

Oral and mental starters for week 4

See bank of starters on page 246. Oral and mental starters are also on the CD-ROM.

73 Count in 2s

74 Count in 5s

75 Count in 10s

Overview of progression

Children begin the week with doubling and halving, and link this to counting in twos. They then make groups of five for given numbers of cubes and check by counting in fives to find out how many there are in total. They share out given quantities of cubes between 2, 5 or 10 plates and check their sharing by counting up in 2s, 5s or 10s, keeping a tally with their fingers to see how many groups they count. In lesson 5, the children make arrays with cubes, and complete grouping and sharing sentences for each array.

Watch out for

Where children have difficulties 'reading' arrays, provide interlocking cubes for them to model the arrays. For example, for a 5 × 2 array, they make two towers of five cubes, each tower in a different colour. Then they make a 2 × 5 array, with each tower of 2 in a different colour.

Creative context

Encourage the children to talk about sharing fairly in different contexts, such as sharing out sweets so that everyone in the group has the same number. Talk about how the children feel if something is not shared out fairly.

Vocabulary

array, counting in fives, counting in tens, counting in twos, grouping, sharing

■SCHOLASTIC

Curriculum objectives
● To solve one-step problems involving multiplication, calculating the answer using pictorial representations with the support of the teacher.

Success criteria
● I can work out double facts.

You will need
Photocopiable sheets
'Ladybird doubles'

Equipment
Scissors

Differentiation
Less confident learners
Decide whether to use just the double 1–5 cards at this stage.

More confident learners
Challenge the children to work quickly and to try to recall the answers.

Lesson 1 — Oral and mental starter 73

Main teaching activities

Whole-class work: Remind the children of the work they have previously done on the subject of doubles and halves. Show the children the cards from photocopiable page 'Ladybird doubles' from the CD-ROM. Hold up a card that shows 6 to 10 double spots, and cover one wing or fold the ladybird in half. Ask: *How many spots can you see? So what is double …? How did you work that out?* Praise those children who just 'knew' the answer. Discuss ways of working out the answer, such as counting on in ones, keeping a tally on fingers from the original quantity. Unfold the ladybird and count on in ones to demonstrate that this card represents a double number. Repeat this for another card.

Paired work: Provide each pair with photocopiable page 'Ladybird doubles' and a pair of scissors. Ask the children to cut out the cards, then to fold them so that just one wing shows. Now ask them to shuffle the cards and to take turns to show a folded ladybird. Their partner says how many spots there are and what the double of that quantity is. They unfold and count on to check the answer.

Progress check: Invite pairs to explain how they worked out the double fact. Ask questions such as: *What is double 4? So what is half of 4? What is double 10? So what is half of 10?*

Review

Say: *I'm thinking of a number. Half of it is 4. What is my number?* Repeat this for other numbers from 1 to 10, out of counting order, to encourage rapid recall.

Curriculum objectives
● To solve one-step problems involving division, calculating the answer using pictorial representations with the support of the teacher.

Success criteria
● I can work out half of a quantity.

You will need
Photocopiable sheets
'Ladybird doubles'

Equipment
Scissors

Differentiation
Less confident learners
Decide whether to work as a group to find the half numbers. Encourage the children to use the vocabulary of fractions appropriately.

More confident learners
Decide whether to extend this to even numbers greater than 20. Children can draw their own ladybird wings and spots, then cut these out.

Lesson 2 — Oral and mental starter 73

Main teaching activities

Whole-class work: Use the cards from 'Ladybird doubles' from the CD-ROM, and show a card with both wings open. Ask: *What number does this show? So what is half of that? Fold the card to show the half number.*

Paired work: Ask the children to work in pairs, and to find the half number of the opened-out ladybirds. (If the children are using new copies of 'Ladybird doubles, give them scissors to cut out the cards.) The children write a 'halving' sentence for each ladybird. For example, 7 is half of 14.

Progress check: Ask pairs questions such as: *What is half of 18? So what is double 9? What is half of 14? What is double 7?*

Review

Ask questions such as:
● *I'm thinking of a number. I have halved it and the answer is 7. What was my number? How do you know that?*
● *I'm thinking of a number. I've doubled it and the answer is 16. What was my number? How did you work that out?*
● *I'm thinking of a number. It is half of 4. Now I add one to my number. What is double this number?*

Invite four children to come to the front of the class. Count out eight counters. Ask each of the children at the front of the class to hold out a hand. Invite another child to see if the counters can be shared out equally by putting counters into the outstretched hands. Repeat for 12, then 16 counters. Now put out 15 counters and repeat. Discuss how it is not always possible to share equally between four – into quarters.

Curriculum objectives

● To solve one-step problems involving multiplication, calculating the answer using pictorial representations with the support of the teacher.

Success criteria

● I can use pictures to show equal groups.

You will need

Photocopiable sheets

'Equal groups'

Equipment

Interlocking cubes

Differentiation

Less confident learners

If children are unsure, provide cubes for modelling the grouping questions.

More confident learners

Encourage the children to try to give the answers quickly, either by counting or by fast recall.

Lesson 3

Oral and mental starter 74

Main teaching activities

Whole-class work: Put out ten cubes and ask a child to make groups of two. Say: *How many groups of two are there? Yes, five. How many cubes are there altogether? Count in twos to find out. So five groups of two is* ☐*? Yes, five groups of two is ten.* Repeat this for other quantities, such as making two groups of five, two groups of ten, and so on.

Independent work: Provide photocopiable page 'Equal groups' from the CD-ROM. Ask the children to make groups by circling with their pencils.

Progress check: Ask the children questions such as:

● *How many groups are there?*
● *How many are there in each group?*
● *So ... groups of ... is* ☐*?*

Review

Repeat the main activity, asking for example, for three groups of five, nine groups of two, and so on. Ask questions such as: *How many groups are there? How many are there in each group? So how many are there altogether? How did you work that out?* Again encourage the children to count in twos, fives or tens in order to find the solution.

Curriculum objective

● To solve one-step problems involving division, calculating the answer using pictorial representations with the support of the teacher

Success criteria

● I can use pictures to show equal sharing.

You will need

Photocopiable sheets

'Sharing equally'

Equipment

Interlocking cubes; paper plates

Differentiation

Less confident learners

If children need more support, provide cubes so that they can model the questions with these.

More confident learners

Encourage the children to use counting up to help them to check their answers.

Lesson 4

Oral and mental starter 74

Main teaching activities

Whole-class work: Put out two paper plates and 16 cubes. Do not tell the children how many cubes there are yet. Now invite a child to count the cubes and to say how many there are. Ask the child to share the cubes equally between the two plates. Then say: *How many cubes are there altogether? How many are there on each plate? So 16 shared by two is how many?* Ask the children to count in twos to 16, keeping a tally with their fingers. Repeat this for other quantities, such as 10 and 5 plates, and 20 and 10 plates.

Independent work: Ask children to complete photocopiable page 'Sharing equally' from the CD-ROM. They share the fruits onto plates, then complete a sharing sentence for each picture.

Progress check: Ask questions children such as:

● *How many are there altogether? How many plates are there? So how many fruit go onto each plate?*
● *Have you shared them equally between the plates? How many are on each plate?*
● *Say the sharing sentence for me.*

Review

Put out 30 cubes. This time invite a child to share the cubes into five piles. Ask another child to make a tower with each pile of cubes. Show the children the five towers of six cubes and ask: *What is 30 shared by 5?* Ask the children to count up from 0 in 5s to 30, keeping a tally with their fingers. Repeat this for, for example, 28 shared by 2, and 25 shared by 5.

Curriculum objectives

● To solve one-step problems involving multiplication and division, calculating the answer using arrays with the support of the teacher.

Success criteria

● I can use arrays to show equal groups and equal sharing.

You will need

Photocopiable sheets

'Arrays'

General resources

Squared paper

Equipment

Blu-Tack®; interlocking cubes; blackmarker

Differentiation

Less confident learners

Decide whether to work together as a group to complete photocopiable page 'Arrays'.

More confident learners

When the children have completed photocopiable page 'Arrays', they can use squared paper to make their own rectangles and squares, and write grouping and sharing sentences for each one.

Main teaching activities

Whole-class work: Provide the children with interlocking cubes and ask them to make two towers of five cubes. Say: *How many groups of five are there? So two groups of five is how many?* Say together: *two groups of five is ten.* Now say: *There are ten cubes altogether. How many towers of 5 do you have? So ten shared by five is two.* Now stick up the enlarged version of squared paper. Use a black marker to outline a 5 × 2 array. Invite a child to count how many squares there are inside the black lines and agree that there are ten. Count together along the 'five' side and agree that there are two lines of five squares. Repeat this counting along the 'two' side and agree that there are five lines of two squares. Ask: *How many groups of two are there? So five groups of two is ten. And how many groups of five are there? So two groups of five is ten.* Say: *What is 10 shared by 2?* (Point to the '5' side.) *What is 10 shared by 5?* (Point to the '2' side.)

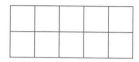

Paired work: Ask the children to work in pairs but give each child their own copy of photocopiable page 'Arrays' from the CD-ROM. They work together to complete the grouping and sharing sentences.

Progress check: Check pairs of children's work. Ask questions such as:

● *How many groups of ... are there?*
● *How many squares are there altogether?*

Review

Stick the A3 version of photocopiable page 'Arrays' onto the board. Work through the photocopiable page together to complete the grouping and sharing sentences. Ask questions such as:

● *How many squares are there here?*
● *How many in this column?*
● *How many in this row?*
● *Tell me a grouping sentence for this?*
● *Who can tell me another grouping sentence?*
● *Tell me a sharing sentence for this?*
● *Who can tell me another grouping sentence?*

Time and using standard units

Expected prior learning

Children should be able to:

- say o'clock times.

Topic	Curriculum objectives	Expected outcomes
Measurement	**Lesson 1**	
	To recognise and use language relating to dates, including days of the week, weeks, months and years.	Know the names of the days of the week and the months of the year.
	To tell the time to the hour and half past the hour and draw the hands on a clock face to show these times.	Tell the time to the hour and half hour.
	Lesson 2	
	To recognise and use language relating to dates, including days of the week, weeks, months and years.	Know the names of the days of the week and the months of the year.
	To tell the time to the hour and half past the hour and draw the hands on a clock face to show these times.	Tell the time to the hour and half hour.
	Lesson 3	
	To measure and begin to record the following: • lengths and heights • mass/weight • capacity and volume • time (hours, minutes, seconds).	Begin to use standard units: metres; 100g and kg; 100ml and litre. Use a simple ruler to measure a short line.
	Lesson 4	
	To measure and begin to record the following: • lengths and heights • mass/weight • capacity and volume • time (hours, minutes, seconds).	Begin to use standard units: metres; 100g and kg; 100ml and litre. Use a simple ruler to measure a short line.
	Lesson 5	
	To measure and begin to record the following: • lengths and heights • mass/weight • capacity and volume • time (hours, minutes, seconds).	Begin to use standard units: metres; 100g and kg; 100ml and litre. Use a simple ruler to measure a short line.

Preparation

Lesson 2: ensure pairs of children have access to a PC or laptop

Lesson 3: copy 'Wormy lengths', one per child; prepare a tray of items that are about 10cm in length, or shorter

You will need

Photocopiable sheets
'Wormy lengths'

General resources
'Clock faces'; interactive activity 'Telling the time'

Equipment
Teaching clock; independent whiteboards and pens; interlocking cubes; metre sticks; 10–12cm rulers (as available); tray of items measuring 10cm or less; ribbons or paper strips which measure less than, more than, or about the same as a metre; 20ml containers, 100ml containers, 1 litre containers; sand or water for pouring; 100g and 1kg weights; small lightweight plastic boxes with lids, such as margarine tubs; bucket balance; sponge cake ingredients – see activity 7

Further practice

As the work this week is practical, repeat the activities to reinforce the children's measuring skills.

Oral and mental starters for week 5

See bank of starters on page 247. Oral and mental starters are also on the CD-ROM.

79 Make 10 and add

80 Add to make 20

81 Subtract from 20

82 Add and subtract to 20

Overview of progression

Children begin the week by reviewing days of the week and months of the year. They order the months of the year. They read o'clock and half-past times, then draw the hands onto clock faces to show these times, being careful to draw the hands to appropriate lengths and to show what happens to the hour hand for half-past times. They then measure lengths with a 10cm ruler. They use metre rules to estimate and compare lengths. They estimate and measure with 20ml, 100ml and 1 litre, and with 100g and 1kg.

Watch out for

Check that the children are confident with which is the hour hand and which is the minute hand and that they draw these appropriately. Check also that they understand what happens to the hour hand for half-past times. Provide a geared clock for them to turn the hands to observe what happens to both hands as time passes.

Creative context

Find stories which refer to days, months, seasons, so that children hear these words in context. Also, children will enjoy baking cakes using the recipe for activity 7 in lesson 3. This involves weighing out accurately 100g of ingredients.

Vocabulary

afternoon, balance, block graph, capacity, centimetre (cm), **clock**, comparatives such as longer/longest, container, day, days of the week, deep, depth, diagram, evening, graph, guess, hands, heavier/heaviest, height, high, holds more/holds most, hour, information, label, length, list, long, low, measure, measuring jug, metre (m), metre stick, midnight, month, months, morning, narrow, night, pictogram, ruler, scales, shallow, short, size, table, tall, tape measure, thick, thin, time, title, unit, week, weigh, weight, wide, width, year

SUMMER 2 · WEEK 5 · Time and using standard units

SCHOLASTIC

100 MATHS LESSONS · YEAR 1 ■ 235

Curriculum objectives

● To recognise and use language relating to dates, including days of the week and months of the year.
● To tell the time to the hour and half past the hour and draw the hands on a clock face to show these times.

Success criteria

● I can say the names of the days of the week.
● I can say the names of the months of the year.
● I can read o'clock and half past times.

You will need

General resources

'Clock faces'; interactive activity 'Telling the time'

Equipment

Teaching clock; individual whiteboards and pens

Differentiation

Less confident learners

Lesson 1: Decide whether to ask an adult to work with this group and to encourage the children to say where each hand goes for each time.

Lesson 2: Decide whether to ask an adult to work with the group. The adult says an o'clock or half past time, then the children draw the clock hands. The adult sets the teaching clock for the children to compare with their drawing.

More confident learners

Lesson 1: When the children have completed 'Telling the time' challenge them to take turns to set the teaching clock to o'clock and half-past times for the others to say the time.

Lesson 2: Ask the children to be as accurate as possible with the placing and length of the hands and to select other times that they can work with.

Lessons 1 and 2   Oral and mental starter 79

Main teaching activities

For each of these lessons, carry out the whole-class activities, and then ask the children to do that lesson's pupil activity.

Whole-class work: Explain that during this week children will be learning more about time and measuring. Begin by saying the days of the week in order. Ask questions such as: *What day is it today? What day was it yesterday? What day will it be tomorrow? What day will it be the day after Friday...?* Provide individual whiteboards and pens and ask the children to write on them what you say and hold their boards up when you say *Show me.* Say, for example: *Write today's day on your board. Write the day before Sunday... the day after Monday....*

Now invite twelve children to stand at the front of the class. Give each of them a month to write, then hold up, on their whiteboards. Ask the other children to say where each child should stand to put the months in order. Now invite the other children to follow your instructions: *Caroline, pick the month that reads February; Mark, write the month before... after July....*

Hold up the teaching clock, set to an o'clock time. Ask questions, such as: *What time does the clock show? How do you know that? Where is the hour hand? Where is the minute hand? Which hand is the longer hand ... shorter hand?* Now set the clock to a half-past time and say: *What time does the clock show now? Where is the hour hand?* Check that the children see that it is between two hours. *Where is the minute hand?* Repeat this for another half-past time.

Lesson 1

Independent work: Provide the interactive activity 'Telling the time' on the CD-ROM and ask the children to match the times in words to the clock faces. Ask each child to read through the times before selecting them.

Progress check: Observe independent children at work. Ask questions such as:
- *Which is the longer hand?*
- *Where does it point for o'clock... half-past times?*
- *Where does the hour hand point for half-past times?*
- *Where does the minute hand point for half-past times?*

Lesson 2

Paired work: Provide each pair with general resource 'Clock faces'. They take turns to say an o'clock or half past time for their partner to draw the hands on a clock face. The other child checks to see if they agree.

Progress check: Ask pairs questions such as:
- *What time did you say?*
- *Where will the hour hand be?*
- *Where will the minute hand be?*

Review

Ask the children to say the times that you show on the teaching clock. Set several o'clock times, then several half past times. Now ask:
- *Where would the hour hand point for 8 o'clock?*
- *Where would the hour hand point for half past 4?*

Now invite the children to recite, with you, the days of the week in order. Ask questions such as:
- *What day comes before/after Sunday...?*
- *Which days do we come to school?*

Repeat this for the months of the year. Invite children to take a month card, and stand at the front of the class with it, out of order. Now invite children to offer to take the January card, and stand at the left hand side. Repeat for the other cards, until they are in order.

■SCHOLASTIC

Curriculum objectives
● To measure and begin to record the following: lengths and heights; mass/weight; capacity and volume.

Success criteria
● I can use a ruler and a metre stick to measure lengths.
● I can weigh out 100g and 1kg.
● I can pour out 100ml and 1 litre.

You will need
Photocopiable sheets
'Wormy lengths'

Equipment
Interlocking cubes; metre sticks; tray of items measuring 10cm or less; ribbons or paper strips which measure less than, more than, or about the same as a metre; 10–12cm rulers; 20ml containers, 100ml containers, 1 litre containers; sand or water for pouring; 100g and 1kg weights; small lightweight plastic boxes with lids, such as margarine tubs; bucket balance; sponge cake ingredients – see activity 7; ruler

Differentiation
Less confident learners
The children will benefit from opportunities to discuss what they are doing with an adult, so that they can experience hearing and using the vocabulary of measurement. They may also need more help with recording, such as a fuller explanation (with examples) of what is expected.

More confident learners
In activity 6, challenge the children to make different sand weights such as 50g, 100g and 300g. They should then find items in the classroom that they estimate weigh about the same as each of these.

Lesson 3
Oral and mental starter 81

Main teaching activities
Whole-class work: Explain to the children that in this lesson and in lessons 4 and 5, they will be learning more about measuring. Provide each child with a small (10–12 cm) ruler. Explain that this can be used for measuring things in centimetres. Ask the children to point on their ruler to the 1cm, 3cm... marks.

Now ask them to compare their ruler to their pencil. Ask: *Is your ruler longer or shorter than your pencil?* Provide everyone with an interlocking cube and ask them to place the cube against the ruler, lining up the beginning edge of both ruler and cube. Ask: *How long is the cube?* Write onto the board 2 centimetres. Explain that there is a short way of writing this and write underneath 2cm. Explain that this stands for 2 centimetres.

Put out a metre stick on each table and ask the group to place their rulers along the metre stick, again lining them up carefully. For a group of four children using a 10 cm ruler, this should measure 40cm and for 6 children 60cm and so on. Remind children that a metre stick measures 100cm.

Group work: Choose from the following activities for lessons 3, 4 and 5. If appropriate, after a short interval, ask them to move to a different activity.

1 Wormy lengths
Provide photocopiable page 'Wormy lengths' from the CD-ROM. Children estimate then measure the worms in centimetres.

2 Metre measure
The children work in pairs to estimate then compare strips of paper or ribbons with the metre stick. They record their estimate (shorter than, longer than or about the same as a metre) then their measure (shorter than, longer than, or about the same as a metre).

3 20ml and 100ml
Provide 20ml container, such as a medicine measurer, and a 100ml container. Ask the children to estimate, then find out by pouring, how many 20ml measures of sand or water will fill the 100ml container. Children record their estimates and measures on paper.

4 100ml and 1 litre
Repeat activity 4, this time to estimate then find out by pouring from a 100ml container into a 1 litre container.

5 100g and 1 kg
Provide a 100g weight. Ask the children to fill small boxes with lids with sand until they weigh the same as 100g. They then find how many boxes are needed to balance 1kg. They record their estimates and measures on paper.

6 Sponge cakes – this will need adult supervision
100g self raising flour, 100g butter or margarine, 100g caster sugar, 2 medium eggs, ½ teaspoon vanilla extract. Use a normal recipe method for sponge cake. The children weigh out the ingredients as accurately as they can.

Progress check: As groups work ask questions such as: *How did you make your estimate? Did you make a good estimate? How did you decide that?*

Review
Review one of the length activities, and ask questions such as: *Which was the longest... shortest worm? Do you all agree? Which items were about 10cm in length? Which items were shorter... longer than 10cm? What did you find in the classroom that was about 1 metre long? What was longer... shorter than a metre?*

(For lessons 4 and 5)

Curriculum objectives

● To measure and begin to record the following: lengths and heights; mass/weight; capacity and volume; time (hours, minutes, seconds).

Success criteria

● I can use a ruler and a metre stick to measure lengths.
● I can weigh out 100g and 1kg.
● I can pour out 100ml and 1 litre.

You will need

Equipment

Metre sticks; tray of items measuring 10cm or less; ribbons or paper strips which measure less than, more than, or about the same as a metre; 20ml containers, 100ml containers, 1 litre containers; sand or water for pouring; 100g and 1kg weights; small lightweight plastic boxes with lids, such as margarine tubs; bucket balance; sponge cake ingredients – see Lesson 3 activity 7; teaching clock; metre sticks

Differentiation

Less confident learners

Give children opportunities to discuss what they are doing with an adult, so that they can experience hearing and using the vocabulary of measurement.

More confident learners

Challenge the children to work out how many 100ml of water will fill a ½ litre container.

Lesson 4 — Oral and mental starter 82

Main teaching activities

Whole-class work: Show the children the 20ml, 100ml and litre containers. Ask questions such as:

● *Which do you think holds the most/least?*
● *Why do you think that?*

Explain how much each holds and write the shortened form onto the board: 20ml, 100ml, 1*l*.

Group work: Choose from the circus of activities in lesson 3 for each group. If appropriate, after half the available time, ask the children to move to a different activity.

Progress check: Ask questions such as:

● *How did you make your estimate?*
● *Did you make a good estimate?*
● *How did you decide that?*

Review

Review the capacity activities. Ask questions such as:

● *How many 20ml lots of water filled the 100ml container?*
● *How many 100ml lots of water filled the 1 litre container?*

If the more confident children have investigated how many 100ml fill a ½ litre container, ask them to explain to the others what they did and what they found out.

Lesson 5 — Oral and mental starter 82

Main teaching activities

Whole-class work: Show the children the 100g and the 1kg weights. Write onto the board 100 grams and 100g, and 1 kilogram and 1kg and explain that the g is short for grams and kg is short for kilograms.

Group work: Choose from the circus of activities in lesson 3 for each group. If appropriate, after half the available time, ask the children to move to a different activity.

Progress check: Ask questions such as:

● *How did you make your estimate?*
● *Did you make a good estimate?*
● *How did you decide that?*

Review

Review the 100g and 1kg activity. Ask: *How many 100g sand boxes balanced the 1kg?* If appropriate, ask the more confident children how many 100g sand boxes balanced ½ kg and how they found this out.

Remind the children that this week they have learned more about time, telling the time, and measuring lengths, weights and how much something holds. Ask the children to think about what they have learned this week and to discuss with their partner which areas they feel confident in, and in which areas they need further help.

2D and 3D shape recognition

Expected prior learning

Children should be able to:

- name some 2D shapes and 3D shapes.

Topic	Curriculum objectives	Expected outcomes
Geometry: properties of shape	**Lesson 1**	
	To recognise and name common 2D and 3D shapes, including: • 2D shapes [such as rectangles (including squares), circles and triangles] • 3D shapes [such as cuboids (including cubes), pyramids and spheres].	Name 2D shapes. Combine 2D shape tiles to make pictures and patterns.
	Lesson 2	
	Recognise and name common 2D and 3D shapes, including: • 2D shapes [such as rectangles (including squares), circles and triangles] • 3D shapes [such as cuboids (including cubes), pyramids and spheres].	Name 2D shapes. Combine 2D shape tiles to make pictures and patterns.
	Lesson 3	
	To recognise and name common 2D and 3D shapes, including: • 2D shapes [such as rectangles (including squares), circles and triangles] • 3D shapes [such as cuboids (including cubes), pyramids and spheres].	Sort 2D shapes. Recognise and talk about the properties of 2D shapes.
	Lesson 4	
	To recognise and name common 2D and 3D shapes, including: • 2D shapes [such as rectangles (including squares), circles and triangles] • 3D shapes [such as cuboids (including cubes), pyramids and spheres].	Name 2D and 3D shapes. Recognise and talk about the properties of 2D and 3D shapes.
	Lesson 5	
	To recognise and name common 2D and 3D shapes, including: • 2D shapes [such as rectangles (including squares), circles and triangles] • 3D shapes [such as cuboids (including cubes), pyramids and spheres].	Name 3D shapes. Recognise and talk about the properties of 3D shapes.

Preparation

Lesson 3: prepare sets of shapes by copying 'Shape tiles (1)' and 'Shape tiles (2)' onto card, one set per group and also one set per child; copy and enlarge 'Work mat' to A3, one per child; provide blank labels

Lesson 5: copy 'A house with a garage and a tree', one per child

You will need

Photocopiable sheets

'A house with a garage and a tree'

General resources

'Shape tiles (1)'; 'Shape tiles (2)'; 'Work mat'

Equipment

2D shape tiles of square, circle, rectangle, triangle for each small group; coloured paper or coloured sticky paper; scissors; glue sticks; A3 paper that can be photocopied; 3D shapes, including cubes, cuboids, pyramids, spheres, cylinders, cones; construction kits; building bricks, Plasticine®; pictures of buildings

Further practice

Photocopiable sheets

'Name these 2D shapes'; 'Name these 3D shapes'

Children can work in groups with shapes and a feely bag. They take turns to describe the shape they can feel, without saying its name the other children say the name.

Oral and mental starters for week 6

See bank of starters on page 247. Oral and mental starters are also on the CD-ROM.

79 Make 10 and add

80 Add to make 20

81 Subtract from 20

82 Add and subtract to 20

Overview of progression

Children begin the week naming 2D shapes and making repeating patterns with them. They see that 2D shapes can be placed in different orientations and that this does not alter the shape, its name or its properties. They name the properties of 2D shapes, such as number of sides or corners, straight or curved sides. They name 3D shapes and their properties such as the shape of faces, number of faces, and so on. They build with the 3D shapes, then make a sketch of their building as accurately as they can. They name shapes they can see in a picture of buildings, then copy a picture of buildings, making these with 3D shapes.

Watch out for

Some children may still confuse 2D and 3D shapes. For example they may call a cube a square. Ask them to hold a cube, and to feel the faces. Explain that a cube has square faces, and ask the children to count the faces. Repeat this with any other shapes where there is confusion, such as a sphere being called a circle.

Creative context

Children can draw and paint pictures of buildings. Ask them to name the shapes used in their buildings.

Vocabulary

build, **circle**, **cone**, corner, **cube**, **cuboid**, curved, **cylinder**, draw, edge, face, flat, hollow, make, **pattern**, point, **pyramid**, **rectangle**, shape, side, solid, **sphere**, **square**, straight, **triangle**

Curriculum objectives
● To recognise and name common 2D shapes.
Success criteria
● I can make pictures and patterns with 2D shapes.
● I can say the names of 2D shapes.

You will need
Equipment
2D shape tiles of square, circle, rectangle, triangle for each small group; coloured paper or coloured sticky paper; scissors; glue sticks; A3 paper that can be photocopied

Differentiation
Less confident learners
Use single shapes, rather than combinations of shapes, to make their pattern.
More confident learners
Suggest that the children make an ABCABC repeating pattern.

Lesson 1 — Oral and mental starter 79

Main teaching activities

Whole-class work: Explain to the children that this week they will learn more about 2D and 3D shapes. Hold up a rectangle and ask: *What shape is this? How do you know it is a rectangle?* Repeat with a circle. Now place the rectangle with the long sides vertical and the circle on top and ask: *What does this look like? Yes, a tree.* Repeat, using a square and a triangle to make a house. Make a repeating pattern of tree, house, tree, house. Ask: *What comes next after the house? What comes before the tree?*

Paired work: Provide children with 2D shape tiles (squares, rectangles, triangles, circles), scissors, coloured paper or coloured sticky paper, and A3 paper that can be photocopied. The children decide which combinations of shapes to use to make a pattern. They will draw around the shapes on coloured paper or coloured sticky paper, then cut them out. Suggest that they rehearse the beginning of their pattern using the shape tiles before cutting out the paper shapes. Ask the children to show at least two repeats of their pattern. If there's time, they can make another, different pattern.

Progress check: Ask pairs questions such as: *What shapes have you chosen? Why did you choose those? Say your pattern for me. What comes next in your pattern? And next?*

Review

Invite pairs to show the patterns that they have made. Ask of the other children: *What shape is this? And this? How do you know what these shapes are? Tell me something about this shape.*

Curriculum objectives
● To recognise and name common 2D shapes.
Success criteria
● I can make pictures and patterns with 2D shapes.
● I can say the names of 2D shapes.

You will need
Equipment
2D shape tiles of square, circle, rectangle, triangle for each small group; coloured paper or coloured sticky paper; scissors; glue sticks; A3 paper that can be photocopied

Differentiation
Less confident learners
Encourage the children to use the vocabulary of shape to describe their pattern and which shapes they are using.
More confident learners
Challenge the children to make combinations of shapes in different orientations.

Lesson 2 — Oral and mental starter 80

Main teaching activities

Whole-class work: With the children sitting in their groups, and with sets of shape tiles in front of them, say: *Sort out the square tile. How do you know it is a square? Sort out the rectangle tile. How do you know it is a rectangle?* Now hold up an equilateral triangle, with an angle at the bottom. Ask: *What shape is this? How do you know it is a triangle?* Repeat this for a square held by a corner, and similarly a rectangle.

Paired work: Ask the children to make a repeating pattern with the shape tiles. This time, ask them to place them on the paper so that they are not sitting on their bases, but are turned. When the children are happy with the pattern they have made, provide coloured paper or coloured sticky paper, ask the children to cut out paper shapes and glue them to their paper in the pattern they first made. If time, ask the children to make another pattern, again with the shapes in different orientations from how they are usually seen.

Progress check: Ask pairs to explain their pattern. Ask, for example: *What shape is this? How have you turned it? What shape comes next? And next?*

Review

Invite a pair to show their repeating pattern. Ask questions of the class such as: *What shape is this? And this? How do you know that this is a ... shape?*

Curriculum objectives
● To order and arrange combinations of shapes.
● To recognise and name common 2D, such as rectangles (including squares), circles and triangles.

Success criteria
● I can name 2D shapes.
● I can say some properties of 2D shapes.

You will need

General resources
'Shape tiles (1)'; 'Shape tiles (2)'; 'Work mat'

Equipment
Glue sticks

Differentiation

Less confident learners
Encourage the children to name shapes and to explain how they know what the shape is.

More confident learners
Challenge the children to think of various ways of sorting the shapes, and make up their own general statements about shapes.

Main teaching activities

Whole-class work: Explain that today, the children will think about some sentences that describe shapes. Provide each group of about four children with a set of 2D shape tiles from photocopiable pages 'Shape tiles (1)' and 'Shape tiles (2)' from the CD-ROM. Begin by saying: *All triangles have three sides.* Ask the children to work in their groups to sort through their shape tiles and find the triangles. Ask:

● *What shapes are not triangles? How do you know that?*
● *How many sides do rectangles/squares/pentagons/circles have?*

Repeat this with another statement, such as: *All pentagons have five corners.*

Group work: On the board, draw six 2D shapes and number them 1 to 6. Also write appropriate descriptions for each shape and label these, randomly, A to F. Ask the children to match the descriptions to the shapes. Encourage them to discuss all the statements before they decide which shape matches which statement.

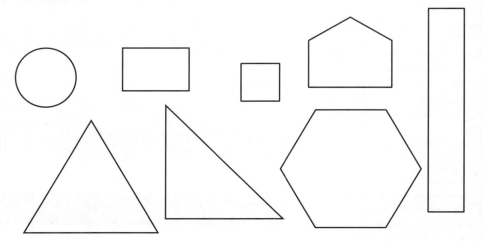

Progress check: Ask, for example: *What is this shape? Tell me something about this shape. Which shape has no straight sides? Which shape has five corners?*

Independent work: Ask the children to work independently with their own sets of shape tiles. They decide how to sort their shapes on the A3 versions of photocopiable page 'Work mat' from the CD-ROM. They could, for example, add labels 'Has 4 sides' and 'Does not have 4 sides' and glue their shape tiles into the appropriate spaces.

Review

Look at the board and read through the statements together. Ask children from each group to say which shape belongs to each statement. Ask:

● *Which sentence does this shape belong to? Why?*
● *How do you know that this shape belongs to this sentence?*

Invite the more confident learners to say general statements about shapes. The other children use their shape tiles to provide examples of the statement.

Curriculum objectives

● To recognise and name common 3D shapes.

Success criteria

● I can name 3D shapes.
● I can say some properties of 3D shapes.

You will need

Equipment

3D shapes, including cubes, cuboids, pyramids, spheres, cylinders, cones; construction kits; building bricks

Differentiation

Less confident learners

Check that the children know the names of the 3D shapes and can sort and recognise them.

More confident learners

Challenge them to make a more complex building of a house, using a range of shapes to do so.

Lesson 4 — Oral and mental starter 82

Main teaching activities

Whole-class work: Hold up each of the 3D shapes in turn and say: *Tell me something about this shape.* Encourage the children to refer to the shape of faces, the number of faces, and to name the shapes. Repeat this for each shape.

Paired work: Ask the children to work in pairs and to make a house from a construction set or building bricks. When they are happy with their model, ask them each to sketch a picture of it as accurately as they can.

Progress check: Ask questions of pairs such as: *What shape is this? How do you know that? Tell me something about this shape. Which shapes are good for building? Why is that? Which shapes are not so good for building? Why is that?*

Review

Ask the children to place their sketches by their model. Now ask the children to look at other children's models and the sketches. When they have done this, ask questions about model making, such as:

● *Which shapes were good for making your house? Why is that?*
● *Which shapes did you try and were not so good? Why was that do you think?*
● *Tell me the name of a shape you used in your model?*

Now discuss sketching the model. Ask:

● *What did you find easy about sketching your house?*
● *What was difficult? Why was that do you think?*

Curriculum objectives

● To order and arrange combinations of objects and shapes in patterns.
● To recognise and name common 3D shapes.

Success criteria

● I can name 3D shapes.
● I can say some properties of 3D shapes.

You will need

Photocopiable sheets

'A house with a garage and tree'

Equipment

3D shapes, including cubes, cuboids, pyramids, spheres, cylinders, cones; construction kits; building bricks, Plasticine®; pictures of buildings

Differentiation

Less confident learners

Ask an adult to encourage the children to describe the shapes that they see in the picture, then to pick out those shapes from a set of 3D shape tiles.

More confident learners

Suggest that children add other features to their model made with 3D shapes.

Lesson 5 — Oral and mental starter 82

Main teaching activities

Whole-class work: Ask the children to look at a classroom cupboard, and ask: *What shape is the cupboard? How do you know it is a cuboid?* Repeat for something else, such as a wall clock (cylinder) or the door (cuboid).

Hold up a picture of some buildings. Look together at the picture and ask the children to name the different shapes and their faces. Ask: *How can you tell that that is a … ?* Repeat this for a different picture.

Paired work: Provide photocopiable page 'A house with a garage and a tree' from the CD-ROM. Ask the children to look carefully at the picture and decide which shapes have been used. Then ask them to copy the picture using a construction kit, building blocks, 3D shapes or Plasticine.

Progress check: Invite pairs to explain which shapes they can see in photocopiable page 'A house with a garage and a tree' and how they know that that is what the shapes are. Ask, for example: *What shapes have been used for the house? How do you know that that shape is a … ? What shapes have been used for the tree/garage? How do you know that?*

Review

Review some of the models that have been made. Ask the children to look carefully at each model made and the drawing it is based on. Ask, for example: *How is this the same as the drawing? How is it different? Have the same shapes been used?*

Now ask the children to think about what they have learned this week. They can talk to their partner about what they have learned, where they feel confident, and what they need next.

Addition and subtraction to 20

Most children should be able to calculate these answers using mental strategies.

Some children will not have made such progress and will require further practice of addition and subtraction bonds to 10 before moving on.

1. Check
82 Add and subtract to 20

Ask children each time to explain the strategy that they used to find the answer. Encourage less confident children to use a number line to help them to find the solution. Challenge more confident children to explain in more detail the strategy that they used.
- *How did you work that out?*
- *What subtraction/addition facts use those numbers?*

2. Assess

Ask the children to work in pairs and provide each pair with two sets of 0–10 number cards. They take turns to turn over two number cards. They both add them and write a number sentence. Ask them to write the other addition and both subtraction sentences for the number trio. Decide whether to provide a number line for the less confident children. Challenge the more confident to work quickly, but accurately. Check that all children use the symbols +, − = correctly. Record the outcomes.

3. Further practice

The suggested OMS will give further practice in using specific mental strategies for addition and subtraction to 20. The photocopiables on pages 248 and 249 give further experience in using mental strategies for addition and subtraction to 20.

Months of the year

Most children should be able to say the months of the year in order and know which month it is now.

Some children will not have made such progress and will require further practice in saying and writing the date, and in ordering the months.

1. Check
83 Months of the year

Check who reads the month cards and who needs further practice with this. Observe who is confident in helping to order the months and which children recognise when their birthday is.
- *When is your birthday? What is the next month after that?*
- *What month is it now? What month was it before this month?*

2. Assess

Ask the children, working in pairs, to position the months from interactive activity 'Months of the year' on the CD-ROM into order. Ask them to write their birth date as a sentence. ask them to choose a month that they like and write a sentence about why they like that month. Record the outcomes.

3. Further practice

The suggested OMS gives practice in reading the names and ordering the months of the year. Use the suggested photocopiable sheet 'Months' on page 250 to provide further experience of reading the months, and recognising in which months key events in their lives occur.

Curriculum objectives
• To tell the time to the hour and half past the hour and draw the hands on a clock face to show these times.

You will need
1. Check
Oral and mental starter

71 Telling the time

2. Assess
'Clock faces'; paper fasteners

3. Further practice
Oral and mental starters

71 Telling the time

Photocopiable sheets
'Clock times'; 'What time is it?'

Telling o'clock and half past times

Most children should be able to read o'clock and half-past times and draw hands on clock faces to show these times.

Some children will not have made such progress and will require further practice in reading o'clock times before moving on to half past times.

1. Check
71 Telling the time

Observe which children are confident and which are not at reading the time. Extend the questions about time passed for the more confident children.

- *Where are the hands on the clock? So what time is it?*
- *What happens to the hour hand when it is a half-past time?*

2. Assess

Ask the children to work in pairs. They take turns to say an o'clock or half past time for their partner to write on their clock faces. They check each other's clock settings. You may prefer for an adult to work with the less confident children at this task, concentrating on o'clock times at first. Challenge the more confident children to work quickly and accurately. Record the outcomes.

3. Further practice

Use the suggested OMS to reinforce o'clock and half-past times. The photocopiable sheets on pages 251 and 252 give further practice in writing the hands on clock faces for given times, and for reading clock faces then writing the times.

Curriculum objectives
• To recognise and name common 2D and 3D shapes.

You will need
1. Check
Oral and mental starter

84 Shape patterns

2. Assess
2D shape tiles per pair; 3D shapes per pair; large book to act as a screen between each pair

3. Further practice
Oral and mental starters

84 Shape patterns

Photocopiable sheets
'Name these 2D shapes'; 'Name these 3D shapes'

Shape patterns

Most children should be able to recognise and name common 2D and 3D shapes, and make repeating patterns with them.

Some children will not have made such progress and will require further practice in naming 2D and 3D shapes, then making repeating patterns.

1. Check
84 Shape patterns

Observe whether children can name the shapes used. Encourage less confident children to say a simple ABAB pattern, naming the shapes each time. Challenge the more able children to make and extend a more complex ABCABC pattern.

- *Which shape comes next? And next?*
- *Look at the pattern now. What is missing from it?*

2. Assess

Ask the children to put the book between them so that they cannot see what is in front of their partner. The children take turns to make a repeating pattern with the 2D shape tiles, then give their partner instructions for making the same pattern. When completed they remove the book to check that the patterns are the same. They can repeat this using 3D shape tiles. Listen to the instructions given, and whether these are followed. Challenge the more confident children to make more complex patterns. Record the outcomes.

3. Further practice

The suggested OMS gives opportunities for children to recognise and extend repeating patterns made with 2D or 3D shapes. The photocopiables on pages 253 and 254 give further practice in naming 2D and 3D shapes.

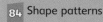

Oral and mental starters

Number and place value

72 Count in 1s

Ask the children to count with you in ones from 0 to 100 and back again. Keep a sharp pace. Now repeat this counting from any number, to 100, back to 0, then up to the starting number. Ask questions such as:

- *What is the fifth number after 40... 51...?*
- *What number comes two before 41... 53... 99...?*
- *If we start on 46..., what would be the next number we say?*

73 Count in 2s

Count together in twos, forwards and back from 0 to 100. Keep the pace sharp. Now ask the children to count in twos from 1 to 19 and back again. Extend this count over time. Ask questions such as:

- *What number in the count of twos comes next after 78...?*
- *What number comes before 50...?*
- *What are the unit digits in the count of twos? (2, 4, 6, 8, 0)*
- *What are the unit digits in the count of two if we start from 1? (1, 3, 5, 7, 9)*

74 Count in 5s

Count together in fives from 0 to 100 and back again, with a good pace. Repeat the count several times. Now ask questions such as:

- *What is the next number in the count of fives after 15... 25... 40...?*
- *If we count back in fives from 100, what is the number we say after 65... 40... 15...?*
- *What are the units digits in the count of fives?*

75 Count in 10s

Count together in tens from 0 to 100 and back again, with a good pace. Repeat this several times, then count around the class, so that each child says a number. If anyone falters, say the number for them to keep the count going. Repeat this several times, starting with a different child each time. Now ask, for example:

- *What number in the count of tens comes after 20... 50... 90...?*
- *If we count back in tens from 100, what number do we say after 70... 40... 10...?*
- *What is the units digit in the count of tens?*

76 1 more and 1 less to 100

Ask the children to write the number that is one more than the number that you say. When you say *Show me* they hold up their individual whiteboards for you to see. Say, for example: *What is one more than 25? One more than 39... 43... 99...?*

Now repeat for the number that is one less than the number that you say, such as: *What is the number that is one less than 20... 43... 70...?*

77 Ordinal numbers

Put ten objects in a line in front of the class so that the children can see them. Point to each object in turn as you say together the first ten ordinal numbers in order: first, second, third, and so on. Repeat this several times. Now add more objects so you have 20 in a line, and say the ordinal numbers to 'twentieth'. Ask, for example:

- *What comes after third... fifth... seventh... ?*
- *What comes before eleventh... fourteenth... seventeenth... nineteenth...?*
- *Look at these objects in front of you. Which is the eighth... twelfth... fifteenth... twentieth... object?*

78 Arrow cards tens and units

Provide each child with a set of arrow cards. Demonstrate how to make a TU number by adding a unit arrow card to the tens arrow card. Explain that you will say a number. Ask the children to make it with the arrow cards and when you say *Show me*, they hold up their cards for you to see. Begin with teens numbers, such as 13, 15, 18, then extend to 20, 25, 34... Ask questions such as:

- *How many tens are there?*
- *How many units are there?*
- *Which is the tens digit?*
- *Which is the units digit?*

Addition and subtraction

79 Make 10 and add

Explain to the children that you will ask some addition questions where the answer is greater than 10. Remind them of the strategy of 'making a ten and adding on what is left'. Ask, for example: *What is 8 + 5? How did you work that out? What is 9 + 4? 8 + 7? 9 + 8? 6 + 5...?*

80 Add to make 20

Explain that you will say a number. Ask the children what number needs to be added to the number to make a total of 20. Begin with, for example: *What do I need to add to 19 to make a total of 20? What do I need to add to 16 to make a total of 20?* Invite children to explain how they found the answer. Continue with adding to a two-digit number. When the children are confident with this, extend to adding to a one-digit number. Here, children could think of adding to make 10 then adding on 10. For example, begin with 6, and 4 makes 10 and 10 makes 20. So 6 + 14 equals 20.

81 Subtract from 20

Ask questions such as: *If I take 5 from 20, what is left? How did you work that out?* Remind the children that for one-digit numbers they can subtract from 10, then add the result to 10. Ask: *What is the difference between 20 and 1? What is 20 take away 3?* When the children are confident with these, extend to subtracting a two-digit number from 20.

82 Add and subtract to 20

Explain to the children that you will ask an addition question. Give them time to find the answer. Ask, for example:

- *What is 8 add 5? How did you work it out?*
- *What is 12 add 7? How did you work it out?*
- *What is 10 add 3? How did you find the answer?*

Ask other, similar, addition questions.

Now ask subtraction questions such as:

- *What is 14 take away 5? How did you work out the answer?*
- *What is 13 take away 5? How did you find the answer?*
- *What is 20 take away 7? How do you know?*

Ask other, similar, subtraction questions.

Oral and mental starters 83–84 continue on the CD-ROM.

Addition and subtraction grids

- Choose two numbers from the grid, which total 20.
- Join the numbers with a line.
- Repeat this until all the numbers are joined to their partner to make a total of 20.

5	2	6	17	11	16
9	13	0	4	14	18
1	20	10	8	19	
15	7	3	10	12	

- Now choose two numbers with a difference of 3.
- Repeat this until all the numbers are joined to their partner to leave a difference of 3.

3	18	2	0	12	9	19	3	16
9	6	4	8	16	7	6	15	10
10	20	15	5	13	11	5	17	11
14	4	1	12	17	14	7	13	8

Addition and subtraction word problems

- Write the answers to these word problems.
- There is space for you to write number sentences to help you to find the answer.

I. Farah buys a pen for 10p and a pencil for 7p.

How much does Farah spend? p

2. How much change will Farah have from 20p? p

3. Manuel buys a carrot for 9p and an onion for 6p.

How much does Manuel spend? p

4. How much change does Manuel have from 20p? [ ] p

5. Amit spends 14p.
How much change does Amit have from 20p? p

I can answer word problems.

How did you do?

Name: _____   Date: _____

Months

- Write the answers to these questions.
- All the answers need a month.
- Here are the months to help you.

January   February   March   April   May   June

July   August   September   October   November   December

1. In which month is your birthday? _____

2. In which month is Christmas? _____

3. When do you go on holiday? _____

4. When does school start after the summer holidays? _____

5. Which month do you like the best? _____

   Tell me why.

_____

_____

_____

_____

I know the months of the year.

How did you do?

PHOTOCOPIABLE   ■SCHOLASTIC
www.scholastic.co.uk

Clock times

■ Draw the hands on the clocks for the times.

1. 5 o'clock

2. 8 o'clock

3. 10 o'clock

4. 1 o'clock

5. Half past 3

6. Half past 7

7. Half past 6

8. Half past 4

I can draw hands on clock faces.

How did you do?

What time is it?

■ Write the time.

1. _____

2. _____

3. _____

4. _____

5. _____

6. _____

7. _____

8. _____

I can tell the time.

How did you do?

Name: _____   Date: _____

Name these 2D shapes

■ Join the shape to its name.

 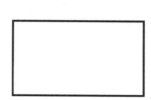 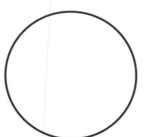 

circle   triangle   square   rectangle

■ Draw these shapes.

rectangle   triangle   square   circle

I can name and draw 2D shapes.

How did you do?

Name these 3D shapes

■ Join the shape to its name.

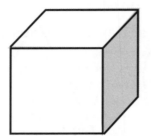  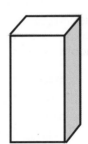

 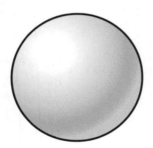 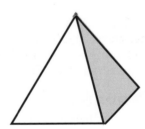

cuboid	cube	cone
pyramid	cylinder	sphere

I can name and draw 3D shapes.

How did you do?

Year 1 equipment list

Number and place value

Abacus (two spikes), Arrow cards, Beads, Buttons, Blank number tracks, Conkers, Counters, Counters per pair, Counting objects, Elastic bands, Interlocking cubes, Marbles, Number cards 21–30, Number word cards zero to thirty, Pasta pieces, Picture (in a big book or a poster) of items that can be counted, Reading books, Straws, Washing line and pegs

Addition and subtraction

Blank number tracks, Box (metal or wooden), Coins (all values from 1p– £2), Containers for cubes, Dice – numbered 1, 1, 2, 2, 3, 3, Dice – numbered 1, 2, 3, 4, 5, 5, Dice – numbered 2, 2, 3, 3, 4, 4, Dice – numbered 1–6, Interlocking cubes, Items for a class newsagent's shop (such as newspapers, comics and sweet boxes), Number cards 21–30, Number word cards zero to thirty, Number lines 0-30, Pad of paper, Paper clips

Multiplication and division

Blank number tracks, Coins – 10p, 5p, 2p and 1p, Counters, Dice – numbered 1–6, Dice – numbered 1, 1, 2, 2, 3, 3, Elastic bands, Interlocking cubes, Number cards 21-30, Number word cards zero to thirty, Number lines 0–30, Paper plates, Hoops – PE or sorting, Shape tiles, Straws

Fractions

Black marker, Hoops, Interlocking cubes, Interlocking cubes, Paper plates, Paper shapes (such as squares, equilateral triangles, circles and rectangles), Paper strips, Shape tiles, Squared paper, String

Measurement

Bucket balances, Clock faces, Coins – 1p, 2p, 5p, 10p, 20p, 50p, £1, £2, Containers – 20ml, 100ml, 1 litre, Containers – different sizes marked A, B, C and so on, Containers – pairs of identical transparent, Containers – six 1-litre containers of various shapes and labelled A–F, Containers for coins, Containers for filling and pouring, Counters, Cups, Dial balances that read in 100g, Dried peas, Egg cups, Elastic bands, Filling material such as sand, water, cubes, Food colouring, Interlocking cubes, Items to be compared such as scarves, gloves and shoes, Jugs, Margarine tubs, Measures vocabulary cards, Metre stick marked in decimetre, Metre sticks, Months of the year cards, Notes: £5, £10 and £20, Number cards 21–30, Pan balances, Paper plates, Parcels for comparing, Plastic bags and ties, Price labels 1p–20p, Reading books of different sizes and weights, Ribbons that measure less than, more than, or about the same as a metre, Rulers, Sand timers – 1-minute, Scale balance, Scarf, Scoops – 20ml and 10ml, Spoons, Stop clocks that mark seconds, Stop watches that mark seconds, Straws, String, Sugar paper – A3, Teaching clock, Tray, Washing line and pegs, Weights – 100g and 1kg, Yogurt pots, 10cm rulers

Geometry: properties of shapes

2D shape tiles – squares, rectangles, circles, triangles, 3D shapes – cubes, cuboids, pyramids, spheres, cylinders, cones, Building bricks, Coloured paper or coloured sticky paper, Commercial packaging materials, Construction kits, Feely bags, Paper that can be photocopied – A3, Pictures of buildings, Plasticine®, Squared paper

Geometry: position and direction

2D shape tiles – squares, rectangles, circles, triangles, 3D shapes – cubes, cuboids, pyramids, spheres, cylinders, cones, Hoops, one per child, Interlocking cubes, Large PE apparatus, Models (a doll's house with furniture, a garage with cars, a farm with animals), Roamer, Squared paper, Sugar paper, Temporary adhesive

General

Blu-Tack®, Coloured pencils, Glue sticks, Individual whiteboards and pens, Interactive whiteboard, Scissors, Sorting tables

Year 1 vocabulary list

Number and place value

after, answer, as many as, before, bigger, compare, count, counting numbers 0 to 100, digit, equal to, equals (=), even number, exchange, explain, fewer, first, greater, hundred, larger, less than, more than, odd number, one less than, one more than, ones, order, **pattern**, read, record, show me, sign, smaller, 'teens' number, ten, **tens**, the same number as, three, two, **units**, write

Addition and subtraction

add, after, altogether, and, answer, as many as, before, calculate, calculation, compare, count, difference, double, equal, equals (=), equal to, explain, first, half, halfway, halve, how many?, how many are left/left over?, how many are gone?, how many fewer is ___ than ___?, how much less is ___?, how many more is ___ than ___?, how many more to make ___?, how many more/less? how many more to make ___?, how much more is ___?, how much less is ___?, leave, leaves, less, make, makes, method, minus (−), more, near double, nearly, number sentence, odd number, ones, operation, order, **pattern**, plus (+), problem, put together, read, record, roughly, second, share, show me, sign, solution, subtract, sum, take away, tens, the same number as, third, total, what is the difference between ___ and ___?, whole, write

Multiplication and division

array, count, counting in fives, counting in tens, counting in twos, counting numbers, double, equal groups, group, grouping, half, halves, share, share equally, sharing, twice

Fractions

equal, **fraction**, half, halves, quarter, share, whole

Measurement

£1 coin, £2 coin, £5 note, £10 note, £20 note, 100 grams, 100 millilitres, 10p, about, add, afternoon, answer, balance, before, block graph, capacity, centimetre (cm), change, **clock**, **coins**, compare, container, cost, count, count on, count up, day, days of the week, deep, depth, diagram, different, estimate, evening, first, graph, guess, hands, heavier, heaviest, height, high, holds more, holds most, hour, information, kilogram, label, last unit, length, list, litre, long, longer, longest, low, measure, measuring jug, method, metre (m), metre stick, midnight, minute, money, month, morning, narrow, next, night, notes, number sentence, order, pictogram, problem, record, ruler, same, scales, second, shallow, short, shorter, shortest, sign, size, table, tall, tape measure, then, thick, thin, time, title, today, tomorrow, unit, week, weekend, weigh, weight, wide, width, year, yesterday

Geometry: properties of shapes

build, **circle**, **cone**, corner, **cube**, **cuboid**, curved, **cylinder**, draw, edge, face, flat, group, hollow, make, **pattern**, point, predict, property, **pyramid**, **rectangle**, repeating pattern, set, shape, side, solid, sort, **sphere**, **square**, straight, **triangle**

Geometry: position and direction

above, back, below, beside, between, centre, clockwise, direction, far, front, grid, half turn, halfway, inside, left, near, next to, on top of, outside, position, quarter turn, right, three-quarter turn, underneath, whole turn